Political Islam and the Invention of Tradition

Political Islam and the Invention of Tradition

Nicholas P. Roberts

Foreword by John O. Voll

Washington, DC

Copyright © 2015 by Nicholas P. Roberts

New Academia Publishing, 2015

All rights reserved. No part of this book may be reproduced or transmitted in any form or by any means, electronic or mechanical, including photocopying, recording, or by any information storage and retrieval system.

Printed in the United States of America

Library of Congress Control Number: 2015930571
ISBN 978-0-9906939-6-3 paperback (alk. paper)

New Academia Publishing
P.O. Box 24720, Washington, DC 20038-7420
info@newacademia.com - www.newacademia.com

For Chiraz

For I say at the core of democracy, finally, is the religious element. All the religions, old and new, are there.

> Walt Whitman
> *Democratic Vistas*

If democracy is as Lincoln defined it – government of the people, by the people, and for the people – then this definition is represented, without doubt, in the system of the Islamic state.

> Muhammad Diya' al-Din al-Rayyis
> *Al-Nizariyat al-Siyasiyya al-Islamiyya*

No man can have in his mind a conception of the future, for the future is not yet. But of our conceptions of the past, we make a future; or rather, call past, future relatively.

> Thomas Hobbes
> *The Elements of Law, Natural and Politic*

Contents

Foreword — xi

Acknowledgments — xv

A Note on Spelling — xvii

Introduction — xix

PART ONE: Context, Framework, and Labels — 1

   The crisis of the Muslim intellectual in the modern era
   Muslim evaluations of the West in the modern era
   Toward truth in labeling: A brief discussion of terms

PART TWO: The Emergence of Political Islam — 35

   The Tanzimat mode of renewal and reform
   The modernist mode of renewal and reform
   Crossroad of history
   The secular-nationalist mode of renewal and reform
   The fundamentalist-style mode of renewal and reform
   The intellectual foundation of Political Islam

PART THREE: Power and Authority in an Islamic State — 87

   Political Islam
   Dīn as dawla
   Tawhid and ḥākimiyya
   'Popular vicegerency'
   Political power and authority in the Muslim community
   Ḥisba and shūra
   Bay'a and 'shūracracy'

PART FOUR: Arabia and the Prophet at Medina　　135

Arab tribal society and communal authority
The Prophet at Medina
Conception of the caliphate

PART FIVE: Conclusion　　157

Political Islam and the invention of tradition

Afterword　　169

Glossary of Non-English Terms　　175

Notes　　179

Bibliography　　217

Index　　227

Foreword

by John O. Voll

Islam, as the faith and worldview of believers for fourteen centuries, has important political dimensions, and it shapes the devotional life of Muslims. The community of believers maintains a distinctive sense of unity despite great diversity and sometimes bitter conflicts among the groups that identify themselves as Muslim. The nature of political systems established by Muslims over the centuries has reflected both this diversity and a sense of shared traditions.

The early community that developed around the Prophet Muhammad in Mecca and Medina during the seventh century CE provides the starting point for the Muslim sense of organized Islamic society. It lays the foundation for the ideals of the community of believers or *umma*. The integrated sense of communal identity included political organization as well as social and religious dimensions. In modern terminology, many people recognize this integration by saying that Islam combines "religion" and "politics" or that "church" and "state" are merged in Islam. How the *umma* should be politically organized became one of the early issues of disagreement among the believers and it continues to be a major subject of significance in the twenty-first century.

Nicholas Roberts provides a clear analysis of how the modern and contemporary Muslim visions of state and religion developed in the past two centuries. He places these modern visions within the broader framework of Muslim intellectual history and the history of modernity. Much has been written about the relationships and interactions between "Islam" and "the West," and between "Islam" and "Modernity." These relations involve tensions and conflict, but, as Roberts demonstrates, these disputes do not represent irreconcilable differences between two totally separate civilizations or two distinct ways of life. Instead, he argues that the important historical development of what has come to be called "Political Islam" is part of what modernity is in the contemporary global community of Muslims (the modern *umma*).

Roberts's approach gives recognition to the history of Muslim political thought and recognizes that modern Political Islam represents a synthesis of reinterpreted Islamic tradition and Western thought, brought together by the conditions of modern global history. It is not advocacy of a Luddite-style opposition to modernity. In many ways it reflects the political realities of world affairs of the past two centuries – adapting, redefining, creating socio-political visions that work to be both modern and in accord with the ideals presented in the Qur'an, the sunna, and the life of the early community of Muslims. He distinguishes between the ideology of modern*ism* and ideologies and movements that may be anti-modern*ist* but are themselves modern in the way they formulate ideals and organize movements. Discussions starting with assumptions that the basic dynamic of global political and cultural relations is a "clash of civilizations" or a clash between "modernity" and "tradition" miss this significant characteristic of contemporary Muslim life.

Many observers and participants note the continued importance of religion in modern life. The old expectations, articulated as secularization theory, that "religion" would lose influence in the public sphere and become simply a matter of individual choice as a result of modernization have been proven wrong. One of the major articulators of secularization theory as it developed in the 1960s, Peter Berger, argued at the end of the twentieth century that "a whole body of literature by historians and social scientists loosely labeled 'secularization theory' is essentially mistaken."[1] In the twenty-first century, many analysts affirm that, globally, "religion is on the rise... The major world religions are all taking advantage of the opportunities provided by globalization to transform their messages and reach a new global audience."[2]

Muslim thinkers, activists, and organizations are significant actors in world affairs. However, while extremists regularly get headlines for terrorist acts or radical pronouncements, the larger political movements and important intellectuals get less coverage in the mass media. This situation is especially true in terms of the major trends that are included in the label "Political Islam." Militant extremists who advocate one form of Political Islam have high visibility. Roberts provides a corrective to this coverage with a remarkably comprehensive description and analysis of the broader ideas and beliefs that represent non-extremist Political Islam.

The significance of Roberts's study and approach is shown by important responses to the Arab Spring movements, which overthrew or opposed authoritarian, basically secular modernizing regimes. Opposition to dictators like Ben ʿAli in Tunisia, Mubarak in Egypt, and Qaddafi in Libya before the Arab Spring came primarily from groups that represented various forms of Political Islam. However, when these leaders were overthrown in the demonstrations and movements of the Arab Spring in 2011, political scientists argued that the "vast majority of academic specialists on the Arab world were as surprised as everyone else by the upheavals."[3]

In the current events analyses at the time of the Arab Spring, there was little mention of the long history of Political Islam that is presented by Roberts. Even though most scholars agreed that secularization theory had been mistaken and that religion was significant in global and regional political affairs, there was a reluctance to identify religion as an important element in the democratization movements. Political scientists tended to be surprised by the events of the Arab Spring because the perspectives of many were still shaped by an inherent acceptance of the assumptions of secularization theory.

In examining the Arab Spring, scholars across a broad spectrum emphasized the "Arab" nature of the regional movements. Gregory Gause, for example, argued that most "Middle East scholars believed that pan-Arabism had gone dormant.... Academics will need to assess the restored importance of Arab identity to understand the future of Middle East politics."[4] Fouad Ajami, from a different part of the spectrum of scholars, said much the same: "Arab nationalism had been written off, but here [in 2011], in full bloom, was what certainly looked like a pan-Arab awakening."[5] In this context, the series of election victories by Islamist-oriented political parties in Tunisia, Egypt, and elsewhere, came as another surprise to those observers and participants who had underestimated the continuing strength of religious identification in the Arab and Muslim world. However, as Roberts shows, important intellectual and theological foundations for the political appeal of the Islamist groups in the second decade of the twenty-first century had been laid by the development of Political Islam in the preceding two centuries.

An important element in the thinking of historic Political Islam is the recognition of the community of the Prophet Muhammad in the seventh century CE as the model for Islamic state and society. The first generation of Muslims is identified as the *salaf* (the pious "ancestors") and "Salafi" became the term for people who advocated following the example of the salaf. In recent years, journalists have used the term "Salafi" to apply to extremist Muslim militants who are literalist in their understanding of medieval legal teachings, but the term has a broader meaning of working to follow the example of the early Muslim community in Mecca and Medina. As Roberts shows, much of the thinking of modern Political Islam is "salafi" in taking the early *umma* as a model. However, as he also shows, the major articulators of Political Islam are modern thinkers and activists who are not advocates of a violent militancy. They are part of the long tradition of renewal and reform in Muslim history.

Nicholas Roberts provides a clear survey of that stream of modern Muslim political thought that is modern in form and self-identified as Islamic in content that came to be called Political Islam in the second half of the twentieth century. Roberts provides a useful corrective to those theorists who think that the Islamic tradition is primarily not compatible with modernity. He shows how Political Islamists have reinvented tradition or reframed the narrative of Islam to create an effective and powerful worldview for the post-secular world of the twenty-first century.

John O. Voll
Georgetown University

Acknowledgments

Every book, especially one written by a young scholar, is a group effort. I have been fortunate to learn from a succession of dedicated and gifted teachers, who, at varying stages throughout my scholastic and professional development, prepared me for succeeding in the next. Even in the lecture halls of a university such as Georgetown, I often thought back to the first lessons in inquiry, writing, active reading and critical thinking taught to me in high school by my history teacher, Philip Rudolph, and my English teacher, Laura Iodice. They prepared me well for the next stage – college – when I was guided by the sage, patient hand of Bill Smullen, my former boss, mentor, and thesis advisor. Though never actually sitting in her classroom, I have learned more from Professor Linda Loomis than she will ever know. Pertaining particularly to this project, Deina Abdelkader has selflessly provided me with unique perspective and support. I feel honored that I often do not know where the ideas of my teachers end and my own begin.

Though I wrote this book in graduate school, I began thinking about these issues years before, when I was living in Tunisia and studying languages. Living there during the revolution that began the events collectively known as the 'Arab Spring' was an inimitable experience. Chanting *'degage!'* in the jasmine-laced streets of Tunis with my friends, I was, at first, not fully aware of the historical transformation I was witnessing. I would not realize this until years later as a student at Georgetown, where two preeminent world historians, David Goldfrank and John Voll, challenged me to think about these events as part of a grand narrative of the history of a major world civilization.

The conceptual spark for this work came in Professor Goldfrank's comparative history seminar. Professor Goldfrank's caring for his students and his enthusiasm for teaching them is second to none. He challenged me, as he does with all his students, to consider any issue under study from every angle, to account for every exception, to be confident in being a contrarian voice, and to never stop thinking.

It has been an honor to study with Professor John Voll and remain his student even after his retirement. From countless afternoons of class together, long conversations in his office, to my endless questions over e-mail, he has been an inspiration and guide. It is rare to have a teacher who so wisely knows how, with just a few simple words, to keep a student on track and push him to discover new ideas. I have learned from Professor Voll far more than the topics included in this work. An artist in the classroom and the finest of scholars, he is the embodiment of Norman Maclean's eloquent words that all good things come by grace, and grace comes by art, and art does not come easy.

A Note on Spelling

In this book I have tried to minimize the use of non-English words. However, there is a significant amount of Arabic because many of these words, such as shariʿa or ḥisba, represent concepts that are not easily translated into one counterpart English word. For scholars working with alphabets other than English, spelling remains an issue that has not been resolved by a simple and efficient system.

One of the reasons for the difficulty of spelling Arabic words in English is that Arabic contains sounds that do not exist in English (and vice versa). The standard guide for transliterating Arabic into English is the one used by the *International Journal of Middle East Studies* (IJMES). This guide attempts to render into simple symbols and spellings the intricacies of Arabic, as well as Turkish and Persian.

I have followed the IJMES guide as much as possible. Therefore, the reader will see symbols that might appear strange; these symbols are used to represent sounds unique to Arabic. For example, the *hamza* – which, in Arabic, designates a glottal stop – is represented in English by the symbol ʾ. Similarly, the Arabic letter *ayn* indicates a sound not made in English; therefore, it is represented by the symbol ʿ. For persons not versed in Arabic, the prefix "al-" (sometimes spelled in English as "el-") can be confusing. This prefix represents the definite article in Arabic, and most Arabic last names contain a definite article, such as al-Afghani. IJMES requires that the al- prefix be maintained each time the name is used. For flow of language and ease of reading, however, I have chosen at certain parts throughout the book to drop the prefix, simply rendering "al-Afghani" as "Afghani," for example.

I have not changed the spelling of non-English words in quotations or citations. When confronted with confusion applying IJMES guidelines, I have adhered to spellings used by James Gelvin in *The Modern Middle East: A History*, 3rd ed. (New York: Oxford University Press, 2011). Errors in transliterations are my own.

Introduction

Contemporary Western scholarship has largely assumed that despotism or absolutism is inherent in Islam and the political systems of Muslim societies. The historian Bernard Lewis articulated this standard line of thinking when, in 1958, he wrote that the political history of Islam is one "of almost unrelieved autocracy." "For the last thousand years," wrote Lewis, the "political thinking of Islam has been dominated by such maxims as 'tyranny is better than anarchy' and 'whose power is established, obedience to him is incumbent.'"[1]

Granted, depending on how one chooses to define "Islam," Lewis's claims can be supported by history. However, this narrative ignores the vibrant resistance to despotism and absolutism that forms a significant part of modern Muslim intellectual history. The efforts to establish "Islam" as a faith and worldview which contains within it a blueprint for governance that is representative and accountable in nature is an important component of Muslim religious and political activism in the modern and contemporary eras.

For example, in the same year (1958) that Bernard Lewis wrote that, in political terms, Islam knows nothing but "the sovereign power, to which the subject owed complete and unwavering obedience," a source meant to serve as an introduction to Islam for Muslims, printed in the "al-Azhar Official Organ," quoted various Qur'anic verses to reach a conclusion quite different from that of Lewis. "Such were the principles on which the political system of Islam was grounded," concluded the al-Azhar scholars. "It was thoroughly democratic in character. It recognized individual and public liberty, secured the person and property of the subjects, and fostered the growth of all civic virtues."[2]

One theme of modern world history is that the linguistic norms of the West – the United States and most of Europe – form a package from which non-Western societies draw to frame their intellectual debates. Accordingly, many contemporary Islamic activists seek to demonstrate that certain concepts assumed by the West to be Western in origin and nature, such as democracy, are essentially Islamic. The Egyptian writer Ahmad Shawqi al-Fanjari, for example, after presenting what he interpreted as the major rights and liberties of democracy, concluded, "What is called freedom in Europe is exactly what is defined in our religion as justice (*'adl*), right (*haqq*), consultation (*shūra*), and equality (*muwasat*)." He continued: "This is because the rule of freedom and democracy consists of imparting justice and right to the people, and the nation's participation in determining its destiny."[3]

Al-Fanjari's statement is representative of the strand of Muslims who seek to use religious activism to inform their political thought. These activists form the movement of Political Islam. Political Islamists are those Muslims who believe that Islam contains within it a distinctive and comprehensive political program for all aspects of human existence, and thus call for the establishment of an Islamic state. This book analyzes the Sunni Islamic reformist movements beginning in 1798 that helped shape the emergence of Political Islam in the second half of the twentieth century. It explores the ideas of Islamists regarding concepts of power and authority in their theoretical conceptions of an Islamic state to demonstrate that the vision of Islamic government at the core of Political Islam is one founded upon a social contract between rulers and ruled.

A significant part of this book explores the intellectual history of Muslim resistance to despotism and absolutism in the modern era. This historical contextualization refutes the oft-cited cliché that Islam and Islamists are hostile to representative and accountable government and seek a return to some distant, barbaric past. To the contrary, many Islamists (some of whom prefer to be labeled as Islamic activists) have made innovative contributions to Islamic thought and political philosophy by reinventing the ways in which many traditional Islamic concepts are understood in the context of contemporary political issues in Muslim countries. The culmination of this is the invented tradition of an Islamic state founded upon a social contract between rulers and ruled. This vision of government is one framed as indigenous in tradition and Islamic in character – not simply a product of Western imitation.

One of the problems for any scholar attempting a study of this movement is that we do not really have the proper labels for describing persons such as Rachid Ghannouchi or Yousuf Qaradawi.

In this work, I describe the intellectuals under study interchangeably as "Islamists," "Political Islamists," or "Islamic activists." Each of these labels describes the same basic idea. However, it must be clear to the reader that these individuals – though they are "Islamists" in the sense that Islam is their basic conceptual framework for life – are not, in any way, similar to the *takfiri* militants, who – at the time of this writing – refer to themselves as "Islamic State." These *takfiri*, al-Qaʿida -type figures also use Islam as their conceptual framework and are thus often (poorly) described as Islamists; however, they act upon that framework through violent and radical means. To consider al-Ghannouchi the same as Ayman al-Zawahiri or Abu Bakr al-Baghdadi simply because they share the same faith is an insult to scholarship as well as a great world religion and civilization.

One reason why this work's focus on Muslim intellectual history is important is because it is impossible to properly understand the successes or failures of Political Islam in the contemporary, post-Arab Spring Middle East without first understanding the history of ideas from which Political Islam emerged. Accordingly, I begin Part One by contextualizing for the reader the crisis facing Muslim intellectuals and reformers in the modern era. I then build upon this context to establish a conceptual framework linking the four modes of renewal and reform in the modern era to changing Muslim evaluations of the West in that period. Each of these modes was a function of shifting Muslim evaluations of the West and modernity.

Based upon this framework of crisis and shifting evaluations of the West, Part Two is a history of Sunni Islamic reformist movements beginning in 1798, primarily in the Arab Middle East. This is a history that elucidates the Muslim intellectual's sense of crisis and focuses on reformers' resistance to despotism and increasing concerns for representative and accountable government. I then demonstrate in Part Three how prominent Islamists have reinvented certain Islamic concepts to invent the tradition of an Islamic state based upon a social contract.

By nature of their doctrine, Islamists view the Prophet and his companions as the ideal model of human endeavor. Furthermore, all invented traditions are expressed by their inventors as being rooted in a particular place in the past. Therefore, in Part Four I provide examples from the historical period surrounding the Prophet Muhammad at Medina that are drawn upon today by Islamists in providing foundation for their political philosophy and the invented tradition of an Islamic state.

This is a study of Political Islam from the perspective of the movement itself. While any modern Islamic movement should, and must, be interpreted in the context of the interaction of Islam and the West in the modern era, too often this is the only context in which such studies are written. This tendency has led to the proliferation of market-driven, sensationalist, or superficial literature on the subject. Much of this literature is consumed by issues that have little practical significance – such as trying to explain what is "wrong" with Muslims, or whether democracy is compatible with religiously informed political thought, especially Islam. Certainly, some scholars will be unsatisfied that in this work I do not attempt to engage with Western philosophers' concepts of social contract or even democracy.

Granted, that many Islamic activists today claim democracy as Islamic in origin encourages scholars to become mired in comparisons. However, the significance of such claims is not whether they are accurate in terms of history or political theory. Rather, the significance is that they are even being made in the first place, and, furthermore, that they form the basis of a movement that garners massive followings and has a profound impact on the world stage and its players. Political Islam is an innovative and dynamic movement seeking to answer the most pressing issues facing Muslims today, and it continues to play a decisive role in the world; it is, therefore, crucial to understand its actors as they understand themselves.

PART ONE

Context, Framework, and Labels

The Islamic world did not decline because of colonization, it was colonized because it had declined to the point of being colonizable.

-Muslim convert Murad Wilfried Hoffman

The crisis of the Muslim intellectual in the modern era

The world into which Abu Taleb Khan traveled in February 1799 must have seemed strange. He had journeyed far. Born in Lucknow in 1752 of mixed Iranian and Turkish descent, he had built a storied career serving British government officials in colonial India. Fond of the third person, he remains known to historians as "the wanderer over the face of the earth, Abu Taleb, the son of Mohammed of Ispahan." This colorful self-description begins his memoir, in which he recorded: "Owing to several adverse circumstances, finding it inconvenient to remain at home, he was compelled to undertake many tedious journeys, during which he associated with men of all nations and beheld various wonders."[1]

The Travels of Mirza Abu Taleb Khan is significant not simply because it is one of the first accounts of an educated Muslim observing Europe, but also because it reflects important themes of world history in the modern era, a period generally assumed to have begun around the year 1500.[2] One of these themes is the relative nature of the dramatically shifting structure of geopolitical power on the world stage. These shifts in geopolitical power led many Muslim intellectuals of the late modern era to reflect upon the uneven and asymmetric nature of military, political, and economic developments in their own society. Khan's work, then, remains important because it foreshadows the contemporary Islamic resurgence of movements of renewal and reform (*tajdid* and *islah*) that have sought to rehabilitate the place of the *umma*, the worldwide community of Muslims, in history.

"He was of the opinion," noted Khan in his characteristic third person, "that many of the customs, inventions, sciences, and ordinances of Europe, the good effects of which are apparent in those countries, might with great advantage be imitated by the Mohammedans." In his memoir, Khan's praise is reserved almost entirely for material aspects of the West; his critique of Western moral standards forms another important element of his work. Throughout, Khan is revealed as a discerning and objective analyst. He does not pander apologetically to European aristocracy for personal aggrandizement. "The first and greatest defect I observed in the English," he wrote, "is their want of faith in religion."[3]

The critique of the West in moral terms and embrace of the West in material terms foreshadows yet another important aspect of the contemporary Islamic resurgence of renewal and reform. This resurgence was a response to the challenges posed by European powers. In his memoir, Khan presents Europe's power as a function of modernity – secular, materialistic, and industrial. His memoir is thus symbolic of the way in which modernity first challenged the *umma*. Though culminating in the actual physical occupation of nearly all Muslim lands, the challenge of modernity began as an intellectual process aimed at incorporating the Ottoman Empire and other societies into the European-dominated world economy.[4] By the time Abu Taleb Khan was being greeted in the courts of English aristocrats as "the Persian Prince," this process was well under way, and soon there was no denying the military, political, and economic superiority of the Western powers, including Russia, over Muslim states.

The uneven and asymmetric path toward modernization is the core issue behind the crisis of the Muslim intellectual in the modern era. This is a crisis characterized by intense intellectual introspection regarding the place of the *umma* in history and the seemingly inexorable ascension of Western hegemony. Certainly, European hegemony over the world was not the case for all of history; it is perhaps better understood as an exception. At the beginning of the modern era, each of the "Great Powers" was relatively equal. As historian Paul Kennedy wrote in *The Rise and Fall of the Great Powers*, at around the year 1500 "it was by no means obvious to the inhabitants of Europe that their continent was poised to dominate much of the rest of the earth."[5]

In fact, it might easily be concluded that the Ottomans were the "greatest" of the "Great Powers" in the late fifteenth and the sixteenth century. In this period, the Muslim world had the most influence on other societies throughout the world, not only because of its central location, but also because of its military strength, political and religious tolerance, cultural sophistication, and economic prosperity. The superior Ottoman military machine allowed the Empire to rapidly and continuously expand. For example, the lush, strategically placed city of Constantinople, which had been a symbol of European power for hundreds of years, fell to the Ottomans in 1453. This was only one victory during a period that saw the vast expansion of *dar al-Islam*, the House of Islam.

After the conquest of Byzantium the superbly trained and outfitted Ottoman armies conquered Greece and all the Ionian Islands, Bosnia, Albania, and much of the rest of the Balkans – all before 1500. Shortly thereafter, they marched on the European power centers of Budapest and Vienna. To the south, the Ottomans pressed startlingly close to the papacy in Rome. In 1512 they conquered Moldavia; in 1516 they conquered Syria; in 1517 they conquered Egypt; in 1529 the Turks were, yet again, laying siege to Vienna; in 1571 they took Cyprus, expanding their control throughout the Mediterranean; and by 1584 they would re-secure their presence in Crimea and most of present-day Ukraine. The Ottomans thus controlled the all-critical trade routes stretching from the Indies and South Asia, through much of the eastern Mediterranean, and most of the Black Sea.

Even outside the Ottoman Empire the House of Islam was prospering. To the East, the Safavid dynasty under Ismail I (1500-1524) and Abbas I (1587-1629) was experiencing an incredible flourishing of Iranian high culture and geopolitical influence. Most of the fabled Silk Road, the crucial commercial artery connecting East and West, was controlled by an interconnected chain of Muslim Mongol khanates. The most powerful states in West Africa, Bornu, Sokoto, and Timbuktu, all Muslim, were the center of massive trading outposts responsible for rich intercultural exchanges. The Hindu Empire in Java fell to Muslim expansion in the early 1500s, unlocking massive economic potential. On the Indian subcontinent, Babur, the King of Kabul, established the Muslim Moghul Empire in 1526. Under Babur's grandson, Akbar (1556-1605), the Moghul Empire would expand from Baluchistan to Bengal.

In non-military terms, too, the *umma* was thriving. Since long before 1500, the world of Islam had surpassed the world of Christendom in culture (especially political and religious tolerance), technology, and literacy. For hundreds of years, all of the most advanced knowledge in mathematics, medicine, philosophy, and the sciences in general was written in the Arabic language and housed in the ornate libraries of Baghdad and Damascus. Indeed, it was the Arabs, mostly Muslims but some Jews and Christians as well, who translated important works from the ancient classicists, such as Aristotle, that had been long lost in Europe. In terms of expansion by proselytism, the number of converts at the hands of Christian missionaries in this period paled in comparison to the vast increase in numbers of Muslim converts throughout Africa and the Indies.

In no small part, this was due to the enormous cultural attraction of Muslim societies. Cities throughout Muslim lands were, comparatively speaking, superior to those throughout Europe in terms of infrastructure, technology, institutions of higher learning, and libraries. "In mathematics, cartography, medicine, and many other aspects of science and industry - in mills, guncasting, lighthouses, horsebreeding," noted Kennedy, "the Muslims had enjoyed a lead" for centuries. Muslim artists in this period were among the most prolific and internationally renowned. The present-day genre of visual arts known as "Persian miniatures," which began in the fourteenth century, was especially sought after. From this genre would emerge those of formal illustration, pen-and-ink, and fine portraiture. So, too, did Muslims dominate the field of fine architecture. The creativity and artistry that was allowed to flourish in what was the most open and pluralistic society at the time led to breathtaking examples of this, such as the Taj Mahal in India, the construction of which was completed in 1653.[6]

Given all of this, the late world historian Marshall Hodgson, preeminent in his field, was not overstating his case when he wrote that if a visitor from Mars arrived on the Earth in the sixteenth century he might well have concluded that the human world was on the verge of becoming Muslim. "He would have based his judgment partly on the strategic and political advantages of the Muslims," wrote Hodgson, "but partly also on the vitality of their general culture."[7]

Had that same visitor from Mars returned a few hundred years later, however, he would likely have reached a far different conclusion. From its height of socio-cultural and political eminence, the Muslim world's social, political, and military power would begin to decline after about the year 1700. Its decline would continue, its rate increasing, for the next several hundred years. The late renowned historian of Islamic history Albert Hourani put this into perspective. He noted that Ottoman power, in terms of geopolitics, had been so far superior to Europe or China that it was not until the early eighteenth century that they would begin to deal with European states on a level of diplomatic equality, rather than the level of superiority they had been accustomed to for so long. By 1800 the geopolitical power structure of the world had changed dramatically. For the Ottomans, the first sign of this new reality came in the form of the Treaty of Kucuk-Kaynarca. This treaty, following a war with Russia lasting from 1768-1774, forced the Ottomans to surrender to non-Muslims control over a group of Muslim people, the Crimean Tatars, for the first time in the history of Islam.[8]

Already by 1900 the leading European powers dominated all interstate relations – political and economic and intellectual. Marshall Hodgson described this "immediately decisive rise in the level of social power" as "the ability for European enterprises, such as firms or churches or, of course, governments" to exert a level of influence that could not be matched by "even the most wealthy or vigorous peoples in the rest of the world."[9] This sudden disparity in the world balance of power was not completely a blessing for those European states that exercised it. The slow but seemingly inexorable rise of the West had, for centuries, relied upon certain foundations of the Ottoman Empire, such as the trade routes that formed an international commercial nexus. The decline of the Ottoman Empire, and the *umma* more generally, on the world stage was, therefore, a significant point of concern for European powers. The debate over this issue – which included the Ottomans themselves - became known as the "Eastern Question." This was the predominant subject of international affairs throughout the nineteenth century, and it remained so until the conclusion of the First World War.[10]

According to the famous Eleventh Edition of the *Encyclopedia Britannica* (1910-1911), the "Eastern Question is the expression in diplomacy from about the time of the Congress of Verona [1822] to comprehend the international problems involved in the decay of the Turkish [Ottoman] Empire and its supposed impending dissolution." An exchange one January evening in 1853 between Nicholas I, Emperor of Russia, and Hamilton Seymour, Minister Plenipotentiary of the Queen of England to the Court of St. Petersburg, reveals the mindset of the European powers regarding the Eastern

Question. Privately taking aside the Minister, Tsar Nicholas said to him:

> The affairs of Turkey are in a very disorganized condition. The country itself seems to be falling to pieces. The fall will be a great misfortune, and it is very important that England and Russia should come to a perfectly good understanding upon these affairs...Note, that we have a sick man in our arms, a very sick man. It will be, I tell you frankly, a great misfortune, if one of these days he disappears, especially before all of the necessary dispositions are taken.[11]

Though perhaps not entirely conscious of it when he spoke them, Nicholas's words are symbolic to the historian. The Great Powers thought the Ottomans sick and dying because they were not modern; in the arms of the Europeans, the 'sick' Turks would be nursed back to health only if they joined the "political, legal, commercial, scientific, and military culture" of modernity that was presented to the world under the de facto leadership of Great Britain. The example of Russia's role in the debate over the 'Eastern Question' is illustrative of this. Russia was at this point considered part of the European Great Powers because in recent decades it had been reorganized strictly according to the Western European military model and mode of industrial production.

'Sickness' in international politics or societies is a subjective quality and quite relative. Certainly, it does not denote a deficiency in any particular group of people or religion. Rather, it is both a cause and effect of the world historical theme of the asymmetric development of societies throughout all of history. Nor is this concept particular to the Ottoman Empire. As historian David Goldfrank points out, the multinational Ottoman Empire in 1853 was 'sick' for the same basic reasons the multinational Soviet Union was 'sick' in the 1980s. The same might even be said about the Roman Empire in the fourth and fifth centuries, or even China under the Ming Dynasty. The Ottoman economy was neither modern nor remotely competitive in terms of industry or manufacturing; its education system was crumbling and consisted, to a large extent, only of religious learning; its army and navy, though large, were economically and technically incapable of matching those of Europe.[12]

Albert Hourani concluded that, in the centuries leading up to the First World War, which saw the dissolution of the Empire, the Ottomans had made little to no advances in technology, especially when applied to military efficacy, and there had been a steady decline in the level of scientific knowledge. Given the unprecedented ways in which the Europeans were using technology and science to enhance their military power, the relative weaknesses of the Ottoman military were especially important. Indeed, as the late sociologist Charles Tilly once famously observed, "War made the state and the state made war." Each of the most important functions of state power in the eighteenth and nineteenth centuries – commerce, slave trading, scientific exploration, colonialism – depended upon military, especially naval, power. The decline of the once mighty Ottoman military machine was first made evident by the failure of their armies to capture Vienna in 1683, which was followed by the continued collapse of its military in subsequent campaigns, such as the loss of the Crimea in 1774.[13]

The collapse of the Ottoman military coincided with the crumbling of the cultural traits that had once made the Ottomans eminent on the world stage. Though the Muslim community in the form of different empires was at one point in world history the leader of science, the opposite was true in the modern period. The Europeans, long silent under the yoke of the so-called Dark Ages, were now making the most advanced scientific discoveries. "The astronomical theories associated with the name of Copernicus were mentioned for the first time, and then only briefly, in Turkish at the end of the seventeenth century," wrote Hourani, "and the advances in European medicine were only slowly coming to be known in the eighteenth."[14] This reversal in the level of scientific knowledge reflects the theme of uneven and asymmetric military, economic, and cultural development.

A study of world industrialization levels also reflects this same theme. Industrialization is measured in terms of world historical economic factors, which include all sorts of machinery, railroads, steamships, wrought-iron bridges, iron-framed buildings, circulation of newspapers and other printed materials, the telegraph, mass production of rifles and other armaments, artillery, and naval vessels. The late economic historian Paul Bairoch provided the definitive treatment of comparative international industrialization levels between the years 1750 and 1980. Taking into account that Bairoch was writing when the label "Third World" was still feasible in its use and implications, among his conclusions is that, whereas per capita levels of industrialization in Europe and what would become the "Third World" were quite similar in 1750 (8 percent and 7 percent, respectively), by 1900 the latter's was only one-eighteenth of the former's (2 percent to 35 percent).

Furthermore, the total per capita level of industrialization of the entire "Third World" in 1900 was *one-fiftieth* of Great Britain alone (2 percent to 100 percent). By 1850, the weakest of the major European powers was still well advanced in terms of industrialization over any non-Western society, except Japan. By 1860 the members of the future "developed world," whose inhabitants comprised only 28% of the world population, had achieved a level of production far exceeding the total *world* industrial output in 1750.[15]

Returning to Paul Kennedy's observation, it is likely that, in the year 1500, Europeans would never have imagined that, by the twentieth century, there would be in their favor such a disparity in the levels of world geopolitical power. The path toward modernization, as the previous historical contextualization demonstrates, is not one of unitary linear development. The crisis, or crises, of Muslim intellectuals in the modern era, then, is that the place of the *umma* in history tended to be conceptualized within an analytical framework of unitary linear development, rather than the uneven and asymmetric twists and turns toward development that history demonstrates to be the norm, not the exception.

Many important Muslim intellectuals, most of them Arab, have written about this sense of crisis. "For years and even decades," writes Ibrahim M. Abu-Rabi', "Arab intellectuals on the Left and Right had been speaking about 'crisis' (*azmah*), its meaning, causes and ways to overcome it." As will be demonstrated throughout this work, Abu-Rabi' writes that this crisis stemmed from the juxtaposition between the formulations of "tradition versus modernity, *umma* versus nation, secularism versus divine sovereignty, democracy versus dictatorship, criticism versus quietism."[16]

One of the most important intellectuals in this regard was the Algerian scholar Malek Bennabi (1905-1973). The quintessential work, written by a Muslim intellectual, about the crisis of the Muslim intellectual in the modern era is Bennabi's *Islam in History and Society*. First published in French in 1954, Bennabi argued that the uneven development of the *umma* in the modern period is a consequence of factors that do not "come from outside but from within." As he argued, "An analysis of the causes of inhibition that hamper the evolution of the Muslim world would reveal that they are overwhelmingly the result of the internal factors, that is, of colonisibility." Bennabi thus introduced the concept of "colonizability," which he argued was the true essence of the crisis of the Muslim intellectual – not colonization itself. "For ceasing to be colonized," he wrote, "one must cease to be colonisable."[17]

Another important work in this regard is *The Crisis of the Arab Intellectual*, published first in 1974, by the Moroccan historian Abdallah Laroui (1933-). Laroui contextualized his argument within the framework of the competing forces of "traditionalism" and "historicism." For Laroui, the failure of Arab (mostly Muslim) intellectuals to wrestle with the challenge of history had only one consequence: "failure to see the real." He wrote that history, as past and present structure, must be used to inform the present situation. "Ahistorical thinking," as he termed it, has had the effect on Muslim intellectuals of "confirming dependence on all levels." "Dependency, visible or concealed, means not only exploitation, loss of liberty, and damage to the pride and material interests of a nation," wrote Laroui, "but also and above all the continuance and exacerbation of historical retardation."[18]

The concept of a self-created crisis, either Laroui's "dependency" or Bennabi's "colonizability," was not the domain only of Arab intellectuals. Some of the most profound works regarding this concept were written by the Indian-Muslim scholar of religion Sayyid Abu'l Hasan 'Ali Nadwi (1914-1999). Nadwi's most influential work was published in English in 1950 with the title *Islam and the World*. Yet, the English translation of its original Arabic title, *What Did the World Lose with the Decline of Islam?*, is perhaps most illustrative of the content of the work. Only forty years after its publication in English it was already in its fifteenth edition, and it has remained an important contribution to modern Islamic thought. One essay written by Nadwi, "Muslim Decadence and Revival," draws upon portions of *Islam and the World,* and presents an unsparing critique of Muslim society under the Ottomans.[19] "The greatest error the Ottomans made was they allowed their minds to become static," he wrote, before noting that this observation was not peculiar to the Ottomans. "Muslims, universally, had grown inert both mentally and spiritually." He continued:

> Excessive conservatism and servility to tradition also robbed poetry and literature of its freshness. Language became heavy with embellishments. Even personal letters, official notes, memoranda, and royal edicts were not free from defect. The madrasas and other institutions of learning were afflicted with an inferiority complex, which degraded lit-

erature and thought. Classics were gradually expelled from the syllabi, and their place was taken by the compilations of latter-day writers who lacked the originality of thought and were merely blind imitators or interpreters of the old masters. Classical texts written by early scholars were replaced by annotations and commentaries, in the compilation of which the authors practiced extreme economy and reduced them to mere notes.

Nadwi continued to observe that, while Muslim societies throughout the world were experiencing a period of relative decline, Europe "was making colossal scientific and industrial progress." He notes that in terms of shipbuilding, Europe had made enormous technological breakthroughs, and the Ottomans did not begin building ships that could compete with newly outfitted European navies until the sixteenth century. The printing press, the most current medical practices, and military academies were not established in the Ottoman Empire until the seventeenth century. "Toward the end of the eighteenth century," wrote Nadwi, "when a balloon was seen flying over Constantinople, the Turks thought it was a magic trick."[20]

Nadwi's essay, like the work of Laroui and Bennabi, is significant because it demonstrates the concept of asymmetric modernization and development. The preceding historical contextualization of this concept is important because it is impossible to understand the contemporary Islamic resurgence of reformist movements, especially the emergence of Political Islam, without first understanding this sense of crisis.

Muslim evaluations of the West in the modern era

The uneven development of the *umma* and its place in modern world history prompted a resurgence of Islamic reform in the modern era rooted in the long-refined concepts of *tajdid* and *islah*, renewal and reform. Though perennial themes, the quest for authenticity in reform and the continuous renewal of the *umma* have manifested in different ways at different points throughout the Muslim historical experience.

In the seventh century, the Prophet Muhammad and his companions sought to reform the early *umma* according to the revelations of the Qur'an and guard against unnecessary pagan or Jewish influence. In the thirteenth century, the jurist-scholar Ibn Taymiyya sought reforms based on his perception of a more authentic Islam to renew the vitality of the *umma* after the Mongol sacking of Baghdad in 1258. Later, the Ottomans sought to restore the pristine nature of the Islamic caliphate. Each of these examples was the result of a confluence of different world historical circumstances and each spawned unique reformist movements. Renewal and reform in the modern Middle East, though not organizationally linked to these early examples, is, nonetheless, deeply rooted in this important tradition.[21]

Napoleon Bonaparte's invasion of Egypt in 1798 began a new phase in the history of Islamic reform. As Ibrahim Abu-Rabi' put it, "The colonized Arabs and their intellectual elite were bewildered by the progress of their colonizers and at the same time were alerted to their own outdated modes of structure and thought."[22] By opening a new intellectual space that allowed for the unprecedented transmission of European ideas throughout the Muslim world, and by demonstrating the superiority of the French military, the invasion prompted Muslim intellectuals to question why and how they had become colonizable. For the educated elite, the invasion was so bewildering because from the earliest Islamic conquests of the Prophet Muhammad until Napoleon's invasion, the overwhelming majority of the world's Muslims enjoyed relatively linear political, cultural, military, and economic development. Furthermore, the world's Muslims had generally lived free of political and military threats from non-Muslim societies.

Even the Crusades, so firmly entrenched in the Christian historical experience, were peripheral when considered from a Muslim viewpoint within the vast *dar al-Islam*. Though the Crusaders did invade spiritually important lands, these invasions were limited in geographical depth and did not long survive. The dominant political concern for most Muslims during that historical period was the threat from brutal Mongol invasions; unlike the Crusaders, the Mongol invasion of Baghdad in 1258 overthrew the Abbasid caliphate, the seat of Muslim power for more than 500 years. But even then, by the late 1200s the ruling Mongol dynasties in Central Asia and the Middle East (three out of four Mongol khanates) had converted to Islam and embarked upon an age of Islamic expansion from Hungary to Indonesia that lasted roughly 400 years. Even the Spanish *Reconquista*, the expulsion of Muslim rule from the Iberian Peninsula, was a relatively insignificant loss compared to the concurrent Muslim destruction of the Christian Byzantine Empire and the 'Islamization' of Anatolia.[23]

As Albert Hourani wrote in his introduction to *The Modern Middle East*, "All divisions of the continuum of historical time are bound to some extent to be arbitrary, but the changes which have taken place in the Middle East, as in the rest of the world, during the last two centuries have been so great and have gone so deep that they can be regarded as forming a new and distinctive period in the history of the world."[24] Most scholars agree with Hourani that the period of the 'modern Middle East' began toward the end of the eighteenth century – exactly when is sometimes debated. Napoleon's 1798 invasion of Egypt, or simply 1800, is used by many as a convenient starting point for the historical narrative. Of course, this periodization should be assumed in a somewhat generic sense, because the Ottoman military reforms of Selim III in the early part of the century, for example, can be interpreted as an important sign of a new age in Middle East history.[25] The fall of the Safavids in present-day Iran in 1723 could be used as a similar starting point; the same could be said about the decline of the Moghul Empire in India around the same time.

Regardless, renewal and reform gained newfound legitimacy and urgency in the years following Napoleon's invasion because after this point, non-Muslims (Europeans) came to exercise hegemony over all Muslim peoples. Time and again it was demonstrated that the Europeans, should they agree on a policy, had the power to enforce their will in Muslim lands, something unprecedented in the Muslim historical experience.[26] That the Europeans were able to exert complete hegemony over all Muslim peoples might seem an overstatement. However, as the eminent world historian Immanuel Wallerstein concluded, what allows for the correct use of the term *hegemonic* "is that for a certain period [Europeans] were able to establish the rules of the game in the interstate system, to dominate the world-economy (in production, commerce, and finance), to get their way politically with a minimal use of military force (which however they had in goodly strength), and to formulate the cultural language with which one discussed the world."[27]

Before Napoleon's invasion, European development was quite uneven. Its ability to display power in Africa, the Far East and the Middle East had been growing, but was not yet decisive, overwhelming, or regular enough to be considered hegemonic. Napoleon's invasion thus signifies the beginning of the ability of the leading European powers to impose their dominance throughout the world. The decisively unique aspect of the Islamic resurgence of renewal and reform in the modern Middle East, as has been described by the Muslims that have shaped it, is that it occurred in direct response to the challenge of modernity, which was carried throughout the *umma* by the very ships and soldiers it had created.[28]

The intellectual history of Sunni Islam since 1798 is one characterized by transitions and reinventions of traditional Islamic concepts regarding basic questions of identity, loyalty, and sociopolitical organization. The uneven experience of development and modernization for the *umma* in the modern era, coupled with the ascension of European hegemony, led to a growing sense of psychological dislocation for many Muslims between the experience of the *umma* in world history and the Muslim sense of crisis in the modern era. Indeed, already in the earliest years of the nineteenth century there were "alert and respected Muslims to declare that Europeans were leading a better life by Islamic standards than were the Muslim societies themselves." This sense of crisis, expressing itself in different modes, culminated in the years after the First World War with the Western imposition of the secular nation-state as the basic political operating unit in Muslim lands – a concept foreign to the Muslim historical experience – and the abolition of the Caliphate in 1924.[29]

The classic scholarly statement regarding this grand narrative of the Muslim experience in modern world history, that summarizes the general perception of both Muslim and non-Muslim writers from the time, was written by Wilfred Cantwell Smith in 1957. He wrote:

> The fundamental *malaise* of modern Islam is a sense that something has gone wrong with Islamic history. The fundamental problem of modern Muslims is how to rehabilitate that history.[30]

Smith's statement cannot be dismissed as a misguided Orientalist trope because it expresses the very essence of the work of Islamic activists in modern history. It remains the definitive statement at the heart of the contemporary Islamic revival.[31] The efforts of Muslim reformers have taken different forms throughout the past two centuries, and, of course, any periodization of this history is bound to be somewhat arbitrary. Yet, the basic trajectory of the most dominant modes of renewal and reform since 1798 is: the

Tanzimat mode of Westernizing existing institutions; the modernist mode of increasingly discriminatory, Islamically-oriented adaptation; the secular-nationalist mode; and the fundamentalist-style mode prompted by the perceived failure of the West and the package of modernity.

Each of these modes of reform can be broken down into different styles of action and interaction, and each emerged under the auspices of different, perpetually changing local contexts. While understanding the micro-history of the different local social, political, and economic contexts that shaped each individual reformer's thought is important, these different local contexts can be misunderstood – and their broader significance missed – if not placed within a grand narrative of the intellectual history of the Sunni Muslim community in the modern world. As Mansoor Moaddel concludes in his book *Islamic Modernism, Nationalism, and Fundamentalism*:

> These intellectual leaders – be it Islamic modernists, liberal nationalists, national royalists, liberal Arabists, Arab nationalists, or Islamic fundamentalists – were all part of a larger saga of the systematic cultural encounters between the West and Islam that started sometime around the turn of the nineteenth century and are still going on.[32]

The assumption by Muslim intellectuals of a unitary linear model of development and modernization, subsumed within the Western model, can be nuanced by understanding the evolving evaluation of Muslim attitudes toward the West. To be certain, there never has been a single, monolithic view of 'the West,' and Muslim evaluations of 'the West' have evolved significantly throughout the past few centuries. However, at any given time the most influential reformist visions have dealt fundamentally with an evaluation of the Western experience in the Islamic context. As Ibrahim Abu-Rabi' characterizes this, "To grapple with the meaning of the modern self, that is, the Muslim self, is to grapple by definition with the meaning of the Other, that is, the West."[33] Therefore, the transitions and reinventions of concepts and symbols in modern Islamic reformist movements must be understood as part of a general framework of changing Muslim evaluations of the West.

In the eighteenth century, Muslim attitudes toward the West were generally apathetic. While there certainly had been various strategic threats in the military sense of global geopolitics between

Muslim empires and foreign powers, as a concept or conceptual entity the West played "little or no role in the thinking of the leaders of major movements of renewal."³⁴ The writings of the famous Egyptian historian al-Jabarti, especially his first-hand account of Napoleon's invasion and occupation of Egypt, demonstrate this well. Throughout al-Jabarti's chronicle there are lengthy discussions about the French invasion, occupation, and, ultimately, the French departure from Egypt. Yet it contains very little, if any, engagement with the basic principles of French thought, history, politics, economy, or military power – all-important factors that allowed the French to occupy Egypt in the first place.

Even Nabil Matar, who sought to nuance this historical generalization with his work *Europe Through Arab Eyes*, admits that his scholarship leaves one question unanswered: "Why was it that throughout the early modern period, Magharibi – and generally Arabic – knowledge about Europeans remained by far narrower in scope than European knowledge about the Muslim world?" The same question can, of course, be asked about non-Arabic speaking Muslims. Matar acknowledges the characteristic apathy of Muslim attitudes toward the West, and admits that the majority of sources in his work, which are North African, were the exception. "The reason for the Magharibi emphasis," he writes, "is the distinctive culture that prevailed in that region, dictated by its geographic proximity to Europe and its changing demography after the arrival of hundreds of thousands of expelled European/Christianized Muslims, the Moriscos, throughout the sixteenth century." Matar continues to state: "The separation of Morocco from the Ottoman Empire and the Arabic linguistic continuity and cultural autonomy that persisted in the North African regencies produced a Magharibi interest in, and reaction to, Europe that was quite different from that of the rest of the Islamic world."³⁵

A sense of apathy is also evident in the writings of Abu Taleb Khan. For example, the renowned scholar of South Asia Stephen Hay concluded:

> *The Travels of Mirza Abu Taleb Khan* ... gives us unique insight into the reactions of an aristocratic Indian Muslim to English life. For the most part a careful account of the curiosities and customs he observed, the book is remarkably barren of reflections on the cultural and religious foundations of Western civilization, leaving the impression that as a Muslim he regarded them as unworthy of serious attention.³⁶

The characteristic general apathy toward the West began to change by the end of the eighteenth century. The relative ease with which Napoleon and his troops and sailors were able to occupy Egypt presented Muslims at the time with a vision of a triumphant and successful Western model. For many Egyptians, this model sharply contrasted against their society, especially the inability of the Ottoman government to protect its provinces. The Tanzimat mode of renewal and reform emerged in this period in the context of not only an increasingly favorable attitude toward borrowing the West.

Reformers in this period basically sought to explain the reasons for the apparent strength and superiority of the West on the world stage. This strength was demonstrated to Muslim intellectuals not only by the French invasion and occupation of Egypt, but many other European military advances, such as the case of Russian control of the Crimea. They also sought to demonstrate that Muslims could adopt certain Western ideas and methods while remaining true to their faith. In the Tanzimat mode of reform, then, the West was viewed as an effective partner and guide, and reform in this time sought to improve, by strict Westernization, already existing institutions. As the Muslim scholar Ibrahim Abu-Lughod noted, reformers of the Tanzimat mode tended to operate within the confines of "hoping to obtain a favorable verdict from the invisible jury of the West."[37]

The concept of a Western invisible jury continued to play an important role in renewal and reform throughout the nineteenth century. The modernist mode of reform, which emerged in the second half of the century, fit squarely within the intellectual confines of Western intellectual hegemony. Frequently, its most prominent intellectuals, like Jamal al-Din al-Afghani or Muhammad ʿAbduh, argued defensively and apologetically with Western philosophers and critics of Islam. The most prominent example of such debates was the exchange between al-Afghani and Ernest Renan over the French philosopher's critique of Islam and rational thought.[38] The Modernists thus sought to demonstrate that many of the most vaunted aspects of modernity – like reason, rational thought, constitutionalism, and scientific investigation – were not in opposition to Islam. As the sociologist and historian of religions Charles Kurzman described, "The authors and activists engaged in this movement [Islamic Modernism] saw the tension between Islamic faith and modern values as a historical accident, not an inherent feature of Islam."[39]

As a movement, Islamic Modernism was 'modern' because it was a product of 'modernity'; it was 'modernist' because it propounded 'modernity.' The basic goal of renewal and reform in this mode was thus the modernization of Islam itself, but toward the last years of the nineteenth century, it also became characterized by more discriminatory evaluations of the West and modernity. In this sense, certain aspects of the West were deemed desirable, while other aspects were rejected in whole. It was quite common in this era for Muslim intellectuals to positively regard material or political aspects of the West, but reject aspects of Western morality.[40]

The events surrounding the historical period of the First World War led to significant transitions in Islamic reform. The war caused fundamental physical changes to the nature of the *umma*. The imposition of the secular nation-state and the abolishment of the Caliphate reoriented the basic unit of analysis in Islamic thought from *umma* to *dawla*, an Arabic word that was reinvented in this time to denote the European concept of state. In this context, two new modes of renewal and reform emerged from Islamic Modernism: the secular-nationalist mode and the fundamentalist-style mode. Each continued the growing discernment of Muslim evaluations of the West.

The secular-nationalist mode of reform operated within the confines of the European concept of nation-state, but it was also characterized by more frequent negative evaluations of the West. Jamal ʿAbd al-Nasir remains the most prominent example of this mode of engagement. However, while Nasir and other secular nationalists rejected Western hegemony, they did not necessarily reject Western modernity. Rather, many operated within the framework of what has become known as "alternative modernities." Nasir's actions and rhetoric demonstrated to many that conformity to a prevailing norm does not necessarily mean conformity to the form that norm has taken elsewhere.

The fundamentalist-style mode of renewal and reform was rooted in the growing sense among many Muslims throughout the twentieth century that the Western model was imperfect and not entirely successful. The intellectuals in this mode began to develop a model of modernization and development for their own society that was divorced from the unitary model of the linear experience of the West in the modern era. Rather than thinking in terms of the Western experience with modernity, the fundamentalist-style mode of reformers began to think in terms of a distinctly Islamic modernity. This was augmented by the growing disenchantment of many Muslims with their own governments, many of which were based off Western ideology and allied with Western governments. Many different world historical events between the First and Second World Wars led both Muslims and non-Muslims throughout the world to question whether the West provided the most effective model of modernity.

For example, the savagery and destruction of the two world wars raised basic questions about the Western political and military model. The global economic depressions that occurred in the inter-war period raised questions regarding the model of a capitalist world economy. More present than political and economic condemnations, however, is the persistent theme that the West, and in particular the United States, had lost its moral hegemony. The expert on the history of interaction between Islam and the West Yvonne Haddad characterized this eloquently. In revivalist literature, she wrote, the West and the United States is generally perceived as being bankrupt in terms of morality and social values. She continued:

> The west, therefore, is no longer a model to be emulated. Rising crime rates, race riots, substance abuse, AIDS, pornography, unfortunate consequences of the feminist movement such as the breakdown of the family and pregnancy outside of marriage, social and economic inequality and inequity, and many other ills plague the very structure of American life.[41]

In the fundamentalist-style mode of renewal and reform, even the communist and socialist alternatives to Western modernity were deemed as failures. "From the perspective of global history," wrote John Voll, "communism and radical socialism is as much a Western model as liberalism and capitalism, and Lenin as much a product of the West as Woodrow Wilson."[42] For reformers of the fundamentalist-style mode, this concept was made more apparent in the years following the Second World War, which saw the failure of communism and socialism throughout the world. Furthermore, the fundamentalist-style mode was especially vindicated in the eyes of many Muslims in this period because of the continued failure of many socialist or communist based governments in Muslim countries to deliver event he most basic functions of sound governance to their citizens.

In the years after the Second World War, the fundamentalist-style mode was further vindicated by the continued success of Israel. Many Muslims perceived the Israelis, having based the identity of their state on their religious heritage, as providing an alternative modernity to the original, Western model, which was generally quite secular. Israel's apparent superiority over its Muslim neighboring countries ostensibly proved correct those fundamentalist-style reformers who postulated that God was punishing Muslims for turning their backs on the Islamic faith and placing it instead in alien systems like nationalism, socialism, or communism. The 1967 and 1973 wars, as well as the world oil boycotts led by Saudi Arabia, strengthened this perception. Henry Kissinger stated that these events altered irrevocably the world as it had grown up in the postwar period.

For many Muslims in the 1970s, Kissinger's observation was especially true. "The oil boom had shown the vulnerability of the West more dramatically than anything in the past five centuries. By confirming Islam in the eyes of many, it prepared the way for the Islamic movements of the 1970s" that questioned not whether Muslims could survive in the contemporary world, but whether *the West* could survive in the contemporary world.[43]

As the events surrounding the First World War had reinvented the basic analytical framework of Islamic reform, so too did the concept of 'the failure of the West.' No longer was it necessary for renewal and form to take place within the confines of Western thought; therefore, the basic project of reform in the late twentieth century no longer sought to modernize Islam, as had been the case since the Tanzimat era. Rather, the goal of renewal and reform in the fundamentalist-style mode was the Islamization of modernity. From a global perspective, this shift was part of changing understandings of modernity itself. "Modernity in the age of empires and nationalisms was conceived as the modernity of Western Europe and North America," wrote John Voll. "However, by the 1960s, it was clear that modernity could take many different forms."[44]

Political Islam emerged as a function of this particular world historical context. The intellectuals who label themselves "Islamists," "Political Islamists," or even "Islamic activists" view Islam as providing a total and comprehensive alternative to Western modernity and a complete blueprint for socio-political organization. As such, they argue that Islam is a system encompassing all aspects of life – including a particular form of state and government. Therefore, the basic conceptual framework of Western thought can be, although is not always, disavowed. The continued failure of Western-style secular governments throughout the last decades of the twentieth century in the Middle East and elsewhere in the Muslim world augmented the positions of Political Islam. Many Muslims began to consider their own governments illegitimate for being insufficiently Islamic in character. When Khalid Islambouli shot and killed Egyptian President Anwar al-Sadat in 1981, for example, he shouted, "I have killed Pharaoh." This was a direct reference to the *jahiliyya*, or age of ignorance that plagued the world before the revelation of Islam. Political Islam, as Nazih Ayubi concludes, is thus properly understood as a reaction to the perceived failures of the formulae associated with Western modernity.[45]

Accordingly, Political Islam is a modern phenomenon. It is as modern as the Internet or the iPhone, and as much a human creation as democracy or socialism. The Islamist contention that Islam contains within it a complete, definitive system of government, that it is both "church" and "state," is, in many ways, a new argument in the history of Islam. This contention, at the core of Political Islam, rests upon a series of reinvented understandings of traditional Islamic concepts and symbols. By using new reinventions of old concepts and symbols, Islamists seek to imply, through rhetoric and action, continuity with the past. However, no such past has ever existed in the history of Islam. There never has been an "Islamic state" as contemporary Islamists conceptualize one, with the possible example of the Prophet's community at Medina.

Political Islam is, therefore, an invented tradition. The concept of invented traditions was first articulated by the historians Eric Hobsbawm and Terence Ranger. All traditions are rooted in some sort of historic past. However, Hobsbawm and Ranger demonstrated that, insofar as there is such reference to a historic past, the peculiarity of 'invented' traditions is that the continuity with it is largely factitious. "In short," they wrote, "they [invented traditions] are responses to novel situations which take the form of reference to old situations, or which establish their own past by quasi-obligatory repetition."[46]

As an invented tradition, Political Islam is only one manifestation of the fundamentalist-style mode of reform. Its intellectual origins lie with the Muslim Brotherhood and its chief ideologues, Hassan al-Banna and Sayyid Qutb. While al-Banna founded the actual organization, Qutb articulated for it a vision of reform that called for radical social, moral, and political transformation. This was a vision founded in the conceptualization of the West and modernity as having failed. In political terms, this meant that the secular nation-state could be disregarded as a basic unit of analysis. This freed Islamists to begin calling for the establishment of an "Islamic state," whereby the state would no longer be identified by a particular nation, but rather by Islam itself.

As was previously noted, the Islamist concept of an "Islamic state" traces its intellectual origins to the middle of the twentieth century at the earliest. Properly understanding Political Islam as an invented tradition elucidates that its doctrine is not really a return to the ways of the past. As an invented tradition, therefore, Political Islam is part of "a search for new and effective social formula, that, because it is not simply imported (and thus alien and ineffective), might stand a better chance of being authentic and of producing results as well."[47]

There is a vigorous scholarly debate over Political Islam. Some scholars have disregarded the concept in whole. The French political scientist Gilles Kepel, for example, argued that, "'Islamism' is in effect nothing but a name among others" and that it is "in reality very contradictory." Olivier Roy, also by chance a French scholar, was bold enough to title one of his books *The Failure of Political Islam*, in which he claimed: "Islamism has not significantly altered the political landscape of the Middle East. Political Islam does not pass the test of power ... It no longer offers a model for a different society or a brighter future."[48]

Even a superficial scan of news headlines since the beginning of the Arab Spring (and, indeed, well before this) indicates that Roy's categorical statements are not based in historical reality. As a non-Arab and non-Muslim, Roy's contention that Political Islam no longer inspires hope in Muslims for a brighter future is particularly troublesome, especially given the widespread success of Islamist parties in recent years. Furthermore, and of more importance, even if particular Islamist political parties fail in various political processes, the fundamentalist-style mode of renewal and reform remains. And, it remains a credible mode of engagement with contemporary issues for many Muslims throughout the world.

Political Islam has, in fact, changed political dynamics in Muslim countries and international relations and its activists have made unique and innovative contributions to modern Islamic political thought, especially as it fits into a contemporary world of nation-states. Yet, as many non-Islamist Muslims like Aziz al-Azmeh rightfully point out, the fact remains that "Political Islam itself routinely resorts to notions borrowed from the modern ... ideologies of European origin that pervade contemporary Arab culture and politics."[49]

It is precisely al-Azmeh's critique that demonstrates the dynamic themes of transition and reinvention in modern Islamist thought. In sharing conceptual labels, Islamists frequently seek to demonstrate an essentially Islamic intellectual origin to words used in the discourse of European liberal philosophy. Furthermore, they argue that they only use these words to remain relevant in a global intellectual discourse dominated by a European linguistic toolbox. This is especially apparent with the concept of a social contract. This concept, though historians can and do argue that it has appeared in different forms in different governments throughout history, received its most complete articulation in the thought of the French intellectual Jean-Jacques Rousseau, which, in turn, rested upon the earlier works of philosophers such as Thomas Hobbes and John Locke.

No translation, however rough, of the words *social contract* exists anywhere in the Qur'an or Islamic jurisprudence. Yet, the Islamic concept of social contract as articulated by Political Islamists is not quite a reproduction of Rousseau's thought, or that of Hobbes or Locke, or any other Western philosopher. Certainly, many aspects of European Enlightenment thought and practice cannot be reconciled with Islamic thought, and *vice versa*. Regardless, when synthesized together, it is evident that contemporary Islamist political thought is one rooted in a vision of an Islamic state founded upon *a* social contract between rulers and ruled, not *the* social contract of Rousseau, or Hobbes, or Locke.

There are many other examples of Islamists borrowing conceptual labels from European philosophy while arguing that the conceptual origin lies in Islamic history. The Islamist Kemal al-Saʿid Habib claims that it is perfectly, fundamentally Islamic to use the term *taʿadudiyya* – a word that entered the Arabic language when it was first used by Arab nationalists in the mid-1980s – to denote the English word *pluralism* because Islam and Muslims "taught mankind pluralism" in the first place.[50]

In this regard, other traditionally Islamic concepts such as *shūra* (consultation), *maslaha* (public interest), *ijmāʿ* (consensus), and *bayʿa* (oath of allegiance) have been reinvented by Islamists to form a contemporary Islamic political philosophy.⁵¹ This discourse might be aligned with the guiding principles of European political philosophy, but that is because Political Islam emerged during a period of European intellectual hegemony, which allowed the Europeans to create a cultural language that all peoples have used to discuss the world. An important aspect of the Islamist project, therefore, is presenting these ideas as being Islamic in character and indigenous in tradition. Whether one agrees with this argument or finds it baseless does not matter as much as seeking to understand Islamists as they understand themselves. For, as nearly any newspaper headline from the past decades confirms, the political interpretation of Islam remains a strong and vibrant force on the stage of international politics.

Toward Truth in Labeling: A brief discussion of terms

> Words strain,
> Crack and sometimes break, under the burden,
> Under the tension, slip, slide, perish,
> Decay with imprecision, will not stay in place,
> Will not stay still.
>
> -T.S. Eliot, *Burnt Notion*

The following is a brief and general discussion aimed at bringing to light certain issues regarding labeling that are most pertinent to the Muslim historical experience in the modern era in the context of interaction with the West. Indeed, the language we use, especially binaries such as "Islam and the West," reflects the world we live in. It also structures our experiences in it. This discussion is not exhaustive and it is not meant to satisfy political theorists or those scholars who work on issues like modernity or linguistic relativity. Nor is it meant as an attempt to define sublime concepts like modernity. Rather, the following discussion is meant to introduce some of the most important ideas *in terms of intellectual history*, not political theory as such, that have influenced the way Muslim intellectuals in the modern era have developed reform projects in the context of changing evaluations of the West and modernity.

All language is relative. As his famous painting *La trahison des images* suggests, the French artist René Magritte would likely have agreed with T.S. Eliot that words and labels are relative, ultimately arbitrary constructs that tend to decay over time from imprecise use. Precision of language becomes especially important in any discussion involving some of the major themes of world history. In any such discussion, certain broad and complex concepts or entities often need to be expressed with a simple label, if not simply to serve as basic building blocks of complex and multifaceted arguments, then simply for clarity and flow of concise sentences.

But what, after all, is "the West"? Can such a geographic label be contrasted with "Islam" – a religion, not a geographic area – without reifying either? What is "modernity" and is "modernity" itself inherently linked to the West or being Western? Such issues regarding labeling are not only the problem of the world historian. In fact, ambiguous, imprecise language is found throughout centuries of writings by Muslim and non-Muslim peoples – especially when writing about each other.

As Marshall Hodgson concluded in his definitive discussion of labels in world historical analyses, these labels persist - despite the obvious problems - because they are, in fact, useful. A scholar uses labels to construct his propositions and analysis. Often, simple labels are used for no other reason than to simplify convoluted concepts into basic units of analysis. In this way, the labels chosen are useful and constructive so long as any particular label chosen is understood never to be monolithic or unchanging over historical time. This is especially the case with loaded terms like 'modernity,' 'Islam,' or even 'the West.' Each of these terms can be understood as embodying a particular great world-view tradition that arose in times of different societal and cultural transformations. While 'the West' might have certain constant and unchanging features, it has never been monolithic. The same can be said for 'modernity,' a concept that has changed as rapidly as the ways different peoples interacting with it have changed.[52]

The most common label used throughout this book is probably "Islam," and even this label has meant different things to different Muslims in different times. Indeed, as Aziz al-Azmeh argues in his book *Islams and Modernities,* throughout history there have been as many different "Islams" as there have been situations that sustained them.[53] For example, the Muslim reformist Jamal al-Afghani – whose writings are drawn upon by Muslims of all different schools of thought – would conceptualize "Islam" in an essay targeted for an audience of British imperialists differently from how he would in an essay targeted for an audience of Indian Muslims. Each was a different situation with different forces sustaining it.

Furthermore, al-Afghani, like many other intellectuals, would often use language far more ambiguous than "Islam," like when he addressed a particular passage in one of his essays to "sons of the East." Of course, "sons of the East" encompasses myriad peoples of incredibly different ethnicities, languages, religions, and customs. So what, then, did al-Afghani mean?

The answer goes back to al-Azmeh's statement of different situations sustaining various understandings of different labels. In simplest terms, "sons of the East" or "the West" or even "Islam" meant to al-Afghani, or any other writer, whatever it is he wanted it to mean at the exact time and circumstance in which he wrote it. When al-Afghani addressed his 1879 essay on despotism to "sons of the East," for example, he was referring to Muslim peoples under the despotic rule of the Ottoman Empire, in specific contrast to Christian Europeans living under constitutional, representative government, as he witnessed in his travels there. In terms of intellectual history, therefore, it is most beneficial not to try and define the labels used by these writers, but rather to understand these labels as the writers themselves used them in the particular contexts of various historical circumstances. It is equally important to not superimpose present-day constructs or understandings upon analysis of historical writings.

That being said, however, certain suppositions can be applied to these labels to aid the reader in properly understanding them in the context of world history. To begin, take one of the most common descriptive labels used in historical studies: "the West." Without taking great care, the use of this label can presuppose the notion of a uniform piece of geography, even though it encompasses numerous ethnic and social substrata. If one assumes the continent of Africa as a center point of a map, this label has been used throughout centuries of historiography by persons living in the actual Western part of the world and persons living in the actual Eastern part of the world. As Hodgson described and many other historians have confirmed, the use of this label by actual Westerners and non-Westerners throughout history has created the sense of confined civilizations that find it bafflingly difficult to comprehend each other despite being inescapably enmeshed. This is the bewilderment found in the famous words of Rudyard Kipling: "East is East and West is West and never the twain shall meet."[54]

Studying the usage of this label over time elucidates important concepts. That the term was and continues to be accepted by many non-Westerners indicates their continuing cultural dependence upon the West. Just as Immanuel Wallerstein stated, it demonstrates the ability of the leading European powers to create a dominant linguistic culture. This major concept of modern world history becomes especially important in the context of modern Middle Eastern or Islamic history. In this period, the concept of "the West" was as intrinsic to movements of renewal and reform as the Arabic language or even Islam. As the late Fouad Ajami eloquently described it, "The Arab world had long seen itself in Western mirrors, judged itself by Western standards" because "no political-cultural movement had given it the distance from the outside world that political orders need if they are not to break down and lose their autonomy."[55]

Usage by Muslim persons of "the West" and other labels of European origin was a direct consequence of European encroachment – physical and intellectual – into Muslim lands. As Nabil Matar stated, for example, Muslims in North Africa (geographically the closest Muslim peoples to Europeans) did not know what to call the first Europeans they encountered, except *salibiyyun*, which means "cross-bearers." This is because Europeans exhibited the sign of the cross on their naval and merchant vessels and, of course, in battle.[56] The concept of a nation-state with a unique label to identify it, such as Germany or France, was also foreign to the Muslim historical experience. While certain present-day names of Muslim countries are exhumed from antiquity, such as Syria or Palestine, the use of these words to label a territorially confined nation-state was a result of Western imposition. Some names of Muslim countries, such as Pakistan, are entirely new creations. Even the name Turkey, wrote historian Bernard Lewis, is a modern introduction from the West that, despite the ancient history of the Turkish people, was not used by them as a self-descriptive label until 1923.[57]

The adoption of Western labels by Muslims is an elucidating function of the challenge of modernity. Especially in a world historical discussion regarding the interactions of Muslim peoples with modernity, "the West" almost always refers to the intellectual traditions of French and English thought and practice. This remains true even if the particular concept in question is a French or English refinement of an idea stemming originally from the Italian Renaissance or ancient classicists. It was, after all, predominantly the English, but also, to a slightly lesser extent, the French, who carried the package of modernity aboard their naval vessels and with their troops to Muslim lands. This is not to say, however, that modernity is or ever was inherently Western, though some scholars have argued just this.

The German philosopher Max Weber (1864-1920) was among the first intellectuals to link the West with modernity and confine both terms primarily to certain northwestern European states, which, he argued, were exceptional. Originally printed as a journal article in 1904, he argued in his 1920 book *The Protestant Ethic and the Spirit of Capitalism* that certain innate features of Protestantism transformed "the soul of mankind" by fueling in its European followers a world-view based on materialism and industrial output that resulted in modes of production aimed at maximizing profit.

Weber argued that this unique world-view – a consequence of the Protestant Reformation – created a capitalist economy that transformed certain European states from agricultural, feudal societies into industrial, capitalistic ones. As he wrote in an essay years after the publication of *The Protestant Ethic*, "Such a powerful, unconsciously refined organization [the Protestant ascetic community] for the production of capitalist individuals has never existed in any other church or religion." Yet, he also argued that the exceptional peculiarity of the West was due to more than simply its Protestant ethic. In a later series of essays, he argued that certain economic, political, legal, and scientific patterns of action led to "the characteristic uniqueness of modern Western rationalism." This was a development that was of *"universal* significance and empirical validity" and could be found "in the West, and only in the West." The Weberian model of modernity is, therefore, one bound by geography and temporality.[58]

To some extent, at least, Weber was drawing upon the earlier work of his fellow German philosopher Immanuel Kant (1724-1804), especially in advocating for the temporality of modernity.[59] Much later, the French philosopher Michel Foucault (1926-1984) argued against this long-standing line of analysis. Foucault argued for understanding modernity as a world-view that was not tied inherently to Europe or the consequence of a confined period of time. For example, in his essay "What is Enlightenment?" Foucault wrote, "Modernity is often spoken of as an epoch, or at least as a set of features characteristic of an epoch" that is "situated on a calendar" between "a more or less naïve or archaic premodernity, and followed by an enigmatic and troubling 'postmodernity.'" But Foucault was not pleased with this. Instead, he wondered:

Whether we may not envisage modernity rather as an attitude than as a period of history. And by 'attitude,' I mean a mode of relating to contemporary reality; a voluntary choice made by certain people; in the end, a way of thinking and feeling; a way, too, of acting and behaving that at once and the same time marks a relation of belonging and presents itself as a task.[60]

For Foucault, modernity was not the result of any particular thing, such as a Protestant ethic that emerged during a particular period of time, as it largely was for Weber. Rather, Foucault argued that modernity was a loosely evolving "mode of being" that can and has taken "various guises" over the past two or three centuries because, ever since its formation, it "has found itself struggling with attitudes of 'countermodernity.'"[61] As will be demonstrated, Foucault's concept of a struggle between the attitude of "modernity" and "attitudes of 'countermodernity'" is particularly useful in understanding the evolution of Islamic activism in the modern era and the emergence of Political Islam.

Before Foucault, Marshall Hodgson argued along a similar line of analysis. Hodgson's treatment of modernity and its role in modern world history was the first and most comprehensive articulation of modernity, from its outset, as a global process. Contemporary scholarship on issues of 'modernity' rest to some degree or another upon his conceptual foundation. As historian Edmund Burke III pointed out, some of Hodgson's concepts, such as *technicalism*, can be problematic from the perspective of a twenty-first century scholar.[62] Regardless, the refinement of contemporary scholarship on modernity is the result of grappling with issues like those raised by Hodgson; his work remains the conceptual foundation for contemporary scholarship.

One of Hodgson's conceptual breakthroughs was his use of a new label for modernity, namely, the "Great Western Transmutation" (GWT). With this label, Hodgson sought to displace modernity from within the confines of the Weberian geo-temporal model and instead analyze it from a genuinely world-historical viewpoint. He chose to use the label *Western* to qualify the word *transmutation* because the decisive shift in the way humans experienced life did, in fact, occur in the West – albeit circumstantially. Though not constituting modernity in itself, the Industrial and French Revolutions were the most obvious early consequences of this "momentous, glacial-like shift" in the human experience of world history that

that ultimately caused a "third and almost equally unprecedented event: the establishment of European world hegemony." This hegemony, although it did not manifest itself immediately in physical domination over the world, did immediately allow the Europeans to dominate all interstate relations – political and commercial and intellectual.[63]

Hodgson noted that the transmutation itself was relatively sudden when compared to other human history and that, with proper care, it can be discussed as a single, though vast and complex, event. The GWT cannot be considered a consequence of historical events contained within a unitary linear model of development and modernization, one that assumes an unbroken ascending curve from ancient Greece, to Christendom, to the Renaissance, to modern times. The GWT was essentially the accidental consequence of a series of unique historical experiences throughout several centuries that shifted man's world-view from moral and ultimate questions, such as salvation, to the material questions in the present.[64] Like Foucault and in contrast to Weber, Hodgson deemed problematic the linking of modernity to any particular century. Although he acknowledged that the modern pattern of development was already established *in nucleo* by about the year 1800, it was "the transformations of the seventeenth and eighteenth centuries that served to decisively set off Westerners from the rest of the world."[65]

The aspect of the GWT that set off Westerners from the rest of the world, according to Hodgson, was "technicalism." Though by circumstance it affected Westerners first, technicalism did not derive from particular characteristics unique to certain humans. Technicalism refers to the patterns of thought or activities appropriate to or functionally associated with technicalized processes. Hodgson defines technicalized processes as:

> Technical development not only in manufacturing but in agriculture, administration, science, and so on ... [that] characterize the several sectors or the whole of a society in which the dominant elements are on a level of social organization where in intellectual and practical activity, calculatively rationalized and specialized technical procedures form an interdependent and preponderant pattern.[66]

Moral or social questions surrounding modernity, Hodgson notes, might have been necessary to launch technicalization in the first place, but they cannot be subsumed under the label *technicalism* and are, therefore, considered part of the "age" of technicalism. The "age of technicalism," in turn, forms part of the general world-view of modernity. During the age of technicalism, there arose a mode of social organization sufficiently diverse and intricate enough to remove an individual person from within the broader processes of which he was but one part. "Goethe, the greatest writer of the generation in which the Transmutation culminated," wrote Hodgson, could not "have hoped to follow minutely all the technical processes in which the tools were cast which made the machines to service his theatrical innovations." There is, therefore, a 'de-individualizing' implication in technicalism, thus strengthening the element of the accident nature of Hodgsonian modernity, and refuting the Western-exceptionalist model of Weberian modernity.[67]

At the same time, however, Hodgson acknowledged that Western peoples in the course of the GWT did represent a "tremendous human achievement ... An immense triumph" that was "to the credit ... of the Occidental peoples." But inherent in this argument there remains the problem of alluding to completely bifurcated world civilizations, which has never been the case in all of human history.[68] Even the cultural fluorescence that was the European Renaissance borrowed heavily from Islamic philosophy and the work of Muslim scientists in the High Medieval period. Furthermore, many of the most decisively formative elements of the GWT did not originate in the West: the famous trio of gunpowder, the compass, and the printing press – which symbolize the three greatest themes in the relative rise of the West – originated in China. Even the global world market that allowed capitalism to flourish emerged almost entirely under Muslim auspices.

In this global context, "the West" emerges by accident as somewhat of an "unconscious heir" of the formative elements of modernity itself. To conclude this line of analysis, Hodgson wrote, "Without the cumulative history of the whole Afro-Eurasian Oikoumene, of which the Occident had been an integral part, the Western Transmutation would be almost unthinkable."[69] With Hodgson's conceptualizations, then, modernity is thus understood as a non-national phenomenon, within which historical events take place in an unprecedentedly close-drawn global context.

One of the aspects of this new global context is the quickening of historical time. When combined, both of these aspects served to provide the framework for the emergence of the theme of relative societal decline (backwardness) or ascension. With modernity, humans produced in decades what would have taken centuries to produce before. World historical concepts like "the Eastern Question" or the "military revolution and the rise of the West" are then inherently linked to the basic underlying framework of modernity. This framework made it so that "all non-Western peoples were faced with the problem of coping as outsiders with the new order of civilized life as it was emerging in the Occident."[70]

In his award-winning monograph *Defenders of God*, historian of religions Bruce Lawrence synthesizes Hodgson's analyses, as well as the works of a cast of other historians and sociologists, to provide definitions of the primary sense of modernity and its ideology, modernism. His concise definitions are unmatched. Lawrence defines modernity as:

> The emergence of a new index of human life shaped, above all, by increasing bureaucratization and rationalization as well as technical capacities and global exchange unthinkable in the premodern era.

He continues to describe the ideology associated with modernity:

> *Modernism* is the search for individual autonomy driven by a set of socially encoded values emphasizing change over continuity; quantity over quality; efficient production, power, and profit over sympathy for traditional values or vocations, in both the public and private spheres. At its utopian extreme, it enthrones one economic strategy, consumer-oriented capitalism, as the surest means to technological progress that will also eliminate social unrest and physical discomfort.[71]

The world-view and ideology – or countermodernity – that opposes modernity, then, is fundamentalism. Though it opposes modernity and modernism, fundamentalism is still modern. It is because of the confusion that arises from this conundrum, and the term's widespread use and misuse, that there has been a strong debate among scholars over its continued use, especially its use outside its original historical setting. As the academic and journalist Malise Ruthven summarizes the debate, "Academics are still debating the appropriateness of using the 'F-word' in contexts outside its original Protestant setting. ... 'Fundamentalism' originated in the very specific theological context of early twentieth century Protestant America, and its applicability beyond its original matrix is – to put it mildly – problematic."[72]

Despite acknowledging the problems associated with the term *fundamentalism*, most historians agree that the term can, and should, be extended beyond its original meaning to be applied toward other phenomena today, if for no other reason than that there is simply no other single word that describes the themes behind this broad phenomenon.[73] Bruce Lawrence summarized this best. He wrote:

> Fundamentalism is a multifocal phenomenon precisely because the modernist hegemony, though originating in some parts of the West, was not limited to Protestant Christianity. Through the Enlightenment it affected significant numbers of Jews, and due to the colonization of much of Africa and Asia in the nineteenth and early twentieth centuries, it touched the lives and destinies of many Muslims.[74]

In *Defenders of God*, Lawrence goes on to demonstrate that modernity is the key category to consider when interpreting fundamentalism or fundamentalist movements. Fundamentalism, as he argues, is a general style of social, political and religious contention that draws upon particular interpretations of religious traditions to oppose modernity, but it is still thoroughly modern. As with the concepts of the "separation of church and state," Marxism, the Internet, or even an iPhone, fundamentalism is a product of modernity. "Without modernity there are no fundamentalists, just as there are no modernists," Lawrence concluded. "The identity of fundamentalism, both as a psychological mindset and a historical movement, is shaped by the modern world."[75]

Fundamentalism, then, is somewhat paradoxical. Al-Qaʻida fighters using satellite phones and laptops while operating out of caves in the mountains of Afghanistan or Pakistan are modern even though they detest modernity and modernism. The Taliban might reject modernity and despise the West, but they still engage in "Twitter Wars" with the United States.

In the Islamic context, the fundamentalist-style mode of reform, from which Political Islam emerged, has obtained significant successes because it is interpreted by many Muslims as being the least Western of the various global responses to Western hegemony. In Foucaultian terms, it is the strongest and most viable countermodernity. As John Voll has repeatedly demonstrated, Islamic fundamentalism and the concept of the 'failure of the West' is a unique phenomenon because it has made it possible to divorce modernity from Western models and precedents. His conclusions continue the Foucaultian and Hodgsonian line of analysis that refutes the more classic Weberian model of modernity. As he concluded:

> Non-Western modernity becomes both intellectually conceivable and practically possible. ... Now Islamic modernity competes with Western modernity, and the concept of the failure of the West strengthens the affirmation of Islam as the more effective model for modernity.[76]

Finally, for the specific purposes of any work regarding Islamic intellectual history in the modern era, terms such as *Muslim, Islamic, Islamism* or *Islamist* are used expressly to denote fact. A "Muslim country," therefore, is a country in which the majority of the population is Muslim. The "Muslim world" denotes the large part of the world that is predominantly Muslim. A "Muslim intellectual" is an intellectual who is Muslim in origin and religion. The term *Islamic* denotes the intent of certain persons to consciously organize a vision, outlook, or argument within the common words, symbols, and traditions of the religion of Islam, such as in the concept of an "Islamic state." The use of the term *Islamist* refers exclusively to those individuals who self-identify with Political Islam and seek to affect change through peaceful means. It should never be understood as an umbrella term that includes Wahhabists, violent *takfiri* militants of the al-Qaʿida variety, and so forth.

Some might critique this book for using the label "Political Islam" without providing a definition for it. There is no definition of "Political Islam." In understanding this phenomenon, it is useful to keep in mind what Political Islam is not: it does not refer to any generic use of the religion of Islam for political purposes – as a tribal shaykh might do on local levels, for example. Rather, it refers to the particular belief of certain activists who claim Political Islam as a decisively unique ideology that contains within it a system for all aspects of life and a blueprint for socio-political organization. It is a somewhat sublime and, as Islamic scholar Ibrahim M. Abu-Rabiʿ observes, certainly a bewildering and multifaceted hybrid between a social movement and a political movement with a clear religiously oriented world-view.[77]

One of the reasons there is no definition of this phenomenon is because one activist's "Political Islam" is different from another's, just as one Muslim's "Islam" is different from another's. Furthermore, given the contemporaneous nature of this phenomenon and its perpetual role in shaping current events, to conclude a definition for it is to shortly be made wrong. All that is of true practical significance is an understanding of what "Political Islam" means to the activists who use the term as a self-descriptive label and what change they desire the movement to affect. The same can be said for the concept of social contract; it is not the social contract of Rousseau or Locke or Hobbes. Rather, it is the social contract of Ghannouchi or Qaradawi or Howeidy.

By synthesizing the works of several prominent contemporary Islamists to demonstrate their vision of an Islamic state founded upon an indigenously Islamic notion of social contract between rulers and ruled, and by firmly rooting this synthesis in a historical narrative, this book provides an addition to the small but growing body of literature that seeks to understand Political Islam as its actors understand themselves. As such, Political Islam is but one element of the vibrant pastiche of ideas that is Islamic thought today. It should never be considered a dominant or monolithic function of the contemporary Muslim experience; rather, it is an expression of the diversity found among the world's Muslims and within Islam itself.

Part Two

The Emergence of Political Islam

> The Westernization experiment has decisively failed. Both its variants, the capitalistic as well as the socialistic, have been tried and found wanting.
>
> - Khurshid Ahmad

One of the most decisive displays of the uneven and asymmetric nature of development and modernization in the modern era is the sudden rise of Western naval power. The culmination of a number of factors, European powers had, by 1800, undergone a revolution in the construction of ships, naval warfare strategy, and navigation. As military historian Geoffrey Parker writes in his seminal study linking the rise of European powers to their military capabilities, this revolution "opened the way to the exercise of European hegemony over most of the world's oceans for much of the modern period."[1]

Napoleon's invasion of Egypt in 1798 by way of the Mediterranean Sea is demonstrative of this. According to the firsthand chronicle of the invasion written by the famous Egyptian historian al-Jabarti (1753–1825), the invasion had the immediate effect of demonstrating to many educated Egyptians the apparent weakness of the *umma* in the face of European military power. Al-Jabarti records a prominent shaykh who, upon hearing the news of the fall of Alexandria, exclaimed: "All this is a result of negligence in managing the ports and letting things slide, to such a degree that the enemy could occupy the port of Islam." Indeed, the negligence was complete. Al-Jabarti continues to describe that the Ottoman soldiers entrusted with the defense of Egypt did not even have weapons, "except some broken-down cannons which were useless. It happened once that they needed gunpowder to fire the cannon on the Feast but they could not even find enough to load it once so they had to buy powder from the druggist."²

The French presence in Egypt introduced to Egyptians the political philosophy of the French Enlightenment. Napoleon went to great lengths to package certain concepts that he wanted to take root in Egypt, like representative government and resistance to tyranny, in an Islamic framework. For example, he appealed to natural leaders of the Muslim community – judges, prayer leaders, men of religion – when he declared that his goal was to liberate Muslims from despotism and tyranny, and to restore the natural state of individual freedom that Islam demands. This message resonated with local sentiments, especially among educated Egyptians who were dissatisfied with the despotism of the ruling Mamluk dynasty.

The text of Napoleon's proclamation issued to Egyptians upon his landing in Alexandria remains important because it appears as a conceptual agenda for movements of renewal and reform in Egypt throughout the next several hundred years. In stilted Arabic, it was framed in Islamic rhetoric. Napoleon declared:

> O ye Egyptians, they may say to you that I have not made an expedition hither for any other object than that of abolishing your religion; but this is a pure falsehood...I have not come to you except for the purpose of restoring your rights from the hands of the oppressors and that I more than the Mamluks, serve God – may He be praised an exalted – and revere His Prophet Muhammad and the glorious Qur'an.
>
> And tell them also that all people are equal in the eyes of God and the only circumstances which distinguish one from the other are reason, virtue, and knowledge. But amongst the Mamluks, what is there of reason, virtue, and knowledge, which would distinguish them from others and qualify them alone to possess everything which sweetens life in this world? ... With the help of the Exalted, from this day forward no Egyptian shall be excluded from admission to eminent positions nor from acquiring high ranks, therefore the intelligent and virtuous and learned amongst them, will regulate their affairs, and thus the state of the whole population will be rightly adjusted.
>
> O ye Qadis, Shaykhs and Imams; O ye Shurbajiyya and men of circumstance, tell your nation that the French are also faithful Muslims ... the French at all times have declared themselves to be the most sincere friends of the Ot-

toman Sultan and the enemy of his enemies ... And on the contrary the Mamluks have withheld their obeisance from the Sultan, and have not followed his orders. Indeed, they never obeyed anything but their own greed![3]

Napoleon and his troops and sailors left Egypt after three years. While some scholars contend that his occupation there was too short to leave any fundamental, permanent institutional changes to the country, it did have important lingering effects. With his appeal to traditional Muslim persons of authority (shaykh, qadi, imam), Napoleon, through proclamation and subsequent actions, revealed to educated Egyptians certain ideas such as that of local, representative government. That model of government, entrenched in European Enlightenment thought, was novel in Egypt at the time.[4] His proclamation is therefore symbolic because it opened or, rather, reopened an intellectual space for the transmission and adaptation of ideas between European and Islamic political thought and practice. As al-Jabarti makes clear throughout his chronicle, he, like other members of the Egyptian 'ulama', was critical and distrustful of Napoleon. But the intellectual introspection that is evident in his writing foreshadows the movements for renewal and reform that emerged from the opening of this intellectual space and that sought to reconcile the condition of the *umma* with its experience in Islamic history, all within the dominant intellectual framework of European modernity. In this sense, the intellectual consequences of Napoleon's invasion of Egypt were, in fact, long lasting and monumental.

The Tanzimat mode of renewal and reform

By destroying traditional power structures in Egypt such as the Mamluk armies, the French forces and their eventual retreat left a power vacuum that facilitated the rise of Muhammad 'Ali (1770?–1849) to power. As the late historian of the Middle East P.J. Vatikiotis noted, while Muhammad 'Ali ruled technically in the name of the Ottoman Sultan, in all practical analysis he had detached Egypt from Turkey. With his massive reforms aimed at reorganizing Egypt along the lines of a modern European state, his "New Order" became the basic framework for Egypt's drive toward modernity for the next hundred years. When he assumed power in 1805, Muhammad 'Ali stepped not only into the open political space left after Napoleon's retreat, but into the intellectual space as well. The series of reforms in the Ottoman Empire collectively known as the Tanzimat, or reorganization, were a function of this.[5]

Initiated primarily by the Turks, Egyptians, and Tunisians as a way of strengthening Ottoman society against growing European threats, the Tanzimat reforms were paradoxical in many ways. Seeking to strengthen their society against the growing European threat, the Ottomans sought centralization of the state bureaucracy, registration of land ownership, the building of new armies (often trained by Europeans) and the creation of modern educational systems (influenced almost entirely by European models) - all central characteristics of modern European society. As such, the Tanzimat reforms were initiated to strengthen Ottoman society and defend it against growing European intrusions. Yet, as Roger Owen concludes, they had largely the opposite effect: "Instead of making these states more independent of Britain, France and Russia they made them more dependent, instead of allowing them to control the process of European economic penetration it made the whole process of penetration a great deal more easy."[6]

While the general attitude of Egyptians toward modern Europe was "cautious and ambivalent" before the reign of Muhammad ʿAli, under him Egyptian society was brought closer to that of Europe in almost all areas. The primary concern in the Tanzimat mode of reform was the creation of a modern military modeled after those in Europe. The key to this, however, was education - especially because Muhammad ʿAli was confronted with the basic problem of staffing his burgeoning centralized bureaucracy and growing military with a modern educated native elite in Egypt.[7]

To this end, in 1816 Muhammad ʿAli began sending promising young Egyptians abroad, mostly to Italy, France, and England, for technical and academic training and also for cultural and linguistic immersion.[8] The education system in Egypt at this time was supervised by al-Azhar and the traditional religious establishment. It consisted almost exclusively of schools for the study of the Qurʾan and mosque-based theological centers. By initiating European-style state-based non-religious education, Muhammad ʿAli prompted "the rise of a state-trained, European-influenced native elite of public officials, teachers, technical, scientific and administrative officers." The consequences of the exchanges that took place in the intellectual space opened by Napoleon's invasion in 1798 extended beyond Muhammad ʿAli's practical and immediate concern for staffing his bureaucracy and military, however. As P.J. Vatikiotis put it, "The Pasha was also unwittingly sowing the seeds of an intellectual, cultural, social and political renaissance led by his Egyptian protégés in the second half of the nineteenth century."[9]

Rifaʻa Rafiʻ al-Tahtawi

One of the first and most prominent of the Egyptians sent to Europe by Muhammad ʻAli was Rifaʻa Rafiʻ al-Tahtawi (1801–1871). Formally trained in theology at al-Azhar in Cairo, Tahtawi was sent to Paris in 1826. He remained there, happily, for four years while immersed in studying French language and political philosophy. He wrote in his memoir, *Takhlis al-Ibriz fi Talkhis Bariz aw al-Diwan al-Nafis bi-iwan Baris (An Imam in Paris: Account of a Stay in France by an Egyptian Cleric)*, that among the most important works he studied were those by Condillac and Burlamanqui, especially their works regarding natural rights, and the literature of Voltaire, Racine, and Montesquieu, in particular the latter's *Lettres Persanes*. In addition, he closely studied the writings of Jean-Jacques Rousseau, about which he wrote: "I also read a book called 'The Social Contract', by an author called Rousseau, who says things of great import."[10]

Tahtawi's writings on political thought and issues of governance framed the debate after his death among later generations of reformers. "The thought of the French Enlightenment left a permanent mark on him," wrote Albert Hourani, "and through him on the Egyptian mind." Contemplative and analytical, Tahtawi sought to introduce to Egyptian society certain concepts from his Paris education. One of these concepts was his conviction that "the people could and should participate actively in the process of government." Tahtawi observed that in France, a communal feeling of responsibility and duty to the country itself drove political virtue. He would have observed this first hand, but also studied it in Montesquieu's *L'Esprit des lois: l'amour de la patrie conduit à la bonté des moeurs*.[11] These important themes introduced to Arabs by Tahtawi would obtain increasing importance in subsequent movements of renewal and reform.

After his return to Egypt, Tahtawi wrote two treatises in which he developed his thinking on politics, economics, and social issues in Egypt: *al-Murshid al-amin liʼl-banat waʼl-banin* (*The Honest Guide for Girls and Boys*) and *Manahij al-albab al-misriyya fi mabahij al-adab al-ʻasriyya* (*The Paths of Egyptian Hearts in the Joys of Contemporary Arts*). In these works Tahtawi developed his most significant contributions to modern Islamic thought: *watan* and *hubb al-watan* (or *wataniyya*), fatherland or country and patriotism.¹²

To be certain, Tahtawi was not the first to use the word *watan*. According to Bernard Lewis, the Arabic word *watan*, shared with slight changes in pronunciation with other Islamic languages such as Turkish and Persian, means simply to reside or sojourn in a place or to settle in a particular place. In this sense, the word *watan* is found frequently throughout works of classical Arabic and other Islamic writings, in both prose and verse, symbolizing a person or persons' love of a particular place of birth. Muslims throughout history, for example, have drawn upon the Prophet's familiar hadith in which he stated that love of one's homeland (*watan*) is part of the faith. As Lewis states, then, "The *watan* was thus a focus of sentiment, of affection, of nostalgia, but not of loyalty, and only to a limited extent of identity." Indeed, the concepts of a territorially defined country and patriotism or loyalty to that particular country were alien to the Muslim community. The only possible exception to this in Islamic history until that point is perhaps the Prophet's city-state at Medina. Yet, historically and according to the tenets of the faith, a Muslim was loyal to God alone; besides that, any feeling of patriotism or general feeling of brotherhood or good will was to the *umma*. As one Ottoman Grand Vizier characterized the traditional understanding of loyalty: "The Fatherland of a Muslim is wherever the Holy Law of Islam prevails."¹³

It is thus clear that Tahtawi, while not the first to use the word, reinvented the concept behind *watan*. This marked a major transition in Islamic thought and a reinvention of the traditional Muslim understanding of loyalty precisely because in his writings *watan* acquired "the specific meaning of territorial patriotism in the modern sense."¹⁴ In his *Manahij*, Tahtawi conceded that, according to a famous hadith, "the Muslim is brother of the Muslim," but he qualified this further:

> All that is binding on a believer in regard to his fellow believers is binding also on members of the same *watan* in their mutual rights. For there is a national brotherhood between them over and above the brotherhood in religion. There is a moral obligation on those who share the same *watan* to work together to improve it and perfect its organization in all that concerns its honour and greatness and wealth.¹⁵

But what, then, was the "country" and "love of country" that

Tahtawi was writing about? It was certainly not Ottoman, as Bernard Lewis observes. Nor could it have been the lands of Arabia in whole, since Tahtawi was not concerned with other Arabic-speaking countries, and, furthermore, the ideology of pan-Arab nationalism was still decades away from taking root. Tahtawi was writing about a specifically Egyptian state and patriotism toward one. In a section of *al-Murshid* titled "The Egyptians' Attachment to their Homeland" he wrote, "Nobody doubts that Egypt is an honorable homeland [*waṭan*], even if we refrain from calling it the most honorable place ... It has the right to be respected by all nations and faiths, and the states and kings of the world."[16]

Of course, Tahtawi was an official of this Egyptian *waṭan*, and he was, therefore, concerned with the politics of running it. In this regard, his vision is steeped in the representative and constitutional governance he observed during his years in Paris. It is sharply juxtaposed against the system of despotism he lived under in Egypt. In *al-Murshid*, he describes the rights and responsibilities of Egyptian citizens as he saw them:

> The children of the homeland [*waṭan*] – those who originated in it, or those who came and settled and adopted it as their homeland ... are called 'Egyptian'... This means that they enjoy the rights of their country. The greatest of those rights is complete freedom in social association. Patriots are not characterized by freedom except when they follow the law of the land and assist in its implementation. Their adherence to the rules of the country requires, implicitly, that the country guarantee them the enjoyment of civil rights and civil privileges.[17]

Tahtawi continued to describe five types of freedom that he envisioned in the ideal Egyptian *waṭan*: natural freedom, behavioral freedom, religious freedom, civil freedom, and political freedom.[18] As with his description of different guaranteed freedoms, much of what Tahtawi wrote regarding a political vision for Egypt must be understood in the context of the "unlimited and virtually independent autocracy" that characterized the government of Muhammad ʿAli in Egypt.[19]

As an official of Muhammad ʿAli's government and an al-Azhar trained jurist, Tahtawi was certain to maintain a traditional sense of decorum; he never challenged out right the despotism of Muhammad ʿAli or even problems he saw with al-Azhar. Yet his thinking could not escape the influence of Enlightenment philosophy. Especially regarding what he called the "good relations between rulers and ruled," he believed that "the innovations of the modern age should not be shunned or rejected" if they are conducive to the advancement of the political community (*al-jami'iya al-siyasiyya*). Accordingly, one aspect of European political philosophy that had a profound influence upon him was Rousseau's *Social Contract*, and it inspired him to devise an Arabic equivalent: *'aqd al-ta'annus wa'l-ijtima al-insani.*[20]

Tahtawi thus introduced to the discourse of Islamic political thought important concepts regarding the place of Muslims in a modern state, particularly regarding the concept of loyalty and the relationship between rulers and ruled. The latter theme would take on growing importance in the following decades as the Ottoman Empire continued to disintegrate in the face of growing European encroachment and physical changes to the *umma*.

Khayr al-Din Pasha

Another Muslim reformer operating in the Tanzimat mode was Khayr al-Din (1820?–1890). As in Egypt, broad based reforms aimed at modernization along European lines took place in the Ottoman province of Tunis, and Khayr al-Din was one of the most important figures involved in this. Though born in the Caucasus, he ultimately became chief Ottoman minister in the province of Tunis. In Paris from 1852–1856, he was, like Tahtawi, deeply affected by French political philosophy. As a career military officer and statesman, he was concerned with the practical aspects of governance and politics.

Khayr al-Din looked to Europe as a political ally and guide. He thought that many important European concepts and institutions could be adopted into the Ottoman Empire, and disliked the notion of not accepting a foreign concept or idea simply because it was non-Islamic (European) in name or nature. Though not a prolific writer, he was a keen analyst, and, as a high-ranking Ottoman official, his words carried the special weight of authority. Aside from his memoir, his sole literary work is a political study, *Aqwam al-masalik fi ma'rifat ahwal al-Mamalik* (*The Surest Path*). An expansive work covering a range of important political issues, he explained in the beginning of it why he wrote it. He stated:

After I had long contemplated the causes of the progress and backwardness of nations, generation after generation, relying on the Islamic and European histories I was able to examine, and on what the authors of both groups have written concerning the Islamic *umma* ... I decided to assert what I believe no intelligent Muslim will contradict and no one who has been shown the evidence will oppose.

The object of this book is to remind the learned 'ulama' of their responsibility to know the important events of these days and to awaken the heedless both among the politicians and all the classes of the people by demonstrating what would be a proper domestic and foreign conduct.

He then stated the two goals he hoped to achieve:

The first task is to spur on those statesmen and savants having zeal and resolution to seek all possible ways of improving the condition of the Islamic *umma* and of promoting the means of its development by such things as ... to be seen in the European kingdoms.

The second task is to warn the heedless among the Muslim masses against their persistent opposition to the behavior of others that is praiseworthy and in conformity with our Holy Law, simply because they are possessed with the idea that all behavior and organizations of non-Muslims must be renounced, their books must be cast out and not mentioned, and anyone praising such things should be disavowed. This attitude is a mistake under any circumstances.[21]

Khayr al-Din's time in Paris observing politics and government there profoundly shaped his reformist vision. The starting point for reform, he argued, was the basic style of government in the Ottoman Empire. Of particular concern for him was the nature of a ruler's power and the relationship between rulers and ruled in Muslim government. Of course, Khayr al-Din was writing in the context of Ottoman rulers with absolute authority, and throughout his career he questioned what form power in a Muslim government should take. Accordingly, his basic underlying question in all his writings was how to ensure a ruler was just and equitable.[22]

Khayr al-Din argued that the best Muslim government was one in which limitations on the power of the ruler existed. Furthermore, he argued that a ruler's qualifications and merits should not be based solely upon his knowledge of Islam or apparent piety. The ruler's power, he argued, was of course limited by God's innate sovereignty on Earth, as revealed in the Qur'an. Yet, he also thought that one of the most important concepts in the Qur'an was *shūra*, or mutual consultation between rulers and ruled. As he wrote:

> Among the most important of the *shari'a* principles is the duty of *shūra* [consultation] with which God charged His impeccable Prophet ... although Muhammad could have dispensed with this since he received inspiration directly from God, and also because of the many perfections which God had placed in him. The underlying reason for this obligation upon the Prophet was that it should become a tradition incumbent upon later rulers.[23]

Alluding to the Qur'anic concept of *ḥisba*, he argued that a ruler was bound to consult two classes of people, the 'ulama' and the *a'yan*, who "must be able to speak freely to him, guide him in the right path and prevent him from doing evil." A pragmatic and conscientious analyst, Khayr al-Din noted, however, that the *shari'a* is not a "fixed and detailed code" which outlines everything an individual in power should and should not do. Therefore, "the principle of *maslaha* – of choosing that interpretation or ruling from which the greatest good will flow – must be the supreme guide of the government." Furthermore, with a nod toward the European concept of separation between church and state, he wrote that there must be cooperation in government between "men of religion" and "men of politics."[24]

Khayr al-Din introduced to Islamic thought important questions regarding the relationship between rulers and ruled in Muslim government. Augmented by the writings of Tahtawi, this theme was continually expanded upon by his successors in creating a reformist vision of Islamic governance based on contractual and accountable authority to the people the government was chosen to represent. Both Tahtawi and Khayr al-Din were concerned with practical political issues of how to emulate a European model of statecraft, rather than socio-religio questions over Islam itself. Their reform fit neatly within the Tanzimat mode, in that they sought to improve the effectiveness of already existing Western institutions in their respective societies. Albert Hourani provides the classic observation regarding this: "The main problem of Tahtawi and Khayr al-Din, although expressed by each in a different form, was this:

how to become part of the modern world while remaining Muslim?" This was a "happy interlude" of history in which Europe was still viewed as a sort of guide or source of inspiration, and European thought and practice was something to be emulated with little need for critical discernment. As a high-ranking Ottoman political official, Khayr al-Din was of course cautious about the growth of European influence over the empire he served, but this stemmed from the thinking of a pragmatic statesman. European power in his time was not yet so great as to constitute the central fixation of political thought in his time.[25]

For a time, Egyptian rulers after Muhammad ʿAli perpetuated certain aspects of the Tanzimat reforms. The Khedive Saʿid (1822-1863), who ruled from 1854 until 1863, was a Paris-educated French speaker who continued Westernization; he granted the first land concession for the Suez Canal to the French. His successor, the Khedive Ismaʿil (1830-1895), sought Westernization even more. His stated goal was to make Egypt a part of Europe. As such, he cooperated with Western capital interests by bringing many modern conveniences of any major European city to Cairo. He even built a grand opera house in Egypt for Italian troops to perform their most beloved arias and recitatives. Ismaʿil approached Westernization with not nearly the caution that Muhammad ʿAli had. As Hodgson observed, "At all points, his policies served to hasten and improve on the dependent participation in the European economic and financial nexus which Mehmed-ʿAli [Muhammad ʿAli] had assumed."[26]

The "happy interlude" during which Tahtawi and Khayr al-Din lived and worked would soon end, ushering in a new dimension to the relationship between European and Muslim peoples. By the end of the nineteenth century, many Muslim territories were under direct European control; much of the rest of the Muslim world, though not under direct European control, was dominated by the West.

France occupied Tunis in 1881 and England occupied Egypt in 1882. There was the suppression of the Indian mutiny followed by the disappearance of the last remnant of the Moghul monarchy in India and the consolidation of British power there. The Russians in this time were rapidly advancing throughout Muslim Central Asia. The package of European 'modernity,' as it followed throughout the Muslim world the very ships and armies it had inspired, gradually became synonymous with the specter of danger and defeat. Increasingly, the West began to be interpreted as being in competition with Islamic ideals and the livelihood of the *umma*.

The modernist mode of renewal and reform

Jamal al-Din al-Afghani

On November 8, 1882, in front of a crowded lecture hall in Calcutta, India, the enigmatic Jamal al-Din al-Afghani (1839–1897) declared: "The Europeans have now put their hands on every part of the world. The English have reached Afghanistan; the French have seized Tunisia." Afghani, at this point an esteemed intellectual and preacher, was reflecting upon a new reality for Muslims inside and outside the Ottoman Empire at this time: the ability of Europeans to exert their influence in all Muslim lands. The discourse of renewal and reform in this period was characterized by a growing sense of Europe and modernity posing a threat to the *umma*. The general perception among educated Muslims was that the Tanzimat reforms had failed to strengthen Ottoman society enough to defend against Western encroachment and subjugation. By the time Afghani gave his lecture in Calcutta, European penetration and conquest in the Ottoman Empire and adjacent lands was at unprecedented levels.[27]

With Afghani as its intellectual founder, the movement of Islamic Modernism emerged among Muslim reformers who were largely dissatisfied with the results of the Tanzimat. To be sure, the movement was not monolithic, and not all of its intellectuals agreed in style or vision. Afghani, for example, had particularly vituperative debates with the South Asian reformer Sayyid Ahmad Khan (1817–1898), whom Afghani accused of distorting the Qur'an and calling "openly for the abandonment of all religions." However, each of the intellectuals who were a part of this movement sought to define a *new* conceptual framework for renewal and reform of the *umma*.[28] Amid heightened discernment toward the West, Afghani appealed for Islamic unity and solidarity of all Muslim peoples. A rousing public speaker, Afghani was comfortable conversing in many different languages, which he had learned in his travels stretching from Afghanistan to Mecca. Though certainly not the first to appeal for Pan-Islamic unity, it is precisely because of his experiences observing the political and social condition of his fellow Muslims in such far reaching travels that he became an authoritative voice for Pan-Islam and so closely associated with it.[29]

Inherent in Afghani's calls for unity and solidarity was a reconceptualization of the nature of Islam. In his writings, Afghani reinvented the understanding of Islam to be not just a religion – that is to say, faith to a creed and set of rituals - but as civilization itself. Afghani was particularly impressed by the classical French understanding of 'civilization' as expressed by François Guizot. Guizot argued that 'civilization' had a specific, even urgent meaning "of active, willed progress, of 'a people who are pressing forward ... to change ... their condition.'"[30]

Afghani's conceptualization of Guizot's "active, willed progress" had two goals: social development, or the increase in social power and wellbeing, and individual development, that of man's faculties, sentiments, and ideas. Afghani argued that these goals, and the concept of civilization as a world-view tied to the notion of progress, were actually subsumed within a proper understanding of 'Islam.' He developed this argument in a series of polemical essays published in 1881 under the title *al-Radd 'ala Dahriyyi* (*Refutation of the Materialists*). As he wrote, "Man has come into the world in order to acquire accomplishments worthy of transferring him to a world more excellent, higher, vaster, and more perfect than this narrow and dark world that really deserves the name of the Abode of Sorrows."[31]

Afghani argued that Islam contained within it all of the necessary features of civilization, and that these features alone could empower man to transcend from the 'Abode of Sorrows' into the eternal. Islam was progress in its purest sense, he argued, and progress was Islam. With this new conceptualization of religion, Afghani sought to explain why Islamic civilization was "in such a sad situation." His answer was simple: Muslims had turned away from Islam and instead looked toward Europe for solutions. As he argued in *al-Radd 'ala Dahriyyi*:

> If someone says: If the Islamic religion is as you say, then why are the Muslims in such a sad situation? I will answer: When they were [true] Muslims, they were what they were and the world bears witness to their excellence. As for the present, I will content myself with this holy text: 'Verily, God does not change the state of a people until they change themselves inwardly' [Qur'an 13:11].[32]

Muslims had strayed from the *shari'a*, the straight path, argued Afghani, and forgotten the true nature of Islam, which was a civilization calling its followers toward progress, reason, and perpetual renewal and reform. Furthermore, progress was the natural consequence of science and rational thought, which Afghani argued were foundations of the Islamic faith – not concepts monopolized by Europeans. Accordingly, a fundamental concept of Afghani's thought was that Muslims needed to understand Islam anew in order to rehabilitate their rightful place in world history. As he wrote:

> The first Muslims had no science, but, thanks to the Islamic religion, a philosophic spirit arose among them, and owing to that philosophic spirit they began to discuss the general affairs of the world and human necessities. This was why they acquired in a short time all the sciences with particular subjects that they translated from the Syriac, Persian, and Greek into the Arabic language.[33]

Civilization, for Afghani, and "all the wealth and riches [is] the result of science." It was wrong for Muslims to think that the benefits of scientific investigation and civilization belonged to Europe alone. "Science is not a noble thing that has no connection with any nation," he wrote, "and is not distinguished by anything but itself." Afghani argued that it was wrong for the 'ulama' and other men of religion to isolate Muslims and the Islamic faith from scientific investigation and rational thought. "The truth is where there is proof, and those who forbid science and knowledge in the belief that they are safeguarding the Islamic religion are really the enemies of that religion," he wrote. "The Islamic religion is the closest of religions to science and knowledge, and there is no incompatibility between science and knowledge and the foundation of the Islamic faith."[34]

With his conceptualization that civilization, progress, and scientific investigation were fundamental tenets of Islam, Afghani created a framework that allowed for renewal and reform to take place with heightened discernment toward the West. Afghani thought that previous reforms in the Tanzimat era aimed at arresting the decline of the *umma* were unsuccessful because they borrowed too heavily from European solutions and the emulation of European modernity. Muslims, he argued, were strong in the past because of the fundamentals of Islam when it was properly understood - not because of embracing foreign institutions or concepts. Afghani's writings urge Muslims to resist dogmatic adherence to the faith and return to a purer view of Islam as he conceptualized it. As such, all the basic functions of modernity, he argued, had foundation in the original sources of Islam. His thinking in this regard marks a transition away from the enthusiastic adoption of European ideas and institutions as advocated by reformers in the Tanzimat mode.

The new modernist mode of reform rejected "both unthinking traditionalism and blind imitation of the Christian West." Afghani urged Muslims to interpret Islam in a way that allowed them to organically adapt certain values that were vital for remaining strong in a world dominated by European powers. Nikkie R. Keddie summarized this best when she wrote: "By seeking these values within the Islamic tradition instead of openly borrowing from the heretical West, Afghani was able to attain an influence on believing Muslims which was not shared by those who simply appropriated Western ideas."[35]

By rejecting both dogmatic traditionalism and imitation of the West in seeking ways to revive the strength of the *umma*, Afghani's conceptualization of Islam and the place of Muslims in the modern world influenced many subsequent movements in Islamic thought. Rather than being more concerned with local particularities like Khayr al-Din, his unit of analysis was the *umma* as a whole. When he spoke of the solidarity of the community, it was in the context of his belief that its decline was perpetuated by subservience to despotism. Despotism, allowed to flourish because Muslims had gone astray in properly understanding Islam, made easy the European encroachment into Muslim lands. As he wrote in a letter to the French philosopher Ernest Renan:

> It is permissible, however, to ask oneself why Arab civilization, after having thrown such a live light on the world, suddenly became extinguished; why this torch has not been relit since; and why the Arab world still remains buried in profound darkness.
>
> Here the responsibility of the Muslim religion appears complete. It is clear that wherever it became established, this religion tried to stifle the sciences and it was marvelously served in its designs by despotism.[36]

In this letter, Afghani is talking not about the Islam as a civilization embodying the ideal of Muslim endeavor, but about the despotic and superficial understanding of Islam that had been at the hands of Ottoman rulers. While Tahtawi and Khayr al-Din had brought European concepts of accountable and contractual constitutional government to the attention of Arab Muslims, Afghani argued that their efforts at adapting these concepts wholesale to Muslim societies was ill fated. Such ideas were novel to Muslims because for years they had been subservient to the despotism of unjust Muslim rulers. This experience had fostered a misguided, dogmatic adherence to faith over reason and critical thinking.

The evils of despotism were quite personal for Afghani when he wrote his letter to Renan; he had recently been expelled from his advisory role to the court of Sultan Abdulhamid II. Abdulhamid assumed the Ottoman throne in 1876 and initially used Afghani's concept of Pan-Islam to legitimate his control over the empire. However, and to the dismay of Afghani, he became more and more absolute in his governance. For example, upon his accession to the throne, Abdulhamid arrested Midhat Pasha, his immediate predecessor who had sought to introduce a liberal constitution embodying guarantees of individual liberties. After that, he suspended the Ottoman constitution. Paradoxically, it was the trappings of modernity itself that made his despotism so effective: "He developed a structure of personal control that, with the centralized system of administration created by the Tanzimat, made possible a far more extensive and complete autocracy than anything ever achieved previously by the greatest of the sultans."[37]

Afghani made his views on despotism even clearer in 1879 in a polemical essay published in Adib Ishaq's newspaper, *Misr*, titled "al-Hukumah al-Istibdadiyah" ("Despotic Government"). He began without mincing words:

> Many reasons prevent an Easterner from discussing republican government. The first is the long time which the people of the East have spent under the arbitrary rule of despots who, by reason of the disparity of their passions stemming from the dissonance of their own natures, the deficiencies of their upbringing, along with the absence of anyone to deter or restrain them, or any external force that might obstruct their path, have therefore treated their subjects arrogantly and robbed them of their rights.[38]

Throughout the rest of the article Afghani outlined his critique of despotic governments. He divided his critique into two broad categories: the cruel government (*al-hukumah al-qasiyah*) and the oppressive government (*al-hukumah al-zalimah*). Of the latter, he wrote, "The leading men of this kind of government are comparable to the vile luxury-lovers who unjustly and unlawfully enslave people born free." Afghani was most concerned with the oppressive type of despotism because, as he concluded, "To this category belong most of the Eastern governments of bygone eras and the present as well." In the footnotes of his translation of this piece, L.M. Kenny notes that Afghani's category of "oppressive government" differs little in nature from his first category, "cruel government," except in the fact that its oppression is tempered with a degree of rational self-interest which prompts it to keep its subjects alive in order to exploit their labor. In other words, there was little different between a cruel government and an oppressive government.

Afghani concluded his essay with a daring admonishment of his fellow Muslims. He wrote:

> As for you, oh sons of the East, I shall certainly neither address myself to you nor remind you of your duties, for you have grown used to subservience and have resigned yourselves to a lowly life. You have substituted regrets and longing for strength and become like old women, unable to defend [yourselves], to dare, to acquire, to repel, to restrain or to remove. Verily we belong to God and to him we shall return.

Interestingly, Kenny notes further in his footnotes that the preceding list of infinitives at the end of Afghani's essay illustrates the device in the Arabic language of piling up words for rhetorical effect, or pleonasm. According to Kenny, "In spite of the disclaimer of expectation of any response, the passage is a direct attempt by al-Afghani to incite his readers to resist and overthrow tyranny." This passage demonstrates precisely why Afghani was banished from Egypt in 1879 and, later, the court of Abdulhamid. This, as well as a host of other essays on governance, served as a prescient message for the subsequent debates among Muslims regarding contractual and accountable government that were influenced by Afghani.[39]

Muhammad 'Abduh

Afghani shifted the debate over the place of Muslims in a world dominated by the West from a basic question over whether a Muslim should accept Western thought and practice, to a question over to what extent a Muslim was true to his faith if he did not. As Nikkie

Keddie describes this, "Like other nationalists, and like the Islamic modernists who followed him, his general argument for defending Islam, nationalism, and modernism at the same time was to claim that modern virtues originated with Islam, and that the Muslims who rejected them were acting against the principles of their own religion."[40]

In this sense, perhaps Afghani's greatest strength was that he appealed to so many different Muslims of so many different convictions. As a gifted and charismatic teacher, he attracted equally gifted students who were drawn to his dynamic sermons and ascetic lifestyle. Among these students was Muhammad ʿAbduh (1849–1905). ʿAbduh joined Afghani in Paris and organized a secret society of Muslims with the goal of reforming Muslims' understanding of Islam. Seeking to arrest the fall of the *umma* to the growing threat of European subjugation, they continued to appeal for Afghani's concept of Pan-Islamic unity and solidarity. In 1884, Afghani and ʿAbduh began publishing an Arabic periodical, *al-Urwa al-Wuthqa*. The main themes of this periodical were hostility to European intervention in the Muslim world, advocacy of Pan-Islam, and an "interpretation of Islamic principles to demonstrate their applicability to urgent contemporary needs."[41]

The title, *al-Urwa al-Wuthqa*, translates into English as the "strongest link" or the "indissoluble bond." This title is symbolic: Muslims needed religious and moral reform, it was argued, because collectively they formed an indissoluble bond. This bond, this strongest link, alone could defend the House of Islam against European hegemony. In addition to despotism, Afghani argued that religious sectarianism or factionalism within the *umma* was a primary cause of its decline. In an essay for this periodical called *"Taʾassub,"* or "Fanaticism," Afghani argued that God had revealed to the Muslims that the strength and unity of the *umma* was paramount. Furthermore, Europeans were aware that the *umma* was the strongest link standing between them and all the resources and riches found throughout the lands of Islam. Afghani and ʿAbduh argued that Europeans had set out to destroy the solidarity of the *umma*. And Muslims, in their enthusiasm for Western ideals, had helped destroy Muslim unity by putting European ideals ahead of Islam.[42]

For Afghani, sectarianism in the Muslim community and the evils of despotism went hand in hand; one allowed the other to become stronger and more entrenched throughout Muslim lands. With ʿAbduh, Afghani continued to advocate in *al-Urwa al-Wuthqa* for solidarity of the *umma* and the uprooting of despotism. They stressed these ideas in two essays in particular: *al-Wahda al-Islamiyya* ("Islamic Unity") and *al-Umma wa-Sultat al-Hakim al-Mustabidd* (The Nation and the Authority of the Despotic Ruler"). As Albert Hourani observed, ʿAbduh and Afghani "belonged to the minority of Muslim thinkers who thought the community had a right to depose its ruler if he were not just and the general welfare demanded it."[43]

In many ways, Muhammad ʿAbduh carried on Afghani's legacy after his passing. ʿAbduh's writings are primarily concerned with the inner decay of the *umma* and the need for religio-moral revival in it. Though he had a lively admiration for the achievements of Europe, he did not believe that European concepts or institutions could simply be transplanted into Egypt. Nor did he view Europe as the political guide or ally in the way that Tahtawi or Khayr al-Din had. Accordingly, ʿAbduh's writings augmented his teacher's more discerning attitude toward borrowing from European thought. For a confluence of reasons, there is an important transition in Islamic thought associated with ʿAbduh, though it was, of course, shaped heavily by Afghani. Albert Hourani provides the classic description of this transition. ʿAbduh "was not concerned, as Khayr al-Din had been in a previous generation, to ask whether devout Muslims could accept the institutions and ideas of the modern world; they had come to stay, and so much the worse for anyone who did not accept them," wrote Hourani. "He asked the opposite question, whether someone who lived in the modern world could still be a devout Muslim."[44]

Islamic Modernism emerged at its strongest after this intellectual transition. Using Afghani's conceptual framework of Islam as civilization, the Modernists argued that certain concepts claimed by European intellectuals as their own, like reason and rational thought, were also found within Islamic thought and tradition and could be presented within an authentically Islamic framework. Therefore, the Modernists argued that reason and rational thought should be applied toward understanding the original sources of Islam – the Qurʾan and the sunna – to provide solutions to contemporary problems caused by foreign encroachment. This was not, however, an entirely new argument.

The Muʿtazila were the first to advocate for the rational and critical interpretation of Islam. They "attempted to sketch rational perspectives about religious systems that could work as blueprints for Muslim forms of understanding and social order." These intellectuals and theologians argued that reason (ʿ*aql*) and critical thought were concepts derived from the meaning of the Qur'an, and were thus equally important as religious knowledge in seeking societal or religious reform. Mu'tazila philosophy was rooted in five principles: *al-tawhid* (divine unity), *al-'adl* (divine justice), *wa'd wa al-wa'id* (punishment and threat), *manzilah bayn al-manzilatayn* (the intermediate position), and *al-amr bi'l ma'rūf wa'l-nahy 'an al-munkar*, or *ḥisba* (commanding right and forbidding wrong).[45]

Certain aspects of Mu'tazila thought were reinvented by Muhammad 'Abduh to be applied toward the particular socio-political milieu in which he lived. 'Abduh's reinvention of Mu'tazila thought revived the notions of critical thinking and rational interpretation of faith from a dormant element in Islam to one of the dominant elements in modern Islamic political thought. Before Muslims as well as Europeans, 'Abduh grounded his reformist vision in a synthesis of Islamic history and tradition and European philosophy. As Hourani eloquently put it, "To show that Islam can be reconciled with modern thought, and how it can be, was one of 'Abduh's major purposes."[46]

Before his Muslim audience, 'Abduh authenticated his ideas by appealing for a return to Islam's principles as revealed in the Qur'an and the sunna. His unit of analysis for reform was, like Afghani, the unity of the *umma*, but he called for significant changes within it. He argued that Islam was revealed to the Prophet Muhammad to create the most progressive and supremely virtuous society and civilization. As a faith for all places and all times (*li kulll makan wa zaman*), Islam was relevant to the contemporary world in which he lived.

For 'Abduh, the uneven development of the *umma* was a result of *taqlid*, the blind imitation of ways of the past instead of the constant, new interpretation of the original sources of Islam in seeking guidance in the present. The yoke of *taqlid*, he argued, had allowed the Europeans to dominate the *umma* militarily, economically, and intellectually. As he wrote:

> Weakness has followed corruption in morals, lapses in behavior, and the abasement of souls, so that most of the populace resembles cattle, whose only ambition is to live to the end of their days, eating, drinking, and reproducing, contending with each other in bestiality. After that it was all the same to them whether majesty was with God, His prophet, and His caliph or with whoever else was lord over them.[47]

Echoing his teacher, ʿAbduh argued that this could not be reversed until Muslims re-conceptualized their understanding of Islam itself. He sought to create a new conceptual framework for Islamic reform. For ʿAbduh, the ideal model for emulation was not the West, though that model certainly had important qualities; rather, Muslims should seek answers in the example of the sunna of the Prophet and the Qurʾan. Describing his purpose in life as a reformist intellectual, he wrote:

> To liberate thought from the shackles of *taqlid,* and understand religion as it was understood by the elders of the community before dissension appeared; to return, in the acquisition of religious knowledge, to its first sources, and to weigh them in the scales of human reason ... and to prove that, seen in this light, religion must be accounted a friend to science, pushing man to investigate the secrets of existence, summoning him to respect established truths, and to depend on them in his moral life and conduct.[48]

In seeking to demonstrate that "religion must be accounted a friend to science," ʿAbduh was defending Islam and Muslim society in front of the scorn of his European contemporaries. Accordingly, some of his works have been critiqued as apologetic in nature. Yet, he also sought to place the state of the Muslim community in his time within the context of its own history. He argued that a true understanding of Islam allowed the embrace of scientific investigation, but centuries of despotic leaders had tried to preclude Muslims from seeing this. Despotism and unjust rule flourished under men who "betook themselves to devious by-paths," and, he continued:

> As a consequence a complete intellectual confusion beset the Muslims under their ignorant rulers. Ideas which had never had any place in science found sponsors who asserted things Islam had never before tolerated. Fostered by the general educational poverty, they gained ground, aided too by the remoteness of men from the pristine sources of the faith. They evicted intellect from its rightful place and dealt arbitrarily with the false and the valid in thinking.[49]

ʿAbduh argued that the continuous reinvention of traditional

Muslim concepts and symbols to remain relevant to changing contemporary situations was, in fact, part of Islam itself. As he put it, "Islam will have no truck with traditionalism, against which it campaigns relentlessly, to break its power over men's minds and eradicate its deep-seated influence." The blind imitation of ways of the past was therefore something to be scorned: "Islam raised its voice against these unworthy whisperings and boldly declared that man was not created to be led by a bridle," wrote 'Abduh. Rather, "He was endowed with intelligence" to engage in the fresh interpretation of traditional concepts, *ijtihād*. This was how Muslims could regain their sense of dignity and power in a modern world dominated by the West.[50]

In 'Abduh's conceptualization, the message of the Qur'an appealed to all the ideological components of modernity, especially reason and rational thought. As he wrote:

> The Book gives us all that God permits us, or is essential for us, to know about His attributes. But it does not require our acceptance of its contents simply on the ground of its own statement of them. On the contrary, it offers arguments and evidence. It addressed itself to the opposing schools and carried its attacks with spirited substantiation. It spoke to the rational mind and alerted the intelligence. It set out the order in the universe, the principles and certitudes within it, and required a lively scrutiny of them that the mind might thus be sure of the validity of its claims and message.[51]

'Abduh's creative and dynamic use of the concepts of *ijtihād* and *taqlid* built upon a process begun during the Tanzimat era, that of synthesizing traditional concepts of Islamic thought with the dominant ideas of modern Europe. Because of the English occupation of Egypt and the French occupation of most of North Africa, however, by the end of 'Abduh's life, Western ideas were perceived by many Muslims as threatening the vitality of the *umma*. Many argued that any adaptation to European ways was surrendering to European superiority.

The dominant narrative regarding the binary of Islam and the West in the latter parts of 'Abduh's career was that of Western domination and Islamic subordination. 'Abduh's thought, however, represents an important transition in this narrative because he was able to circumvent the narrative of adaption as surrender. He did this by arguing that Islam itself was a vehicle for change, and that its core tenets encouraged perpetual adaptation and renewal. "Islam reproves the slavish imitation of the ancestors," he wrote, and it encourages Muslims "to move away from their clinging attachment to the world of their fathers and their legacies, indicting as stupid and foolish the attitude that always wants to know what the precedents say."[52]

'Abduh's innovative reinvention of traditional Islamic concepts led to the development of an "Islamically oriented adaptationism" in direct response to the domination-subordination narrative. This was a profound transition in modern Islamic reformist thought. For many Muslims, using this conceptual framework legitimized the integration of European and Islamic concepts, even during a time of growing European colonialism. In subsequent years, many Muslim leaders and intellectuals used 'Abduh's framework to employ Western techniques in the creation of more effective state structures.[53]

Crossroad of history

Muhammad 'Abduh died in 1905. The years following his death were particularly tumultuous for the Muslim world, involving dramatic political and ideological changes. In political terms, growing Western intrusion into Muslim lands led to actual physical changes to the *umma*. These changes culminated in the imposition of the secular nation-state as the basic political operating unit for Muslims after World War One and the dissolution of the Islamic Caliphate in 1924. These political events created a sense of psychological dislocation for many Muslims between their vision of their past and their present situation. These political events led to significant ideological transitions, especially in the nature of reform and renewal. In this new political landscape, two prominent modes of reform emerged from within the modernist mode: the first was rooted in the European concepts of secularism and nationalism; the second concentrated more on the affirmation of Islamic ideals in the face of increasing Western hegemony and "became increasingly fundamentalist in style."[54]

The immediate issues facing Muslims in the historical period surrounding the First World War were subsumed within a dramatic reorientation of the basic unit of analysis in Islamic thought from *umma* to *dawla*, or 'state.'[55] The European concept of 'state' was alien to Muslim historical experience and Islamic thought, and the transition from *ummah*-based analysis to *dawla*-based analysis was a significant transition in Islamic thought and a reinvention of the content included in it.[56]

Historically, Islamic political thought was focused on non-state units of analysis; it concentrated on "the community (*umma* or *jama'a*), justice (*'adl* or *shari'a*), and leadership (*khilafa, imama,* and *sultan*)."[57] Given this, there was even an issue of what word to use to describe the imported European concept of 'state'. The Arabic word used today to denote 'state' in the European sense, *dawla*, comes from the root *d-w-l*. This root indicates something that rotates, alternates, takes turns, or occurs periodically. Granted, the word *dawla* is found throughout the Qur'an and in many works of medieval Islamic political thought. However, as Nazih Ayubi concluded, it was only used to convey the "sense of fortunes, vicissitudes or ups and downs (e.g. *dalat dawlatuhu* = his days have passed)" that any government or community naturally experiences. By the end of the nineteenth century, the word *dawla* had become increasingly linked with the European concept of 'state.' After the First World War, the concept of *dawla* was reinvented to mean expressly the European concept of 'state' that had recently been imposed in many Muslim lands.[58]

Not even the Ottomans serve as a proper example of a European state. The roles of *khilafa* or *sultan*, though perhaps not out right religious in their own sense, were still positions of leadership over the Muslim community; therefore, it was expected that the *caliph* or *sultan* uphold the Islamic faith and rule according to it. The complete political title in Arabic, *khalifat rasul Allah*, means deputy, vicegerent, or successor of God. In perhaps the most important work on the topic of medieval Islamic political philosophy, *al-Ahkam al-Sultaniyya* (Principles of Government), the jurist-scholar al-Mawardi described the political functions of the caliph as enforcement of the laws of the land, expansion of that land, and protection of the people in that land.[59]

Yet, the very 'laws of the land' that the caliph was expected to uphold were God-given. The expansion of the caliph's land was even religious in nature: proselytism and expansion of *dar al-Islam* is a tenet of the faith. Therefore, while not entirely a religious position, the office of *caliph* certainly did not connote any 'state' in the European sense. Nor was the office of *caliph* ever monolithic. John Voll notes that by the time of the Mongol invasion of Baghdad in 1258, the office of *caliph* had ceased to be an effective symbol of political unity and thus certainly not representative of any 'state.' Ottoman claims for the title of *caliph* over all Muslims throughout the world began much later, at the end of the eighteenth century, when Ottoman officials negotiated with the West for lands that had been lost to European powers. Toward the turn of the twentieth century the Ottoman Empire was not immune to the shifting global political landscape, and in the early parts of the twentieth century the 'state' became the major political operating unit in a modern world where effective recognition or loyalty was given not to religious communities or to traditional groupings like tribes, but rather to states.[60]

For Muslims, then, this was a period of intense intellectual introspection. The basic Islamic understanding of loyalty was reinvented in this time to remain relevant in a modern political landscape characterized by "the institutionalization and consolidation of territorial states in the image of the European pattern."[61] This European model, as Baghat Korany points out, was alien to Muslims; now, a state as a piece of geography demanded a Muslim's loyalty, rather than the non-national religious community of the *umma*. Abdullah al-Ahsan summarized the collective Muslim experience at this time:

> With the emergence of nationalism the *umma's* foundation was challenged. Although there is no precise and widely accepted definition of nationalism, it is generally agreed that the concept is represented by nation-states which demand the exclusive loyalty of their citizens. The mere existence of a nation-state, therefore, created a crisis of identity in the Muslim world.[62]

The circumstances leading to the dissolution of the Caliphate and the ensuing emergence of nation-states in Muslim lands occurred as part of the long-running world historical concept of the uneven and asymmetric development of different societies. For the Ottomans, this process of uneven development resulted in their defeat in World War One the collapse of the Empire. The impact of the subsequent dissolution of the Caliphate on Islamic political thought was massive.

For example, the Constitution adopted in the newly created state of Turkey by the Grand National Assembly in January 1921 was placed firmly within the framework of representative, contractual and accountable government. This was novel, though not entirely foreign. Sovereignty belongs unconditionally to the people," declared the new Constitution. "The administration derives from the principle that the people control their destiny in person and in fact." Speaking just before his final decision to abolish the Caliphate in whole, Mustafa Kemal (1881–1938) declared: "The notion of a single Caliph, exercising supreme religious authority over all the Muslim people, is one which has come out of the books, not reality."[63] With this line of analysis, the Caliphate was formally abolished in 1924. This sweeping decision placed the Muslim community at a crossroad in its history and presented new challenges to Sunni Islamic thought. The secular-nationalist mode of renewal and reform emerged as a response to these challenges.

The secular-nationalist mode of renewal and reform

The period of history following the dissolution of the Islamic Caliphate saw the rise of many different ideological movements. For most of the twentieth century, secular nationalism was the dominant ideology in most of the Muslim world, especially the Arabic speaking parts. One of the earliest expressions of this new ideology was the movement of the Young Turks, who captured control of the Ottoman state in 1908. To place the movement in the context of world history, much of the nationalist sympathy from which the Young Turks derived their support had been strengthened by the Japanese defeat over the Russians in their war in 1905, which had been regarded by many in Ottoman territories as an "Oriental" defeat over "Europeans." The Young Turks capitalized on this growing sentiment, and their movement remains the earliest, most organized and successful articulation of the secular-nationalist mode of renewal and reform. Arab nationalism emerged alongside Turkish nationalism, and though it was a distinct movement unto itself, it was, nonetheless, augmented by the apparent success of the Young Turks and their 1908 revolution, which was carried out in the secular-nationalist mode of engagement.[64]

Though Islam was used at times as a framing narrative to legitimate certain aspects of their movement, the Young Turks were generally secular in tone and style. Their political goals, extracted from Western models, were generally framed in an overtly Western discourse: liberal constitutionalism, representative government, secularism, and nationalism. The appeal of this mode of reform and the movement of the Young Turks was strengthened by the success of Mustafa Kemal "Ataturk," who led a vigorously secular reform effort aimed at recreating Turkey as a Western state. The success of this model provided a dramatic example for other leaders, reformers, and scholars in the Islamic world, particularly the Arabs.

The most vituperative debate for Muslims in this time regarded the role of Islam in a European style nation-state. In Marshal Hodgson's words, "The official stance of the Ataturk Modernizers was that religion should be Westernized like everything else. The state should be a 'lay' institution ... and religion a private matter of the individual conscience. This much was achieved by the disestablishment of Islam." The relationship between religion and politics has always been debated in Islamic history, but the debate historically took place in terms of *dīn* and *umma*. After the First World War, the debate transitioned to that of *dīn wa dawla,* and, for some intellectuals, this debate involved a reinvention of the meaning of Islam itself.[65]

ʿAli ʿabd al-Raziq

The starting point of this debate was the turmoil caused by the publication in 1925 of a book by the Egyptian scholar ʿAli ʿabd al-Raziq (1888–1966). In this short book titled *Islam and the Foundations of Political Power*, al-Raziq forcefully argued that Islam was a revelatory message, not a form of government – a religion, not a state.[66]

Albert Hourani argued that al-Raziq's goal in publishing this book was purely practical; he sought to undermine the Egyptian king's claims to the caliphate in the wake of its official dissolution in 1924. Charles Kurzman, however, in his translation of parts of al-Raziq's work, argues that his argument is worded in such general terms that it thereby challenged the holistic view of Islam as comprising both spirituality and politics. Regardless of which perspective one takes, the impact of al-Raziq's work was immediate and profound.

Al-Raziq placed his message squarely within the framework of the new debate over *dīn wa dawla*. The title of the sixth chapter of his book summarizes his thesis: "Islam: A Message from God rather than a System of Government; A religion rather than a State" or "Message not Government, Religion not State." "Muhammad was strictly a Messenger, entrusted with a purely religious mission, uncompromised by any desire for kingship or temporal power," he wrote. "He was not a king, nor the founder of an empire, nor someone preaching in favour of a kingdom."[67]

Al-Raziq argued that there was a clear separation between religious and political rule, and that this was practiced by the Prophet himself. For example, he argued that unity under the Prophet at Medina was religious in nature, not political. "It had none of the aspects of a state or a government. It was never anything other than a religious unity free from any admixture of politics. It was based on a unity of faith and religious dogma, not on a unity of state or a system of temporal authority," he wrote. It is likely that al-Raziq was not aware of the stormy truth behind his next statement. Somewhat flippantly, he wrote: "This point of view is rather uncommon and perhaps unpalatable to Muslims."[68]

Indeed, refutations were immediate, vigorous, and came in droves; they continue in the present. As Abdou Filali-Ansary notes in his introduction to al-Raziq's work, "No work by an Islamist today would be devoid of critical mentions of 'Ali Abdel Razek."[69] Despite the numerous refutations however, al-Raziq's work formed the intellectual foundation for the emerging secular-nationalist mode of renewal and reform.

As has been noted, the concept of nationalism - of allegiance to a territorially bounded nation-state - is alien to Muslim historical experience and Islamic thought. Emerging in the Arab context in the 1860s as a direct result of contact with the West, it was widespread by the 1880s in one form or another. The movement of Arab nationalism was mostly the result of questions over identity generated by the disintegration of centralized Ottoman hegemony over its subjects. Arab nationalism had been strengthened by the growing independence under the Khedives of the Egyptian province from Ottoman control throughout the latter half of the nineteenth century and into the early twentieth. Despite the emergence of growing nationalist murmurs, however, as a political ideology nationalism was not able to take root until the crucial twentieth-century transition in Islamic thought of the basic unit of analysis shifting from the *umma* – as a non-national community – to *dawla*.[70]

Though there is considerable debate regarding the origins of Arab nationalism, some things are certain. First, nationalism would become the leading ideology for most of the Arab – and Muslim – world in the twentieth century. As L. Carl Brown concluded, "The Western concept of 'natural' nations and of nationalism as the normal legitimate policy of any people ... was henceforth the dominant operational framework for political action throughout the Muslim world." Second, Arab Christian intellectuals, like Khalil Ghanim and Butrus al-Bustani, made profound contributions to the development of Arab nationalism, especially by pioneering the use of Arabic printing presses.[71]

This latter point demonstrates another important concept; namely, that the concept of nationalism in the Arab historical experience and Islamic thought was never monolithic, and often manifested itself in different ways. As C. Ernest Dawn remarked, "Ottoman and Egyptian advocates of Westernizing reform [nationalism] had rivals. ... Their opponents charged them with heresy and treason, of trafficking with the hostile alien, and countered with assertions of the adequacy of the community's inherited beliefs, laws, and institutions." Some Arab nationalists, such as Amir Shakib Arslan, even sought to dampen this growing Islamist critique of nationalism by emphasizing the inherently Islamic nature of it.[72]

Though nationalism did ultimately become the dominant ideology in the Middle East, it emerged from Islamic Modernism as just one function of the twentieth century Muslim historical experience. Despite its dominance, there have always been other expressions of this same historical experience, many of which disavow altogether the concept of nationalism. John Voll described this split from within Islamic Modernism: "The more vigorous thinkers within the Islamic modernist group split and moved in two directions. One line built on the adopted Western ideas and emphasis on reason and helped to create the secularist-reformist position; the other concentrated on the reaffirmation of Islam and became increasingly fundamentalist in style."[73]

Some scholars, such as Hisham Sharabi and Bassam Tibi, take issue with the claim that Arab nationalism emerged from within Islamic modernism. Yet, similar to John Voll, C. Ernest Dawn notes that Sharabi and Tibi "have not provided any specific identification" of Arab nationalism's ancestry that is not rooted in Islamic Modernism. "They write of Arab nationalism without Arab nationalists," writes Dawn, "of a movement without participants."[74]

Regardless of these debates, however, the embrace of secular nationalism in the twentieth century was a transition within Islamic thought "of revolutionary significance." The secular nationalists reinvented the ways in which Islam was conceptualized in an effort to make it function more effectively in a modern, secular nation-state. At the core of the secular-nationalist intellectual framework, as demonstrated in the thought of Ataturk and al-Raziq, was the contention that "Society and religion both prospered best when the civil authority was separate from the religious, and when the former acted in accordance with the needs of human welfare in this world."[75] The old style *al-Urwa al-Wuthqa* mode of Pan-Islamic reform thus transitioned to calls for nationalism, or Pan-Arabism. Two of the most prominent intellectuals associated with this transition were the Egyptians Ahmed Lutfi al-Sayyed and Taha Hussein.

Ahmed Lutfi al-Sayyed

Ahmed Lutfi al-Sayyed (1872–1963) argued that a nation was defined not by a shared language, religion, or culture, but rather by territory, and that an Egyptian should be willing to accept Egypt as his first and only mother country. Al-Sayyed, however, was writing before Pan-Arabism or Arab nationalism "became Arab in colouring" and, as Hourani observed, his concerns were therefore distinctly Egyptian. Here, al-Sayyed's concern with British rule in Egypt was paramount. "That government should be based on free agreement was one of Lutfi al-Sayyid's convictions," concluded Hourani. He criticized British rule not so much because it was foreign but because it was despotic. Continuing the theme of the long trail of Muslim reformers before him, al-Sayyed believed that, "the *real* political problem ... was the absence of a moral relationship between rulers and ruled."[76]

Al-Sayyed was one of the most prominent founders in 1907 of *Hizb al-Umma* (Party of the Nation or The People's Party), the first modern political party in Egypt. He also managed the party's official newspaper, *al-Jaridah*. In its first issue of 9 March 1907, al-Sayyed defined the paper as such: "*Al-Jaridah* is a purely *Egyptian* paper which aims to defend Egyptian interests of all kinds. It will guide the nation in its truly vital interests ... The paper will not distinguish or discriminate between religions and races." With this declaration, al-Sayyed and his newspaper emerged at the forefront of Egyptian politics, and he dealt with Egyptian political matters squarely in the secular-nationalist mode of reform. His ultimate goal was to foster an Egyptian national personality independent of extraneous influences – whether British or Ottoman or from other Arab states.[77]

Taha Hussein

Al-Sayyed and his colleagues at his paper had a significant influence on Taha Hussein (1889–1971). Though he would ultimately become one of the most articulate voices among those calling for nationalism and Westernization, Hussein, in the beginning of his career, was most influenced by the thought of the Islamic Modernists, especially ʿAbduh. A student at al-Azhar while ʿAbduh was there, Hussein recalled in his memoir ʿAbduh's "extraordinary qualities." While he never studied personally with ʿAbduh, whom he referred to as "the Imam," he recalled how he "yearned with all his heart" to be among the most fortunate of students who did.[78] There is in Hussein's writings from this period a sense of listlessness: that feeling familiar to many young adults of being pulled between two diverging paths in life, and this would eventually manifest itself in his transition from Pan-Islam style thinking to Pan-Arab style thinking.

Ultimately, Hussein grew disenchanted with the culture of al-Azhar and his life in Egypt. His disenchantment with the culture at al-Azhar had a profound effect on pushing him toward secular nationalism. "The four years I had spent at the Azhar seemed to me like forty, so utterly drawn out they were," he recalled in his memoir. "They wore me down. It was like being in a pitch-black night when heavy piling clouds admit no gleam of light. ... The dismay that filled me gave me the sharpest distress. It enveloped my whole existence and dogged me in every part of my being."[79]

When his education in Egypt was completed in 1915, Hussein happily traveled to France, where he remained for four years. His studies in France "decided the destiny of his mind," to borrow Hourani's eloquent phrase. Hussein thought that Europe represented the highest stage yet in the process of human progress. Accordingly, while in France he embraced a thoroughly secular outlook on the world, especially on Egypt and its history. His thinking in this regard was made clear in 1926 when he published his book *On Pre-Islamic Poetry*. In this work, Hussein argued that Egypt was a non-religious nation with its identity rooted in pre-Islamic history. This contention bothered many of his contemporaries, who argued rather that Egypt received its purest identity as an Islamic society.

More troublesome for Hussein, however, was his application of the methods of modern critical scholarship to ancient Arabic poetry. In this regard, Hussein's work received vigorous critique from those who thought his techniques might be used as a critical method of textual analysis to cast doubt on the authenticity of religious texts, namely the Qurʾan.[80]

Hussein's most controversial work was published in 1938. Titled *The Future of Culture in Egypt*, this work was published only two years after the Anglo-Egyptian Treaty of 1936, which officially ended British occupation and required all British troops to evacuate Egypt (except for those protecting the Suez Canal Zone). Within this context, he began the work by addressing the general feeling among Egyptians that a new period in their history had begun. In introducing his work, he wrote: "The subject to be treated in this discourse is the future of culture in Egypt, now that our country has regained her freedom through the revival of the constitution and her honor through the realization of independence."[81]

The Future of Culture in Egypt presented Hussein's European-influenced vision for Egypt and its proper place as a nation-state in the modern world. In his conceptualization, the Egyptian nation and its society had little to do with Islam. He asked of his readers, "Is Egypt of the East or of the West? Naturally, I mean East or West in the cultural, not the geographical sense. ...We may paraphrase the question as follows: Is the Egyptian mind Eastern or Western in its imagination, perception, comprehension, and judgment?"[82]

Hussein's own answer to these questions was unequivocal: Egypt was Western. He thought it a "weird and illogical conclusion" for Egyptians to view themselves as "being closer to the Hindus, Chinese, and Japanese than to the Greeks, Italians, and Frenchmen." "I have never been able to accept this shocking misconception," he wrote. "What is important is that we demonstrate once and for all the utter absurdity of thinking that Egypt is as Eastern as India and China."[83]

However, Hussein did not advocate a total embrace of European thought and practice. Rather, he continued within the parameters of a heightened sense of discrimination toward the West that had begun with the Islamic Modernists, but still viewed the West as having succeeded.[84] As he wrote:

> In order to become equal partners in civilization with the Europeans, we must literally and forthrightly do everything that they do; we must share with them the present civilization, with all its pleasant and unpleasant sides, and not content ourselves with words or mere gestures. Whoever advises any other course of action is either a deceiver or is himself deceived.[85]

He continued, with an eye toward his critics, to qualify this statement:

> A decent intelligent man is surely qualified to distinguish between the good and bad in secular and non-secular matters. Accordingly, my advocacy of contact with and imitation of the way of life that has brought progress and pre-eminence to the Europeans does not mean that I approve of their evils ... Obviously then I am pleading for a selective approach to European culture, not wholesale and indiscriminate borrowing.[86]

The underlying message contained within Hussein's works fit squarely within al-Raziq's intellectual framework of Islam as *dīn*, not *dawla*. For example, Hussein claimed, "From the earliest times Muslims have been well aware of the now universally acknowledged principle that a political system and a religion are different things."[87] Hussein's arguments in this regard would have a significant influence upon other intellectuals operating in the secular-nationalist style mode of reform.

Khalid Muhammad Khalid

One important figure whose reformist vision was similar to Taha Hussein's was Khalid Muhammad Khalid (1920–1996), who published his most important book, *From Here We Start*, in 1950. As with Hussein's *The Future of Culture in Egypt*, it is evident from Khalid's chosen title that his work was a function of the still pervasive feeling for many Egyptians that a new period in their history was beginning. However, Khalid was writing in an entirely different historical context. The feeling of a new beginning and enthusiastic nationalism had been greatly augmented by the fall of colonialism in the Middle East after the Second World War. Like others before him, Khalid argued that despotism had been a primary cause of the "colonizability" of the Muslim community. For example, he wrote:

> Experience points to a sure agreement that 'despotism is the legitimate father of resistance,' that the suppressed opinion changes within the human soul into a perilous explosive, and that the best means for a fertile, blooming civilization is to open wide the straits of intellectual navigation and to

abolish the sources of fear ... Freedom from fear. That is the point of commencement on our long road and cumbersome trip.[88]

Beginning with this assertion, Khalid's argument in *From Here We Start* continued in the style of al-Raziq's position regarding Islam as *dīn* or *dawla*. Acknowledging his opposition, Khalid conceded, "There is, today, in our community a whole group of people who demand the establishment of a religious government." Khalid disagreed with this group of people, and attempted to base his argument in the example of the Prophet, whom he quoted as having stated: "Prophethood, not empery ... For I am but a blessing given unto you." For Khalid, then, the Egyptian nation was secular. Islam might be the religion of the majority of Egyptians, but Islam was not the blueprint for Egyptian government. He made this conviction clear when he stated: "Religious government is an iron curtain behind which an infernal chaos predominates."[89]

Many years after writing *From Here We Start*, Khalid wrote another important book titled *The State in Islam*. Much of this work was a refinement of the arguments he had made earlier in his career. In this later work, Khalid clearly summarized the argument he had made throughout his life: "I asserted that Islam is a *dīn* and not a *dawla*, and that it was not necessary for it to be a *dawla*."[90]

The fundamentalist-style mode of renewal and reform

Muhammad al-Ghazali

The secular-nationalist mode of engagement, founded in the Ataturk-Raziq-Khalid line of analysis, was frequently the subject of critique. Just three years after Khalid published *From Here We Start*, he received a harsh refutation from Muhammad al-Ghazzali (1917–1996), also an Egyptian. This refutation was the subject of a book he published in 1953, translated most accurately in English as *From Here We Learn*, demonstrating it as a direct response to Khalid's book. Published under the English title *Our Beginning in Wisdom*, al-Ghazali castigated Khalid for continuing in what he perceived to be the erroneous tradition of al-Raziq and the secular nationalists. Al-Ghazali began his work with an allusion to the evils that years of despotic rule have brought to Islam and Muslims. He argued that it was not just foreign powers that had led to the decline of the *umma*:

"Domestic imperialism has contributed continuously to the corruption of religion and the lessening of its significance. It has sought to bring up a generation of men who are Muslim in name only, who are ignorant, superstitious, and dogmatic."[91]

For al-Ghazali, however, religion was the starting point for reversing the damage to Muslim society from years of despotic rule. As he wrote, any effort at reforming Egyptian society "without religion is as possible as to teach an elephant how to fly."[92] Throughout *Our Beginning in Wisdom*, al-Ghazali continued his unsparing critique of the secular-nationalist mode of reform. As such, al-Ghazali articulated the basic premises of the fundamentalist-style mode of reform, which had emerged alongside the secular-nationalist one. As he wrote in his first chapter, titled "Islamic, not national rule":

> Islam is not a theory of geometry which must be merely proved or understood. Nor is it an abstract theory which we may study if we have the inclination. Rather, it is a comprehensive program presented to man for the purpose of a general reconstruction of individual societies and states in accordance with practical as well as spiritual principles.[93]

Al-Ghazali continued his refutation of the secular nationalists with sections titled, for one example, "The Fallacy of Separating State and Religion." In this chapter, he claimed that it is only "the stupid among our leaders, who think that the Egyptian state should abandon religion."[94] In making arguments like this one, al-Ghazali was operating as part of the fundamentalist-style mode of reform. Yet, this mode of reform had actually begun decades before al-Ghazali, with one of Muhammad ʿAbduh's most gifted students, Rashid Rida.

Rashid Rida

Born in Mediterranean port city of Tripoli, in what was Greater Syria and is today Lebanon, Muhammad Rashid Rida (1865–1935) began his career as a student of the most important Islamic Modernists. In Tripoli, he had been a student of Shaykh Husayn Abu al-Jisr, who believed young Muslims should be immersed in both traditional Islamic education and modern Western education. Rida was, therefore, well educated in European languages and thought, but his greatest interest was studying the works of medieval reformers Abu Hamid al-Ghazzali (1058-1111) and Ibn Taymiyya (1263-1328). Profoundly influenced by the works of al-Afghani, he joined Muhammad ʿAbduh in Egypt in 1897, becoming one of ʿAbduh's closest disciples and his biographer.

One of the reasons Rida and his writings ultimately became so influential for so many Muslims was his periodical, *al-Manar* (The Beacon or The Lighthouse), which he published from 1898 until 1935. As an Arabic periodical, *Al-Manar,* like its author, owed much to the precedents set by Afghani and ʿAbduh. Throughout his publications in *al-Manar*, Rida demonstrated his belief in the compatibility of Islam with modernity, and his arguments clearly mirror those of his teachers. However, he would ultimately articulate his beliefs in a mode quite different from that of his teachers.[95]

Throughout the first decades of the twentieth century Rida became increasingly disenchanted with his former colleagues in ʿAbduh's circle of students, whom he viewed as subordinating Islam to Western thought. In his works, there is a clearly identifiable, perpetually strengthening tilt toward religious conservatism. This change in style and tone was the consequence of his growing frustration over the continued expansion of European colonialism throughout Muslim lands.[96] Rida thus approached the problem of "colonizability" from the perspective that Muslims had become colonized because they had turned their backs on their greatest strength: Islam.

Rashid Rida was among the first and most vituperative critics of al-Raziq in the 1920s. Perhaps sensing the growing influence of Kemal Ataturk and the secular nationalists among many Muslims, in 1922 Rida published just before the abolition of the Caliphate his most important political treatise, *The Caliphate*.[97] A comparison of Rida's thought in this work with some of his writings in *al-Manar* yields what may at first appear to be contradictory positions. However, this tension between religious conservatism on the one hand and the desire for change on the other, a constant theme throughout his career, should be interpreted as a function of Rida allowing his thinking to evolve alongside changing socio-political contexts.[98]

For example, in many of his writings it appears as though Rida was devoted to the cause of Syrian nationalism. Indeed, in 1920 he was elected President of the Syrian National Congress, which elected Faysal as King of Syria. Yet, in other writings he was a harsh critic of nationalists, especially those he viewed to be subordinating Islam to Western thought or methods. Two conclusions can be drawn to explain this apparent discrepancy in his thought.

First, as a student of the *al-Urwa al-Wuthqa*-style Islamic unity, Rida occasionally used nationalism simply as a means of resisting foreign occupation. However, although Rida advocated for nationalism as a way to resist colonialism, he did not approve of secular nationalism as an ideological construct. At a time when secular nationalism was sweeping the Arab world, Rida remained a staunch critic of it.[99] This is demonstrated in a letter written in 1933 from an Indonesian Muslim to "the Excellent and Learned Shaykh Rashid Rida."

The author of the letter begins: "In my country, Indonesia, at present there is a strong movement for independence involving a continual struggle against the colonialists." He continued to note that the Indonesian ʿulamaʿ had issued statements forbidding patriotism and had been "making war on patriots in the name of the Islamic religion and its doctrines. They claim the patriots [nationalists] have deviated and are inciting enmity among the masses and their leaders." He then listed six questions for Rida, basically asking him to clarify, in terms of Islamic jurisprudence and history, whether or to what degree a Muslim could identify with secular nationalism.

Rida's response, which is not quite straightforward, is symbolic of the intellectual disarray that characterized the first decades of the twentieth century for Islamic thought. "It is well known that one of the imperatives of Islam is its prohibition of partisanship," responded Rida. "It prohibits enmity and divisions among Muslims." He continued to qualify this concession: "Another imperative of Islam obliges its people to attack and combat the foreigners who attack them. ... This is warding off wrong, so it is shameful ignorance to prohibit it." Rida's response thus demonstrates him as aware of the partisanship which nationalism might inevitably bring to the *umma*, but also aware that nationalism could be used as a tool to combat European colonialism.[100]

Rida's response also demonstrates the second conclusion regarding his thought. His writings must be properly placed within the context of the dynamic and constantly changing intellectual environment that characterized the first decades of the twentieth century in the Middle East, particularly Egypt. As Hamid Enayat wrote, Rida's writings should always be contextualized "against the background of Rida's intellectual development – his change from an advocate of the Ottoman Caliphate in the name of Islamic universalism, to a relatively objective commentator on its decline

– as well as in conjunction with his modernist ideas on the necessity of *ijtihād*, legislation, and fighting ignorance and superstition among Muslims."[101]

One constant theme throughout Rida's "intellectual development" is his perceived ignorance and superstition of Muslims. Perhaps more than his teachers, Rida emphasized the importance of a pristine, modern Islam based on the sunna of the Prophet and his companions (the *salaf*, or ancestors) and the Qur'an. In this way, the contemporary manifestation of the *salafiyya* school of thought and mode of engagement is closely associated with him.[102] Islam was primary to Rida's reformist vision, and it was his foundation for critiquing other modes of reform. His staunch belief that Muslims had subordinated their faith to Westernization is evident from an essay, "Renewal, Renewing, and Renewers" (*al-Tajdid wa al-tajaddud wa al-mujaddidun*) that was published in *al-Manar* in 1931. In this essay, Rida calls for an indigenous, independent renewal that preserves the religion of Islam and its culture, laws, and values. As he wrote:

> [There is] no need for an imitative renewal like that of the Ottoman state, which ended in the disintegration of its vast sultanate, then in its termination and eradication from the world geographic atlas. Nor [do we need] a renewal like that of the Egyptian state, which started independently during the reign of Muhammad 'Ali the Great, then turned to imitation and ended with occupation and the loss of independence.[103]

Rida continued in this essay with an unsparing critique of the basic analytical framework of the Ataturk-Raziq-Khalid style secular-nationalist mode of reform.[104] "Destructive individuals," he wrote, "have assumed the leadership of renewal and monopolized the title of renewers. They urge the nation to abandon the guidance of religion." He continues to declare: "Truth has no sanctity for ... the extremist Turks who have tossed Islam behind them." Instead, he urged:

> The renewal of heresy and promiscuity, laxity and profligacy, espousing depravity in the name of the liberal arts [literally 'naked arts'] and discouraging virtue under the pretext of freedom, liberation of the Oriental woman, and imitation of Western civilization.[105]

While Rida clearly took issue with the secular-nationalist mode of reform, it is often not clear in his critiques of it what his basic unit of analysis was: *umma* or *dawla* or *khilafah*. Hamid Enayat has argued that in his later writings there was a "subtle, and almost imperceptible, transition" from the question of *khilafah* to an Islamic state. Yet, Rida never used the term *al-dawlat al-Islamiyya*, 'Islamic state.' Instead, he used terms such as *al-hukumat al-Islamiyya* ('Islamic government'). In fact, Enayat even admits that Rida never provided a definition of an "Islamic state," instead referring almost always to the Caliphate.[106]

The imprecision of Rida's analytical labels reflects the challenge facing Muslims in the earliest years of the twentieth century of trying to find Islamic models to correspond with the European concept of the nation-state. To be clear, then, the discourse in the fundamentalist-style mode of renewal and reform was not yet characterized by a rejection of the Western conceptual framework of modernity. The concept of 'Islamic state', as a function of the rejection of that framework, was still decades away and would develop not as an extension of the Rida's thought, but as a result of an entirely new conceptual framework begun by Hasan al-Banna and the Society of the Muslim Brothers.[107]

As John Voll observes in this regard, "Rida felt that the full application of Islamic law in society required the restoration of the caliphate at a time when the transition from *umma* to state [*dawla*] made such a restoration impossible, and he and his followers felt that nationalism undermined the sense of Islamic solidarity."[108] Rida preached the idea of Islam as a complete system – one in which all functions of renewal and reform could be found – and called more assertively for religious activism in his vision of renewal. Muslims, argued Rida, must take an active role in restoring the present state of the *umma* to what it had been in the time of the *salaf*, or pious ancestors.

Rida's writings in this sense signify an important transition in the conceptual nature of reform in general. In the nineteenth century, the conceptual nature of reform was reform from above.[109] Even religio-moral reform, as opposed to socio-political reform, followed this mold: Muhammad ʿAbduh, for example, instituted decisive, top-down changes as a member of the Egyptian Court of Appeals and later the Grand Mufti of Egypt. In the first decades of the twentieth century, reform transitioned in the hands of activists and intellectuals who preached Islam as a general system calling for the reform of society from below. This model of reform began with the individual, who would then, in theory, help transform whatever general political system the particular individual was a part of. Two intellectuals in particular, Hassan al-Banna of Egypt and Sayyid Abu'l-A'la Mawdudi of India - played decisive roles in shaping this transition which provided the conceptual foundation for the intellectual origins of Political Islam.

The intellectual foundation of Political Islam

Hassan al-Banna

Hassan al-Banna (1906–1949) was born in the small northern Egyptian village of Mahmudiyya in 1906. A watchmaker and teacher from a humble beginning, he is regarded today as the father of Political Islam. Al-Banna was a charismatic and deeply pious person, and he was involved in religious and social activism from an early age. When he was only twelve years of age and a primary school student, he joined his first religious society, an experience that shaped the rest of his life.

In the 1920s he left Mahmudiyya and traveled to Cairo. Like Rashid Rida, he was dismayed at what he perceived to be the subordination of Islam to westernizing influences in all sectors of Egyptian life. "No one but God knows how many nights we spent reviewing the state of the nation ... analyzing the sickness, and thinking of the possible remedies," he recalled. "So disturbed were we that we reached the point of tears."[110]

In 1927 al-Banna graduated from a teacher training program at a school called Dar al-'Ulum. He received his first teaching assignment in Isma'iliyya, a bustling port town in the Suez Canal Zone. The headquarters of the British-owned Suez Canal Company and location of several camps for British troops tasked with protecting commerce in the canal, Isma'iliyya was also home to a significant population of wealthy European expatriates whose lifestyles juxtaposed harshly against the lives of the native Egyptians who labored for them. Like he was in Cairo, al-Banna was sickened by what he perceived to be the widespread subordination of Islamic values to the Western values of secularism and materialism. Especially repulsive to al-Banna was the sight of his fellow countrymen toiling under poor conditions for the foreign capitalist system of profit-driven values, rather than faith-driven values, embodied by the Suez Canal Company. In his memoir, al-Banna wrote that for him, Isma'iliyya was "the stark embodiment of the evils besetting Egypt and all Muslim societies dominated by foreign capital and cultural influence."[111]

Ever the activist, with a precocious talent for organizing and motivating others around him, al-Banna began to lead Qur'anic study and discussion groups in homes and cafes throughout Isma'iliyya. One of the things he preached in these study groups was that Islam contained within it a total and comprehensive system for life. This complete system, he argued, should be the basis for the complete reformation of Egyptian society. These study groups provided the foundation for the religious activist organization that al-Banna founded, in Isma'iliyya, in 1928: The Society of the Muslim Brothers, known today more simply as the Muslim Brotherhood.[112]

The Muslim Brotherhood was founded by al-Banna just four years after the abolition of the Islamic caliphate, an event that was followed by a particularly tumultuous period in Islamic intellectual history. The most immediate intellectual response, as has been noted, came from 'Ali 'abd al-Raziq, who vindicated the model of Kemal Ataturk in Turkey. Rashid Rida represented the fundamentalist-style opposition to al-Raziq and his followers, and al-Banna saw himself as a continuation of this grand struggle to guide the *umma*. As he wrote:

> Until recently, writers, intellectuals, scholars, and governments glorified the principles of European civilization, gave themselves a Western tint, and adopted a European style and manner; today, on the contrary, the wind has changed, and reserve and distrust have taken their place. Voices are raised proclaiming the necessity for a return to the principles, teachings, and ways of Islam, and, taking into account the situation, for initiating the reconciliation of modern life with these principles, as a prelude to a final "Islamization."[113]

Al-Banna saw the Muslim Brotherhood as an organization to represent the voices of those Muslims who sought the Islamization, rather than the Westernization, of their society. From its inception, al-Banna sought to challenge directly his counterparts in the secular-nationalist mode of reform. His point of departure in this regard was his claim that Islam was religion and state, *dīn wa dawla*. In one of the Brotherhood's first official documents, al-Banna made his position on this matter clear:

> My Brothers: you are not a benevolent society, nor a political party, nor a local organization having limited purposes. Rather, you are a new soul in the heart of this nation to give it life by means of the Qur'an; you are a new light which shines to destroy the darkness of materialism through knowing God; and you are the strong voice which rises to recall the message of the Prophet. If you are told that you are political, answer that Islam admits no such distinction.[114]

Egypt in the first decades of the twentieth century was a pastiche of political and religious activism; there were several powerful secular-nationalist political parties and scores of Islamic associations and groups. Al-Banna argued, with "the eyes of a religious villager," that the rise of secular nationalism provided Muslims throughout the *umma* "orientations to apostasy and nihilism." Furthermore, he argued, this was all strengthened by secularist "literary and social salons" and numerous "books, newspapers, and magazines" which propagated ideas whose primary goal was "the weakening of the influence of religion."[115]

Despite the vigorous religio-political activism in Egypt in the 1920s, the creation of the Brotherhood roused Egyptian society at all levels. Its establishment was met with immediate, profound, and sustained effects on Egyptian society precisely because its message of a total and comprehensive Islam – that Islam was both *dīn wa dawla* – was a startlingly new idea. Indeed, the conceptualization of Islam as total and comprehensive, discerning no difference between religion and politics, is a "modern ideological construction and is not supported by either a historical analysis or an analysis of Islamic political theory."[116]

In al-Banna's vision, politics was Islam and Islam was politics and every other aspect of life. He put forth three arguments to demonstrate this: "First, the rules of Islam and its teachings are comprehensive, organizing the affairs of the people in this world and the next. Second, the foundation of Islamic teachings is the Book of God Almighty and the sunna of His Messenger ... Third, Islam as a general faith regulates all matters of life for every race and community, in every age and every era."[117]

With this affirmation of the universal validity of Islam, the

Brothers placed themselves squarely within the fundamentalist-style mode of renewal and reform begun by Rashid Rida, but also inspired by his predecessors. As Richard P. Mitchell noted in his matchless study, *The Society of the Muslim Brothers*, "The Brothers saw themselves clearly in the line of the modern reform movement identified with the names of Jamal al-Din al-Afghani, Muhammad ʿAbduh, and Rashid Rida." Each of these individuals was interpreted by the Brothers as having contributed to the ultimate establishment of their movement. With great historical accuracy, as Mitchell wrote, the Brothers saw Afghani as having fulfilled the role of the 'caller' or 'announcer' (*mu'adhdhin, sarkha*); Rida was seen as the 'archivist' or 'historian' (*sijal, mu'arrikh*). Al-Banna, however, was seen as "the 'builder (*bani*) of a renaissance, the leader of a generation, and the founder of a nation."[118]

Indeed, al-Banna and the Brothers represent an important transition point in the history of Sunni Islamic renewal and reform since 1798. While the modernist-mode of reform sought to create new intellectual frameworks for renewal, the Brothers sought to create a new intellectual framework *and* implement that framework. Renewal thus began with the revitalization of society from the bottom, beginning with guiding individuals, and ultimately society as a whole, toward a more Islamic way of life. Despite being fundamentalist in style, the Brotherhood was creative and innovative. More than any other organization to this point, the Brothers represented a Foucaultian "countermodernity" because they framed their interpretation of Islam as a complete world-view, attitude, and way of thinking.[119]

The discourse of the Brothers reveals important transitions regarding changing evaluations of 'the West' by many Muslims throughout the twentieth century. Already in 1936 al-Banna was seeking to augment the fundamentalist-style mode of renewal and reform with his argument of the 'failure of the West.' He wrote, "The Western way of life has remained incapable of offering to men's minds a flicker of light, a ray of hope, a grain of faith, or of providing anxious persons the smallest path toward rest and tranquility."[120]

For this reason, al-Banna concluded, "The civilization of the West was in bankruptcy and in decline." However, al-Banna also condemned the Communist challenge to the West as having failed as well, particularly because instead of being a true "countermodernity," it was simply a function of Western modernity. The "peoples' democracies," wrote al-Banna, were equally at fault for failure.

Characterized by "atheism," "political tyranny," and "international dictatorship," Communism was deemed a failure by the Brothers for having denied "freedom of work, speech, and thought" that is guaranteed for all people under the laws of Islam.[121]

The concept of 'the failure of the West' and its variants, like Communism, had grown far stronger by the conclusion of the Second World War. In 1947, al-Banna sent a message to King Faruq I of Egypt titled "Toward the Light." Though it was addressed to the King, its message was meant for "the kings, princes, and rulers of the various countries of the Islamic world, as well as to a great number of civic and religious leaders in those countries." He began his message by placing it in the context of Egypt – as a mirror of the Islamic world. He observed that Egypt was in a period of transition "from one state of affairs to another." As such, he said to the King, "Now you will see two ways before you, each one urging you to orient the nation in its direction and to proceed with it along its path." Describing these two directions Egypt might take, he wrote:

> The first is the way of Islam, its fundamental assumptions, its principles, its culture, and its civilization; the second is the way of the West, the external features of its life, its organization, and its procedures. It is our belief that the first way, the way of Islam, its principles and its fundamental assumptions, is the only way that ought to be followed, and toward which the present and future nation should be oriented.[122]

Al-Banna continued to describe to the King that no other system or ideology could provide Egypt with prosperity as well as Islam could. "No regime in this world will supply the renascent nation with what it requires in the way of institutions, principles, objectives, and sensibilities to the same extent that Islam supplies every one of its renascent nations," he declared.[123]

In this period, al-Banna was not the only intellectual preaching the total and comprehensive nature of Islam in the fundamentalist-style mode of reform. It is generally thought that Political Islam developed in the Arab Sunni Middle East, but in the Indian subcontinent, Sunni Islamist thought found one of its earliest and most articulate advocates.

Abu'l-A'la Mawdudi

One of the most important figures in the modern Islamic intellectual history is Abu'l-A'la Mawdudi (1903–1979). Born in 1903 in the southern Indian village of Awrangabad, his career, like al-Banna, did not begin as a theologian. Rather, Mawdudi was an accomplished journalist. In the 1920s, while al-Banna was preaching and debating in the gritty cafes along the Suez Canal, Mawdudi was the editor of *al-Jami'at*. This periodical was the principle outlet of the Jam'iyyat al-'Uluma-yi Hind, a religio-political organization comprised of prominent Muslim scholars in British India. In 1932, he became the publisher and editor of *Tarjuman al- Qur'an (The Interpreter of the Qur'an)*. He would remain its editor, articulating his ideas in its pages for the rest of his life.[124]

Mawdudi was a prolific writer. His arguments fit neatly within the fundamentalist-style mode reform, and he argued passionately against the secular-nationalists (or even Islamic-nationalists, in the Indian context). In fact, Mawdudi argued that nationalism was an impossible concept for Muslims to believe in. "Islam and nationalism are diametrically opposed to each other," he declared, before writing:

> Those who accept the principles of Islam are not divided by any distinction of nationality or race or class or country. The ultimate goal of Islam is a world-state in which the chains of racial and national prejudices would be dismantled and all mankind incorporated in a cultural and political system, with equal rights and opportunities for all ... As opposed to this, nationalism divides man from man on the basis of nationality.[125]

Mawdudi's thought and actions are indicative of the intellectual transition that took place in the fundamentalist-style mode of reform from intellectual speculation to actual implementation. For example, he argued that the concept of *tawhid* (the unity of God or the oneness of the Divine), instead of being merely a theological tenet was, instead, a political imperative to be implemented. "The necessary implication of Islam's call to affirm *tawhid* is that the sole purpose of all human effort, striving, and struggle becomes seeking the pleasure and fulfilling the will of God."[126]

In this line of analysis, Mawdudi argued that God alone is sovereign on Earth: God alone is the source of all laws, all people must submit to these laws, and it is a religious obligation of Muslims to strive to implement these laws. In this regard, Mawdudi was among the earliest Islamists to call for the establishment of an 'Islamic state,' and he was especially concerned with the nature of political power and the relationship between rulers and ruled in one. "The objective of the Islamic movement, in this world, is revolution in leadership," he declared. "A leadership that has rebelled against God and His guidance and is responsible for the suffering of mankind has to be replaced by a leadership that is God-conscious, righteous and committed to following Divine guidance."[127]

Like al-Banna, Mawdudi was disheartened by the way he saw his fellow Muslims practicing their faith. He argued that no change in leadership, or any other movement toward social, political, or religious revitalization could occur, until Muslims transformed themselves as individuals. "The crucial reason for the Muslims' decline is, in fact, the lack of Islamic morality," he wrote in 1945. "Islamic morality," he argued, consisted of four elements: *iman* (faith in God); *islam* (surrender to God); *taqwa* (God-consciousness); *ihsan* (Godliness).[128] These four principles were the basic elements of many of his speeches and writings. For example, in a speech delivered in 1948 in Lahore, he said:

> If the masses do not profess their faith in Islam with full awareness and acknowledge, in all sincerity, Allah as their Master and Ruler and accept Islam as their way of life, the government can never embrace Islam, recognize Allah as the Supreme Authority, and work according to principles of Islam.[129]

Mawdudi's goal was the establishment of an "Islamic state." But, he argued, before such a state could be established, it was necessary for Muslim society to be reformed from the bottom - up. To begin implementing these reforms, Mawdudi founded the *Jama'at-i Islami* (the "Islamic Group" or "Islamic Society") in 1941. His goal in founding this organization was providing a means of guiding Muslims toward a more pristine understanding of Islam. After this, he theorized, Muslims could then revitalize their society to provide a virtuous foundation for the establishment of an Islamic state.[130] With the particular political dynamics in India regarding the partition and formation of Pakistan, Mawdudi and his *Jama'at* were involved directly in political processes earlier than the Brothers in Egypt. As with the Brothers, however, Mawdudi packaged his vision within the framework of the fundamentalist-style mode of reform; it was an alternative world-view for Muslims – a counter-modernity.

Mawdudi's establishment of the *Jama'at* should not be interpreted as only a reaction to the particular political dynamics at the time in the Indian subcontinent. Rather, it was a reaction in the fundamentalist-style mode of reform to the broader context of the Muslim experience in modern world history. Mawdudi made this clear, when, in 1941 he stated in a speech:

> As for our movement [the *Jama'at*], it is nothing short of Islam itself, whose message is intended for the whole of mankind. That is the reason why we have abstained from involving ourselves in the typical problems of any particular people. Our gaze is rather fixed on global problems – those confronting the entire humanity.[131]

Mawdudi argued that the degradation of Muslim society, as he perceived it, was "the culmination of a gradual process of decay spread over many centuries." This had "culminated in our political breakdown, making many a Muslim country the slave of non-Muslim imperialist powers." Muslims had since "woken up," but had been "incapable of looking at things except through the colored glasses of Western thought ... Thus, they succumbed to the onslaughts of modern thought, adopted the new culture of the West, and began to ape blindly Western modes and manners."[132] Accordingly, Mawdudi sought "the reorganization of human life to accord with the ideals and values revealed by God for the guidance of mankind."[133]

Mawdudi argued that Muslims had gone astray by subordinating Islam and by organizing themselves according to Western thought and techniques. In a speech given in 1950, Mawdudi declared that the Muslim response to Western superiority could be divided in two ways: the dissidents, whom he also refers to as the renegades, and the manipulators. He explained:

> The dissidents made no secret of their deviation from the Islamic norms. They had learnt from the western education and rulers that it was not possible to make any progress by treading on the path of Islam. They ceased to believe in Is-

lam as a system of life at all ... Another group [the manipulators] believes that only the western values, moral standards, culture, education and ideas are worthy of acceptance ... They are busy moulding Islam as they please. In fact, they are creating a new Islam to suit the values of their choice.[134]

Mawdudi was criticizing the intellectual and physical hegemony of the European model of modernity. Indeed, he was the first Muslim intellectual to dismiss modernity not only as being incompatible with Islam, but having failed out right. He forcefully articulated the vision of an Islamic countermodernity that other fundamentalist-style reformers like Rida and al-Banna were also moving toward by the 1930s.[135] He hoped that, beginning with the individual, he could transform the entire human experience along Islamic guidelines. "You should not have a limited conception of the task the Jamaat-e-Islami has to accomplish," he declared before an audience gathered in his home to commemorate the founding of his organization. "But whoever joins the Jamaat ought to bear it in mind that what the party has embarked upon is not an easy task. He has to transform the entire system of human life."[136]

Mawdudi was not subtle in his critique of the secular-nationalist mode of reform or modernity, in which "the dissidents" and the "manipulators" were subsumed. In his words:

> In all those Muslim countries which suffered from foreign domination, the leadership of political and cultural movements fell into the hands of those who were shorn of all Islamic background. They adopted the creed of nationalism, directed their efforts toward the cause of *national* independence and prosperity along secular lines, and tried to copy, step by step, the advanced nations of this age.

The beginning of the most sustained period of popularity for the Islamist cause, as it was articulated by both al-Banna and Mawdudi, coincides almost directly with the historical events associated with the establishment of the modern state of Israel. In the case of the Muslim Brotherhood, for example, increased Zionist immigration to Palestine, which resulted in the Arab revolt of 1936-1939, must surely have played a decisive role in al-Banna's decision in 1939 to officially rebrand his organization as a political one. Part of this transition in the function of the Brotherhood was the internationalization of the Islamist movement itself. Beginning in 1939, it stressed the necessity of a struggle not only to liberate Egypt, but all of "the Islamic homeland" from foreign control and influence. To this end, the Brotherhood's message became more outwardly political. It became the duty of the Brothers "to institute in this homeland a free Islamic government, practicing the principles of Islam, applying its social system, propounding its solid fundamentals, and transmitting its wise call to the people." As Hamid Enayat noted, the Brothers went on to declare in 1939 that, "So long as this government is not established, the Muslims are all of them guilty before God Almighty of having failed to install it."[137]

On May 14, 1948, this position received final vindication for many Muslims when David Ben-Gurion declared the establishment of the Jewish state of Israel.[138] The next day, the first Arab-Israeli War began when the armies of Egypt, Syria, Transjordan, and Iraq invaded the newly formed state. The war concluded roughly a year later with a decisive Israeli victory. In fact, Israel had expanded its land area by about 20 percent; at the war's conclusion Israel covered almost 75 percent of the area of the former Palestine mandate west of present-day Jordan. Dubbed *al-Nakba*, "the disaster," Israel's victory was just that and more for the Arabs. It was a searing embarrassment for the Arabs that 600,000 Jews were able to defeat the combined armies of 40 million Arabs, and that they were unable to prevent the destruction of the ancestral homes of nearly one million Palestinian Arabs.

As Yvonne Haddad characterized the Arab viewpoint: "After thirty years of pain and struggle, of sacrifice and suffering, the Arab cannot fathom why Israel continues to prosper and become stronger while his people are weaker and more helpless. Israel is seen as part of the confrontation and effort at domination of the Arab world by the Western colonial powers."[139]

After the 1948 victory, Israel's continued economic, political, and military success vindicated the position of the fundamentalist-style reformers. For many Muslims, Israel was viewed as traditional Western imperialism under a Jewish guise. While difficult to trace precisely the actions of the Brotherhood during the first Arab-Israel War, its involvement in Palestine did add a new element of political activism to its otherwise religio-moral message. With the new element of the Jewish state in the heart of historical Islam, al-Banna's frequently cited order to "Eject imperialism from your souls, and it will leave your lands" gained newfound legitimacy for many Muslims and the Islamist cause began growing in strength and popularity.[140] Israel's continued position of superiority over its Arab-Muslim neighbors, especially the loss of the holy city of Jerusalem (al-Quds) to Israeli control, ostensibly proved correct those fundamentalist-style reformers who postulated that God was punishing Muslims for turning their backs on the Islamic faith and placing it instead in alien systems.

The total and catastrophic Arab defeat by Israeli forces in the June 1967 War vindicated the position of fundamentalist-style reformers even further. The defeat came at a time of incredible Arab pride, of great hope, and of a feeling of maturity symbolized most prominently by the president of Egypt Jamal ʿAbd al-Nasir (1918–1970). As Haddad describes, "While the Israelis felt bolstered in confidence and powerful in their strengthened position and holdings, the Arab world, defeated, stood once again naked, vulnerable, the laughingstock of the world."

For many Muslims, the scarring defeat in 1967 came as a direct punishment from God because, it was argued, "the Muslims once again had placed their faith in alien systems and devoted their energies to the posited purposes of these systems rather than zealously working for the purposes of God."[141] As conceptualized by al-Banna and Mawdudi, it was argued that only Islam, when accepted fully as a total and comprehensive program for all aspects of life, could rehabilitate the place of Muslims in the modern world.

In a certain sense, one of Egyptian president Anwar al-Sadat's (1918-1981) goals during his time in power was to rekindle the ebullience of the Nasir years before the '67 defeat. Although the war he started in 1973 ultimately ended in another Arab defeat, his ability to propagandize on the exploding Islamist sentiment of the time allowed him to portray the war as a victory for Islam – even if it was a tactical military defeat. According to Yvonne Haddad, "In the religious literature that [was] produced by the Sadat propaganda organization there is a definite indication of an Islamic victory."[142] Epitomized by his public defiance of Henry Kissinger's pleas for a cease-fire during the war, Sadat's boastful statements (many of which were cloaked in Islamic undertones) created a vision for Muslims of a new phase in their historical experience. The rhetoric in official circles (emanating from Sadat) as well as on the street was one frequently referring to Arabs as the world's sixth great power, which appealed to the long-running historical desire for some sort of revenge of 'the West.'[143]

The 1973 War is also seen was an Islamic victory because of its inseparable association with the oil boycott of that same year led by Saudi Arabia. God had awarded Saudi Arabia with victory, it was argued, because Saudi Arabia was the only Muslim country to declare itself truly Islamic and to implement religious law and the tenets of the Qur'an.[144] These events marked the beginning of a decade that saw a significant shift in wealth and power to oil-producing countries, most of which were Muslim, and the Western capitalist model of modernity was especially questioned as self-proclaimed "Islamic" countries like Saudi Arabia saw that they could exert great control over the world economic system through their monopoly of the oil market.

As Henry Kissinger noted at this time, these events "altered irrevocably the world as it had grown up in the postwar period."[145] For many Muslims in the 1970s, Kissinger's observation was quite true, for "The oil boom had shown the vulnerability of the West more dramatically than anything in the past five centuries. By confirming Islam in the eyes of many, it prepared the way for the Islamic movements" that questioned not whether Muslims could survive in the contemporary world, but whether *the West* could survive in the contemporary world.[146]

Strikingly, there emerged in the decades after Israel's establishment as a Jewish state Muslim voices who spoke of Israel with a certain extent of admiration. Though not constitutionally defined as a religious state, Israel was perceived by some Islamists as being strong precisely because of its reliance upon religion. The prominent Muslim Brotherhood intellectual Muhammad al-Ghazali, for example, sharply contrasted his perception of Israel as a defiantly religious state with the non-religious nature, at least in name, of several Arab states:

> Nobody would have been surprised had the Jews called their state...the Jewish Republic, the Jewish Socialist Union, or any other such name corresponding to the actual state of affairs...Their neighbors in Jordan, Hejaz or Yemen [are] ruled by deeply-rooted aristocratic families which give their own names to the states and governments. In Yemen it is the Mutawakkili government. In Jordan it is the Hashemite government. In Saudi Arabia it is the Saudi government. Following their example, the Jewish government would be the "Weizmannite" government!
>
> Yet, the Jews have...returned to their ancient history, dug out its roots and appeared two thousand years after Christ with the name of "Israel". This name is the symbol of

their attachment to their religion and their respect for their sacred memoires. It should be observed that the Jews who have chosen to follow this course are themselves the greatest of capitalists, scientists, politicians, and economists... None of these men felt ashamed to belong to their religion or thought of discarding it.[147]

Of course, in the final legal and political analysis what the founders of Israel had done is draw upon religious heritage to frame their national identity. To be clear, this does not in any way make Israel a "religious state" (whatever ones definition of a 'religious state' might be). But it reveals one of the most important themes in the writings of Islamists in the fundamentalist-style mode of reform: the critique of Muslims for having failed to do precisely what the Jews had done in basing their identity off their religious heritage. The "state" of Israel was identified as Jewish – and all that the Jewish heritage encompasses. Before the Islamic Revolution in Iran in 1979 there was no Muslim country where the state could be identified by the Islamic heritage. Though it was Shi'a in character, the Iranian Revolution demonstrated to Muslims everywhere that Islam could be used politically – and successfully.

PART THREE

Power and Authority in an Islamic State

> We do not view democracy as an alternative to Islam, or as better than Islam. We view democracy as an Islamic principle that was taught and practiced by Prophet Muhammad and his companions.
> Radwan Masmoudi
> *Muslim Democrat*, 1999

Political Islam

The decade of the 1960s was a period of significant change in the Arab world, and many of these changes strengthened the fundamentalist-style mode of reform. Pan-Arabism, or Arab nationalism more generally, ceased to be a major ideology after the collapse of Nasir's experimental United Arab Republic in 1961. The Arab League Summit, held in Cairo in 1964, brought no solutions to revive the failing United Arab Republic, despite Nasir's best attempts. Pan-Arabism, for all practical purposes, was dead.

The decline of Arab nationalism as a unified ideology coincided with transitions within the secular-nationalist mode of reform. Reforms in this mode had generally taken place as a function of middle-class, popular civilian support. However, during the 1960s secular nationalism was used by military strongmen as a tool to legitimate and enforce their despotic governance. Ben Bella's deposition by military coup in Algeria in 1965 and Sukarno's deposition in that same year by military coup in Indonesia marked the end of old-style secular nationalism in the Muslim world. "Since 1967," writes Ibrahim Abu-Rabi', "the Islamist movement, reemerging as the most viable socio-religious force, has leveled a sustained and popular critique to the Arab political elites, the failure of their modernization program, the loss of political and civil freedoms and the ossification of political leadership."[1] As the Arab world was going through this period of dramatic change, the fundamentalist-style mode of reform and the Islamist project received its most cogent and enthusiastic articulation from the Egyptian intellectual Sayyid Qutb.

Sayyid Qutb

Sayyid Qutb (1906–1966) remains one of the most prominent figures in Islamic intellectual history. His writings continue to inspire a wide caste of Muslims, from radical militants to peaceful activists. Born in 1906 in a small village in Upper Egypt, Qutb began his career as an elementary school teacher who frequented Cairo's elite cafes, where he was fond of discussing literature, poetry, and international politics. One of his biographers, Muhammad Tawfiq Barakat, divides Qutb's intellectual career into three phases. In the first phase, from his birth until around 1948, Qutb's writings are characterized by a generally positive tone, (or, at least, not hostile) toward the West. In the 1930s, Qutb was a respected literary critic and a frequent participant in bourgeois debates over pressing matters for Egyptians at the time. Although certainly a pious person, in this period of his life his mode of engagement fit within the secular-nationalist one, as was the case for most educated Egyptians.[2]

A series of personal crises during this period of his life had a transformative effect on Qutb. He became increasingly dismayed with what he perceived to be the unabashed and unchallenged British domination of Egyptians. This feeling of Western or foreign domination over Muslims was made worse by the opening of Palestine to mass Jewish immigration after the Second World War. These events led to a radical transformation of his religious and political commitments. Barakat notes the year 1948 as the beginning of the second phase of his intellectual career. In this phase, his writings are characterized by an increased interest in Islamic topics.[3]

Qutb had built a reputation for himself as a respected intellectual and skillful literary critic and he had an influential voice among educated Egyptians. He used his stature to make arguments about Egyptian life and international affairs that were increasingly radical in tone and style. Since by this time he was working for the Egyptian Ministry of Education, the government became concerned with his growing radicalism and sent him to the United States. Under the auspices of cultural exchange, Qutb was told that his task was to study the American system of education. Yet, as Euben and Zaman note, "The assignment was largely a pretext; the trip was designed to quell the increasingly strident moralism of Qutb's writing by exposing him to the attractions of a world he hated but had never directly experienced. The effort backfired."[4] His time in America catalyzed his move toward Islamism.

Qutb's time in America convinced him that he was witnessing a great clash between Islam and a Western-dominated world. He perceived Westerners as anti-Muslim, morally bankrupt, materialistic, and spiritually impoverished. He made his thoughts clear when, upon his return to Egypt in 1951, he published in the Egyptian magazine *al-Risala* an article titled "The America I Have Seen." His account is unsparing. He notes that while America might indeed represent "the peak of advancement," it is also stuck in "the depth of primitiveness." He wrote that there were many reasons for the primitiveness of Americans. "It seems the American is primitive in his appreciation of muscular strength and the strength of matter in general." He continued:

> This primitiveness can be seen in the spectacle of the fans as they follow a game of football, played in the rough American style [in which] each player attempts to catch the ball with his hands and run with it toward the goal, wile the players of the opposing team attempt to tackle him by any means necessary, whether this be a blow to his stomach, or crushing his arms and legs with great violence and ferocity...The sight of the fans as they follow this game, or watch boxing matches or bloody, monstrous wrestling matches... is one of animal excitement born of their love for hardcore violence.
>
> Their lack of attention to the rules and sportsmanship to the extent that they are enthralled with the following blood and crushed limbs, crying loudly, everyone cheering for his team. Destroy his head. Crush his ribs. Beat him to a pulp. This spectacle leaves no room for doubt as to the primitiveness of the feelings of those who are enamored with muscular strength and desire it.[5]

Describing America as primitive allowed Qutb to cast America, as harbinger of all things Western and modern, as having failed. Perhaps more than Mawdudi, Qutb provided a sustained, cogent articulation of 'the failure of the West' and its world-view of modernity. Furthermore, his position resonated with the legitimate sentiment of many Muslims who perceived America and the West as militaristic and a grave threat to their very existence. "Indeed, the American is by his very nature a warrior and loves combat," wrote Qutb. He continued, hoping to dash the misguided understanding of America as a benevolent, isolationist country, and wrote, "The idea of combat and war runs strong in his blood...The period of isolation passed, and its politics ended, when America entered the First World War. Then it entered the Second World War. Now it is starting a war in Korea, and a third world war is not far behind!"[6]

Qutb's depiction of a primitive, militaristic America did not rely upon physical evidence alone; it also extended to matters of spirituality and morality. For example, he wrote that the feelings of Americans toward religion were primitive. "There is no one further from the American from appreciating the spirituality of religion and respect for its sacraments, and there is nothing farther from religion than the American's thinking and his feelings and manners." As evidence for his argument, Qutb recalls "a hot night at the church." For its significance in how he used it to contrast against the purity of Islam and Muslims as well as for its levity, which Qutb surely did not bring intentionally, it is worth reproducing here. He recalled:

> One night I was in a church in Greeley, Colorado...After the religious service in the church ended...we proceeded through a side door onto the dance floor that was connected to the prayer hall by a door, and the Father jumped to his desk and every boy took the hand of a girl...The dance floor was lit with red and yellow and blue lights, and with a few white lamps...and the dance floor was replete with tapping feet, enticing legs, arms wrapped around waists, lips pressed to lips, and chests pressed to chests. The atmosphere was full of desire.

Qutb then continued to recall that the minister, recently arrived in the dance hall, dimmed all of the white lamps, and thus "the place really did appear to become more romantic and passionate." He continued to describe that the minister and the Father went to the gramophone to choose a new song:

> And the Father chose. He chose a famous American song called "But Baby, It's Cold Outside," which is composed of a dialogue between a boy and a girl returning from their evening date. The boy took the girl to his home and kept

her from leaving. She entreated him to let her return home, for it was getting late, and her mother was waiting but every time she would make an excuse, he would reply to her with this line: but baby, its cold outside!

And the minister waited until he saw people stepping to the rhythm of this moving song, and he seemed satisfied and contented. He left the dance floor for his home, leaving the men and women to enjoy this night in all its pleasure and innocence![7]

Qutb's time in America galvanized in him a conviction that Muslim society, beginning in Egypt, needed total reformation before it could emerge from under the yoke of Western hegemony. He viewed the world as lodged in a cosmic battle between the defunct, godless West and pristine Islam. Only Islam, he argued, provided the model for Muslims to emulate because its mission "is always to propel life to renewal, development, and progress and to press human potentialities to build, to go forth, and to elevate."[8] The ultimate goal of the radical social transformation that he envisioned was Islam taking over the rightful leadership of the world. As he wrote in one of his most famous works, *Social Justice in Islam*: "Islam is a faith of achievement, of work in the sphere of practical life; it is not a religion of mere words or abstract guidance existing only in the world of the imagination."[9]

Social Justice in Islam was published in Egypt while Qutb was in the United States. In this work, Qutb provided an extensive analysis of the practicalities of using Islam as a total and comprehensive system for social transformation, and it was here that Qutb first propounded his idea of the "universal theory of Islam." The leaders of the Muslim Brotherhood took a keen interest in it and it earned their immediate approbation. His arguments in this work marked a significant transition in the nature of Muslim reform. Speaking clearly about previous, Westernizing modes of reform, he wrote:

> Some Muslim writers, discussing the Islamic political system, labor to trace connections and similarities between it and the other systems known to the ancient or the modern world...And some of them believe that they find a strong support for Islam when they can trace such a connection between it and one of the other ancient or modern systems. In reality this attempt represents nothing but an inner conviction that the Islamic system is inferior to those of the Western world.[10]

Qutb scorned reform, renewal, or any attempts at social transformation that sought inspiration from anything other than Islam. He questioned such efforts at their most basic level: "For Islam altogether presents to mankind an example of a complete political system, the like of which has never been found in any of the other systems known to the world either before or after the coming of Islam."[11] This "complete political system," as Yvonne Haddad has identified, consisted of the following basic elements: Lordship of God (*rabbaniyya*); constancy (*thabat*); comprehensiveness or totality (*shumūl*); balance (*tawazun*); positiveness (*ijabiyya*); pragmatism (*waqiiyya*); and unicity (*tawhid*).[12]

For the Brotherhood, Qutb's logically presented affirmation of the totality of Islam (*shumuliyyat al-Islam*) was particularly refreshing. Their founder and spiritual guide, Hasan al-Banna, had been killed in 1949, and Qutb's preaching and writings provided a great sense of intellectual reassurance. Though not yet a member of the organization in 1949, he recalled in his memoir his positive disposition toward the cause of the Muslim Brotherhood. The day al-Banna was killed, Qutb was in a hospital in the United States, and he recalled in his memoir the sickness he felt when he observed the ecstatic reception with which the Americans around him greeted the news of al-Banna's death. For Qutb, experiences like this one confirmed in his mind that the Brotherhood was the vanguard of Islam.[13]

Qutb officially joined the Muslim Brotherhood soon after his return to Egypt in 1950, and it was not long until he was imprisoned for his preaching and writings. The third phase of Qutb's intellectual career began during his first imprisonment. This phase is characterized by complete fidelity to the Muslim Brotherhood and the radical Islamization of Egyptian society.[14] It was in this period that he wrote his two most famous works, *Ma'alim fi al-Tariq*, translated into English usually as *Milestones*, *Milestones Along the Way*, or *Signposts Along the Road*. Written in prison and later published in 1964, much of the content in *Milestones* was first written in Qutb's even more influential and massive Qur'anic commentary, *Fi zilal al-Qur'an* (*In the Shade of the Qur'an*). As with *Milestones*, Qutb wrote much of *In the Shade of the Qur'an* between brutal torture sessions in Nasir's prisons.

For the Brothers, al-Banna could never be replaced, but after writing these two works Qutb became their intellectual guide and the main source of inspiration for their call to action, or *daw'a*.

Zainab al-Ghazali, a leading female advocate of the Brotherhood, recalled in her memoir, *Return of the Pharaoh: Memoir in Nasir's Prison*, the zeal with which she and other members studied Qutb's works. "Sweet, glorious days and Allah's bounties passed by while we studied and taught ourselves," she wrote. She was particularly impressed with *Milestones*, as was Hassan al-Hudaybi (1891-1973), who assumed the position of *Murshid*, or supreme guide of the organization after al-Banna's death. In her memoir, al-Ghazali recalled Hudaybi's response when asked his opinion on *Milestones*. He said: "With Allah's benediction, this book has confirmed all my trust in Sayyid [Qutb], may Allah preserve him. Sayyid, Allah willing, is now the awaited hope for *da'wah*."¹⁵

In *Milestones* and *In the Shade of the Qur'an*, Qutb indicted the West as a failure. Furthermore, by spreading the world-view of modernity throughout the world, Qutb argued, the West had led the world into *jahaliyya*, a Qur'anic word that originally referred to the period of ignorance before the revelation of Islam. "If we look at the sources and foundations of modern ways of living, it becomes clear that the whole world is steeped in *jahaliyya*," he wrote.¹⁶ Qutb argued further that Islam is not merely a creed to be faithful to, but a total system of life that must be implemented to reverse the ignorance that had beset all of mankind. Any world-view that was not expressly Islamic, he argued, such as modernity, was a failure. As he wrote:

> If materialism, no matter in what form, is given the highest value, whether it be in the form of a 'theory,' such as in the Marxist interpretation of history, or in the form of material production, as is the case with the United States and European countries, and all other human values are sacrificed at its alter, then such a society is a backward one, or, in Islamic terminology, is a *jahili* society.¹⁷

Like al-Banna, Qutb argued that the world was divided between the West and Islam; the West had failed and only Islam provided the required solutions. He placed this argument at the beginning of *Milestones*, where he declared:

> Mankind today is on the brink of a precipice...because humanity is devoid of those vital values which are necessary not only for its healthy development but for its real progress. Even the Western world realizes that Western civiliza-

tion is unable to present any healthy values for the guidance of mankind...It is essential for mankind to have new leadership![18]

Qutb concluded that Islam is the only system capable of providing mankind with the requisite new leadership. Inherent in Qutb's condemnation of the West is his conclusion that modernity itself had failed. In this regard, Qutb provided the most complete intellectual framework for a distinctly Islamic countermodernity because, unlike Mao's cultural revolution in China, Soviet communism or even Nasir's radical Arab nationalism, Islam was not a product or function of modernity.

"Islam's way of life is unique," he wrote, because "it is not a product of Western invention nor of European genius, whether eastern or western." As Qutb argued, Islam was unique because it was not a "man-made individual or collective theory" like nationalism. "Those who deviate from this system [Islam] and want some other system, whether it be based on nationalism, color and race, class struggle, or similar corrupt theories, are truly the enemies of mankind!"[19] As he wrote of the failure of modernity:

> The period of the resurgence of science has also come to an end. This period, which began with the Renaissance in the sixteenth century after Christ and reached its zenith in the eighteenth and nineteenth centuries, does not possess a reviving spirit.
>
> All nationalistic and chauvinistic ideologies which have appeared in modern times, and all the movements and theories derived from them, have also lost their vitality. In short, all man-made individual or collective theories have proved to be failures.[20]

Yet, Qutb argued that in many ways the Muslim community had failed as well. "The Muslim community has long ago vanished from existence and from observation, and the leadership of mankind has long since passed to other ideologies and other nations, other concepts and other systems," he wrote. It was vital, then, "to revive that Muslim community which is buried under the debris of the man-made traditions of several generations, and which is crushed under the weight of those false laws and customs which are not even remotely related to the Islamic teachings." In this, Qutb was placing himself firmly within the fundamentalist-style mode of reform and the *Salafiyyah* school of thought that emerged with Rashid Rida. As he wrote, referring to the "unique Qur'anic generation" of the Prophet and his companions:

> It is therefore necessary – in the way of the Islamic movement – that ... we should remove ourselves from all the influences of the *jahaliyyah* in which we live and from which we derive benefits. We must return to that pure source from which those people derived their guidance, the source which is free from any mixing or pollution. We must return to it to derive from it our concepts of the nature of the universe, the nature of human existence...From it we must also derive our concepts of life, our principles of government, politics, economics and all other aspects of life.[21]

To be certain, Qutb was not just engaging in intellectual speculation. Consistent with the stated goals of the Muslim Brotherhood, he sought to implement a radical social transformation inspired by the model of the *salaf*. "Our foremost objective is to change the practices of this society," he wrote. "Our aim is to change the *jahili* system at its very roots." The starting point for Qutb, then, was the *shahada*, the Muslim declaration of faith: *la ilaha illa Allah, wa Muhammadar Rasul Allah* ("There is no god but God, and Muhammad is the Messenger of God"). This declaration of *tawhid*, the oneness of God, established Islam as a complete system of life. "A Muslim community can come into existence only when individuals and groups of people reject servitude to anyone except God...and decide that they will organize their scheme or life on the basis of this submission."[22]

Like the intellectuals before him in each mode of reform, Qutb was writing under despotic government, and the evils of despotism are a central characteristic of his thought. In Qutb's vision, despotism was antithetical to Islam, because Islam "seeks to liberate people from subjugation so that they may serve God alone."[23] As he wrote:

> When, in a society, the sovereignty belongs to God alone, expressed in its obedience to the Divine Law, only then is every person in that society free from servitude to others, and only then does he taste true freedom ... In a society which bases its foundation on the concept, belief and way of life which all originate from the One God, man's dignity

is respected to the highest degree and no one is a slave to another, as they are in societies in which the concepts, beliefs and way of life originate from human masters.[24]

Qutb's assertions here are important because they demonstrate his disregard for modernity and its system of secular nation-states. Indeed, the concept of state sovereignty was invented as a feature of modernity. As the historian Immanuel Wallerstein put it, "The modern state is a sovereign state. Sovereignty is a concept that was invented in the modern world-system."[25] Qutb wrote that assigning all authority to God "represents a challenge to all systems that assign sovereignty to human beings in any shape or any form. It is, in effect, a revolt against any human situation where sovereignty, or indeed Godhead, is given to human beings."[26] By relegating sovereignty only to God, and by rejecting any organizational system that does not derive from *tawhid*, Qutb was in his most decisive manner yet rejecting modernity itself.

With his disavowal of modernity, Qutb created a conceptual framework for intellectuals in the fundamentalist-style mode of reform to enact an indigenously Islamic "countermodernity." By operating within this Islamic countermodernity, it was no longer necessary for Muslims to operate within the confines of Western thought. While reformers before Qutb accepted the basic analytical framework of Western thought as the definition of the ground rules for reform and renewal, Political Islamists after Qutb were free to disagree with even that basic framework.[27] For Islamists, the intellectual point of departure is Islam itself. The goal of Political Islamists, as described by Mawdudi's protégé Khurshid Ahmad, is: "The restructuring of their society, individual and collective life and rebuilding socio-economic life on the foundations of Islam."[28] The Islamist restructuring of society is meant to affect the establishment of an Islamic state, which is the basic unit of political analysis in the Islamist countermodernity. As such, the 'state' is no longer identified by any particular nation; rather, it is identified by 'Islam' itself.

In 1966, Sayyid Qutb was accused and convicted of partaking in plans to assassinate President Nasir. He was hanged shortly thereafter. In the years after his death, his writings presented many Islamic activists in the fundamentalist-style mode with a new framework for reform. Political Islam emerged from this framework in the second half of the twentieth century as a function of the increasing sentiment of many Muslims that the West had failed in providing a model for modernization of the state, inspiration for reform, and blueprint for social transformation.

Political Islam is a condemnation of the present and a critique of the world-systems that created it. The concept of the failure of the West and modernity - a product of increasing Muslim discernment toward those concepts over the past two centuries - freed Islamists to experiment with new modes of renewal and reform that were not tied to the intellectual hegemony of the West. At the core of Political Islam, then, is the search for new methods of religious, social, and political transformation that can be presented as authentically Islamic in character and indigenous in tradition. For many Muslims, the Islamist interpretation of the faith as a "comprehensive, integrated way of life" provided a compelling framework for organizing the experiences facing the *umma* into a popular narrative that assembled past, present, and future into one accessible package.[29]

Dīn *as* dawla

The expression of Islam as a normative function of the state is a new concept in the history of Islam. This historical transition involved a dramatic reinvention of the very content of Islamic thought.[30] In Political Islam, the role of religion in public life is not debated in the old-style of *dīn* and *umma*, or even *dīn* and *dawla*. Rather, Islamists argue that in their Islamic countermodernity *dīn* is *dawla:* Islam and the state, or any other aspect of human experience, are one.

The Sudanese Islamist Hasan al-Turabi (1932–) describes this concept as a universal characteristic of Islamic government. "The state is only the political expression of an Islamic society," he wrote. "An Islamic state evolves from an Islamic society."[31] The effort to establish an Islamic state rests upon the Qutbian argument that Islam is more than a moral commitment and set of theories and ideas. Islamists argue that Islam contains within it a coherent strategy from which specific, actionable political conclusions can be drawn. Political Islam is therefore a distinct, comprehensive political ideology that is framed as an alternative world-system to the perceived failure of the West and modernity.

According to Sayyid Qutb, Islam in this conceptualization presented "to mankind an example of a complete political system, the like of which has never been found in any of the other systems known to the world."[32] Islamists argue that previous revivalist movements subordinated the faith to a Western world-system that

Muslims had mistakenly perceived as eternally successful and all-powerful. The decisively new and unique aspect of Political Islam is that it seeks to affirm "the primacy of Islam in the efforts of social transformation and communal identity."[33]

Another new aspect of Political Islam is the attachment of personal piety and individual duty with facilitating the establishment of an Islamic state.[34] The Moroccan scholar of Islam Abdelilah Belkeziz concludes that the roots of this new conceptualization lie with Hasan al-Banna. For example, in a Muslim Brotherhood-sponsored periodical, al-Banna argued: "Any person who is pleased with the current affairs and who dedicates his life fully to worship while leaving society and politics in the hands of the undeserved, the sinners, the infiltrators, and to the colonialists, cannot be considered a true Muslim!"[35]

In this line of analysis, al-Banna argued that rule (*al-hukm*) and political authority in general were matters not simply of *fiqh* (jurisprudence) but of creed, *al-'aqīda*. This was a transition of profound significance because attached to it was the notion that it was obligatory (*fi'l wājib*) for a Muslim to work to establish an Islamic state. Al-Banna argued that establishing an Islamic state for a Muslim was no less than a matter specified by the requirements of Islamic commandment. Mawdudi was among the most prominent Islamists to argue this. As he put it: "The struggle for obtaining control over the organs of the state, when motivated by the urge to establish the *dīn* and the Islamic Shari'a and to enforce the Islamic institutions, is not only permissible but positively desirable and as such obligatory."[36]

Departing from this new conceptualization of Islamic commandment, contemporary Islamists argue that Muslims cannot be true to the faith unless living in an Islamic state. The Islamist Muhammad al-Mubarak characterizes this as such:

> The state is necessary in Islam because it is not possible to execute the rulings of the Qur'an without a state ... because in the Qur'anic understanding of existence, there is no doubt that there must be a social sphere in order for it to be realized and that is the Islamic state; and secondly, because the Prophet himself set up a state.[37]

Tying the Islamist project to individual Muslim duty is a theme in nearly all contemporary Islamist writings. Muhammad Ibrahim Mabruk, for example, states: "The establishment of the state for

Muslims is a religious obligation (*wājib dini*) incumbent upon the Islamic *umma* and the affairs of their religion and their life cannot be conducted except by it."[38] The Tunisian Islamist Rachid Ghannouchi put it more succinctly: "A concept of an Islamic government does exist, and ... it is the religious duty of Muslims ... to work for the establishment of such a government."[39]

Political Islam is thus cast as a participatory movement in which individual salvation is only possible by active participation in political affairs aimed at establishing an Islamic state. In Weberian terms, Islamism is not an "other-worldly" orientation in which salvation requires withdrawal from political and worldly affairs, like many traditional Salafi or Sufi movements. Rather, Islamism is a social, political and religious orientation that functions "within the institutions of the world, but in opposition to them."[40]

Opposition is an important theme in understanding Political Islam. In the context of the modern Middle East, intellectuals, reformers, and activists who have used religion as a frame of reference have faced harsh repression under secular, despotic regimes.[41] The best example of this is the "Islamic Tendency Movement" (*Harakat al-ittijah al-islami*), which Rachid Ghannouchi (1941–) founded in Tunisia in 1981. The name of the group is symbolic. Ghannouchi and his colleagues sought social, economic, and political reforms of the Tunisian state, but tended to frame their discourse in Islamic labels and concepts. Tunisian President Habib Bourguiba (1903–2000) banned the group soon after it was founded and Ghannouchi, after being imprisoned and tortured several times, spent most of his life living in self-imposed exile in Britain. Repression and imprisonment for members of Ghannouchi's organization, renamed *Ennahda* ("Renaissance") in 1988 after Ben ʿAli (1936–) succeeded Bourguiba as President, continued while Ghannouchi was in exile.

Hassan Turabi, once the leading Islamist ideologue of the Bashir regime in Sudan, has been imprisoned many times, most recently in 2011. Hassan al-Banna, of course, was gunned down in the streets of Cairo and Sayyid Qutb was hanged very publically by the Nasir regime. Even Mawdudi was imprisoned throughout his life by authorities in India and later Pakistan.[42] Opposition to despotism and absolute power is therefore a fundamental tenet of the Islamist critique. Yousuf al-Qaradawi of Egypt (1926–) provides perhaps the most eloquent expression of this:

> Whatever has come to afflict Islam and Muslims in the present age has come from despotism, imposed on people with

the carrot and the stick. It is only through coercion and tyranny, the resort to fire and sword, that the shari'a has been suspended, secularism imposed, and people forced to westernize. It is only through the power of despotism – sometimes brazen, at other times concealed in spurious democratic claims; sometimes openly controlled by anti-Islamic forces, at other times from behind the scenes – that the call to Islam and the Islamic movement have been suppressed and those associated with it tortured and banished.[43]

For contemporary Islamists, their experiences of torture and imprisonment play an important role in shaping their political philosophy, a central characteristic of which is the attempt to devise a political system, in line with the guiding elements of the *shari'a*, and in which no one person has absolute power. Islamists argue that a Muslim can only truly live in freedom, with servitude to none but God, in a system such as this.

Tawhid *and* ḥākimiyya

The vision of renewal and reform contained in Political Islam and the conceptualization of social contract-based Islamic government is one that formed in opposition to the repression of secular and despotic rulers who wielded absolute power. In her memoir, *Return of the Pharaoh*, the Egyptian activist Zainab al-Ghazali (1917–2005) described how "Nasir's despotism" only served to "increase our persistence to please our consciences and live for the fulfillment of our mission, the mission of *tawhid*."[44]

As al-Ghazali indicates, Islamist critique of and opposition to despotism begins with the concept of *tawhid*, the oneness of God. This is confirmed throughout Islamist writings. Turabi, for example, declared: "The ideological foundation of an Islamic state lies in the doctrine of *tawhid* - the unity of God and of human life – as a comprehensive and exclusive program of worship." *Tawhid* is interpreted as precluding despotism and absolute rule in Islamic government: "The freedom of the individual ultimately emanates from the doctrine of *tawhid*," wrote Turabi, "which requires a self-liberation of man from any worldly authority in order to serve God exclusively."[45]

Coming from the Latin word *absolutus*, "absolute" power means not so much that the ruler is all-powerful (as the endless succession of coups in the history of the Middle East or similar events in British monarchical history demonstrates), but that the ruler "is not subject to (and is absolved from) the laws and therefore cannot be legitimately constrained by any human being doing what the ruler thinks best."[46] A central component of Political Islam is that absolutism is antithetical to Islamic government because authority belongs ultimately with none but God. As Turabi puts it: "An Islamic state is not an absolute or sovereign entity. It is subject to the higher norms of the shari'a that represent the will of God. Politically this rules out all forms of absolutism."[47]

Islamists argue that the unity of God and His power as expressed in the Qur'an provides natural limits on the power of rulers. As the Qur'an reveals, "Authority (al-hukum) belongs only to God. He commands you not to surrender to anyone save Him" [12:40]. Many Islamists, such as Sayyid Qutb, use this Qur'anic verse to form the basis of their argument about political power and authority. For example, Qutb argued that: "The declaration of faith [There is no god but God] provides the foundation for a complete system of life for the Muslim community in all its details." Stressing the importance to Islamists of individual, active participation in political affairs, Qutb also wrote: "These values are not idealistic but are practical values which can be attained through human effort, by applying the teachings of Islam correctly." Similarly, for Qutb as with other Islamists inspired by him, the original sources of Islam clearly portray Muslims living in a state of freedom. As he argued:

> Universal declaration of the freedom of man on the earth from every authority except that of God, and the declaration that sovereignty is God's alone and that He is the Lord of the universe, is not merely a theoretical, philosophical, and passive proclamation. It is a positive, practical and dynamic message with a view to bringing about the implementation of the Shari'a of God and actually freeing people from their servitude to other men to bring them into the serve of God, the One without associates.[48]

Islamist conceptualizations of political power and authority on earth depart from the concept of *ḥākimiyya*, or sovereignty. Islamists deal with this concept in the context of determining a system of government that affirms God's ultimate sovereignty on earth while also maintaining man's natural state of freedom under His rule. This stems from several Qur'anic verses, which demand that humans rule according to what God revealed [5:44, 45, 47; 6:57, 62; 12:40, 67; 28:70, 88]. Mawdudi was the first Islamist to spend considerable time writing on this concept. Mawdudi wrote that Muslims must first decide who enjoys the right to sovereignty in an Islamic state. Then, he wrote: "An unequivocal reply to this question is furnished by the Qur'an itself when it says that sovereignty, in all its aspects, is only for GOD.[49]

Mawdudi continued to note that the concept of sovereignty (*ḥākimiyya*), in terms of a modern state, is generally viewed through a legal framework. "In the terminology of modern Political Science, this word is used in the sense of absolute overlordship or complete suzerainty," he wrote. "If a person or a set of persons or an institution is to be Sovereign, it would mean that his or their or its word is law." Mawdudi dismissed the "legal sense and meaning of sovereignty prescribed by lawyers and jurists" as having "no practical existence" without political sovereignty. If legal sovereignty is the creation of law, "Political Sovereignty thus naturally means ownership of the authority of enforcing legal sovereignty." But Mawdudi concluded that no such sovereignty actually exists "in the bounds of humanity." "Whenever the experts of Political Science ... have endeavored to locate the possessor of such sovereignty in human society, they have invariably failed." He argues that this is because sovereignty belongs to none but God:

> Sovereignty belongs to God and God alone. He is Omnipotent, i.e. He can do whatever He likes; He has to refer to none and to render account to none; He is the source and fount of all authority; He is the only one whose authority and power nothing can limit or restrain; and He alone is above all aberration and error."[50]

Sayyid Qutb reached similar conclusions regarding *ḥākimiyya*. He argued in *Milestones* that complete freedom on earth, as well as natural limits against persons with absolute power, can only be achieved by a political system that is in accordance with God's design for man. In his words:

> When, in a society, the sovereignty belongs to God alone, expressed in in its obedience to the Divine Law, only then is every person in that society free from servitude to others, and only then does he taste true freedom ... On the other

hand, in a society in which some people are lords who legislate and some are slaves who obey them, then there is no freedom in the real sense, nor dignity for each and every individual.[51]

In Qutb's view, all political power and authority on Earth must allow for the supremacy of God's sovereignty, *hakimiyyat-Allah*. The expert of Islamic jurisprudence Deina Abdelkader points out that this term is often incorrectly translated to mean "God's rule."[52] However, *hakimiyyat-Allah* is not meant to denote a theocratic government in which God rules directly or through the agency of any person or group with privileged access to His word, such as, for example, in the Islamic Republic in Iran. Rather, as Qutb wrote, *ḥākimiyya* ensured the "universal declaration of the freedom of man from servitude to other men." Continuing, he wrote that *hakimiyyat-Allah* is "A challenge to all kinds and forms of systems which are based on the concept of the sovereignty of man ... Any system in which the final decisions are referred to human beings, and in which the sources of all authority are human, deifies human beings by designating others than God as lords over men."[53]

Here, Qutb demonstrates a central theme in Islamist thought. Not only do Islamists critique the absolute authority of rulers over ruled, they also critique forcefully and with constancy the concept of theocracy. As he wrote:

> The way to establish God's rule on earth is not that some consecrated people – the priests – be given the authority to rule, as was the case with the rule of the Church, nor that some spokesmen of God become rulers, as is the case in a 'theocracy.' To establish God's rule means that His laws be enforced and that the final decision in all affairs be according to these laws.[54]

In this case, when Qutb refers to "His laws," he is referring to certain Qur'anic verses that deny privileged access of any person or group of persons to political power and authority. For example, the Qur'an reveals that, "The command belongs to God alone. He commands you not to worship anyone except Him. This is the right way of life" [12:40]. Similarly, the Qur'an instructs humans to "not take lords from among ourselves besides God" [2:64]. The evolution of these basic concepts in Islamist thought regarding *ḥākimiyya* demonstrates Islamists' efforts to provide foundation of an Islamic state in which the community, as the representative of God and His laws, is the depository of political power and authority on Earth.

'Popular vicegerency'

The evolution of the concept of the community as the depository of God's sovereignty on Earth departs from a fundamental paradox in both Qutb's and Mawdudi's writings on *ḥākimiyya*. Each was suspicious of the notion of human agency on Earth. Yet, from a purely practical point of view, neither Qutb nor Mawdudi ever described fully how God, who is transcendent, could rule people directly.[55] In fact, Mawdudi went so far as to conclude, "Authority, whenever and wherever invested in a human agency, has invariably resulted in injustice and maladministration of the most contagious type."[56]

Mawdudi recognized this paradox, and attempted to reconcile it with his concept of "popular vicegerency." This concept remains central to Islamist thought. Mawdudi argued that the Qur'an resolved the inherent tension between acknowledging the reality of human agency on Earth and God's complete sovereignty. Accordingly, he wrote he Qur'an itself had resolved this difficulty. "It describes this position [of human agency] by the term '*Khilafat*,' which means that such an agency is not sovereign in itself but is the vicegerent of the *de jure* and the *de facto* Sovereign, viz., God Almighty.[57]

For Mawdudi, "popular vicegerency" allowed humans some degree of agency in their affairs, yet it also affirmed the ultimate sovereignty of God over those affairs. He argued that humans are only representatives of God, entrusted by Him to establish His laws for them on Earth. Mawdudi described this in a paragraph that provides the basic underlying framework for an indigenously Islamic notion of social contract:

> It must be noted that Islam vests all the Muslim citizens of an Islamic State with 'popular vicegerency.' This establishes democracy in an Islamic State just as 'popular sovereignty' does it in a secular state. In the Islamic polity, the term 'vicegerency' has been adopted purposely, because the authority in its case is delegated by Allah and can be wielded only within the limits prescribed by Him. It is, however, delegated to the Muslim community of the State as a whole and not to any particular individual or group. As a result of

this, the government can be formed only with the consent of the Muslims and can function and remain in power only as long as it enjoys their confidence.[58]

The premise of this concept lies in Qur'anic verses that indicate each Muslim's capacity to rule in God's stead. For example, *Surat an-Nur* reveals, "God has promised those of you who believe and do good works to grant them vicegerency in the land" [24:55] and *Surat al-Baqarah* reveals that God places a vicegerent (*khalifa*) on Earth [2:30]. Similarly, verses 27:62, 35:39, and 6:165 each refer to God appointing Muslims as his successors, vicegerents, or deputies – *khalifa* – to rule on Earth in His stead by implementing a system of government grounded in the power and authority of the Muslim community, which lives according to His laws.

Of course, notions of "community" or "the people" have throughout history presented political thinkers and intellectuals with many different problems. 'Community' is a concept that denotes inclusion, but it can quickly become a concept of exclusion, particularly in a religious setting. Many leading Islamists seek to dispel this fear among their followers, especially regarding the role of women in politics. To provide one instructive example, Hasan Turabi argues that an Islamic state is not government by male members of society only. As he writes, "Women played a considerable role in public life during the life of the Prophet; and they contributed to the election of the third caliph." He continues to declare: "In principle, all believers, rich or poor, noble or humble, learned or ignorant, men or women, are equal before God, and they are his vicegerents on earth and the holders of his trust.[59]

A comprehensive treatment problematizing the role of women in Muslim politics and Islamic activism is mostly outside the scope of this work and deserves a future work of its own. Suffice it to say, the Islamists under study here tend not to differentiate between men and women in their theoretical conceptualization of the community of Muslims as the ultimate depository of God's authority on Earth. The differences arise in discussions of cultural matters, such as domestic roles, that are framed in individual religious interpretations. Islamists generally argue that gender discrimination stems from social constructs rather than from Islam itself. To be certain, however, the evidence for the popular Islamist argument that Islam, properly understood, "restores to women the egalitarian status they once had and again deserve" is ambiguous at best.[60]

However, many women have played decisive roles in the Islamist movement and in formulating the concept of community in Islamist thought. The success of some women in Muslim politics and Islamic activism has disrupted the conventional, unwritten assumptions regarding gender and Islamism. These assumptions tend to be quite patriarchal. The relative success of women in Muslim politics is demonstrated by a history of several heads of state: Megawati Sukarnoputri was president of Indonesia; Benazir Bhutto was twice prime minister of Pakistan; two women, Khaleda Zia and Sheikh Hasina have been prime minister of Bangladesh.

In terms of Political Islam, Zainab al-Ghazali founded the powerful *Jamaaʿat al-Sayyidaat al-Muslimaat*, the Muslim Women's Association, which played a prominent role in opposing absolutism in Egypt. In her memoir, she recalled how Hasan al-Banna wanted to merge her organization with the Muslim Brotherhood. Despite al-Banna's best attempts, al-Ghazali refused because she wanted to maintain an autonomous voice for women within the movement. Maryam Jameelah was a Muslim convert who moved to Pakistan and joined the *Jaamat-e-Islami* political party. Jameelah was one of the most articulate voices arguing for the failure of the West and modernity.

Another similar example is the Malaysian organization "Sisters in Islam," a powerful Islamic advocacy group for women, run for over twenty years by the prominent Islamist Zainah Anwar. Nurul Ibrahim, also Malaysian, is the daughter of Islamist Anwar Ibrahim. She maintains a prominent position as a Muslim activist. Nadia Yassine from Morocco is a leading Islamist voice and a senior official of the Justice and Spirituality Association. The Islamist organization Hamas appointed a Western-educated, English speaking woman, Isra al-Modallal, as an official spokesperson in 2013. And, in Yemen the Nobel Laureate Tawakkol Karman is a powerful member of the leading Islamist political party, *Islah*.

Islamist conceptualizations of "popular vicegerency" are therefore rooted in a Qur'anic vision of communal authority that does not segregate between women and men; rather, it gives "agency, responsibility, and a set of goals to the entire community, and not merely a set of rules to the individual."[61] One Islamist who sought to develop this concept is the late Ahmed Yassin, the founding ideologue of Hamas. In an interview with Jeroen Gunning, he described his interpretation of the Qur'anic vision of popular vicegerency. "God has created the human being and provided him with a brain, thus increasing his value above that of other creatures ... so that he can be vicegerent [*khalifa*] of God on earth," explained Yassin. "God has made him a *waqil* [authorized agent] to do his work – just as a merchant appoints a trustee to do his business in another country."[62]

By this line of analysis, God's vicegerents on Earth are chosen to represent the people in order to implement the collective endeavor of the *umma* in instituting a system of government according to God's laws; they are not religious representatives of God with any sort of privileged access to the faith. Another former Hamas ideologue, the late Ismail Abu Shannab, described this. "In the Islamic system, the head of state [*al-khalifah*] represents the nation, not God," wrote Shannab. "The community does not choose *al-khalifah* except to be their representative [*na'ib*]; so he does not derive his authority except from representing the community which has ... the right to watch him and forbid him from getting beyond the borders of his brief.[63]

Hamas, of course, is an offshoot of the Muslim Brotherhood. While some of Hamas's ideology and practice is unique to their particular setting, much of it borrows from the standard Muslim Brotherhood-influenced Islamist ideology. Accordingly, Shannab and Yassine's statements resonate with statements made by other Muslim Brotherhood activists, such as Yousuf al-Qaradawi of Egypt. A paradoxical figure, Qaradawi is symbolic of the dynamism of Political Islam. Despite his gray beard and traditional robes befitting his title as a shaykh of the classic Azhari tradition, Qaradawi is, in fact, a savvy user of social media and the first Islamist with a thriving online presence and personal website.

Qaradawi is somewhat of a difficult figure to associate with any one particular mode of renewal and reform in Islamic thought.[64] Though a member of the Muslim Brotherhood, his thought is innovative and independent, and many of his arguments are responses to or refinements of the thought of Mawdudi and Qutb. Qaradawi describes his particular mode of engagement with contemporary political and religious issues as the *wasatiyya*, or the middle ground.[65]

In seeking a middle ground between different Islamist positions, Qaradawi's thought represents "a cross-section of the views of the traditional religious intelligentsia in the Arab world." Qaradawi's ultimate goal is the radical transformation of Muslim society in the modern world. His point of departure for making his arguments is the failure of existing Arab and Muslim political systems. As Ibrahim Abu-Rabi' points out, Qaradawi, in rooting his vision as an alternative to the failed projects of secular-nationalists, represents a natural evolution of the reformist vision of Hassan al-Banna.[66]

Qaradawi indicted the contemporary Arab political system as having failed in three major works. In these works, he implicitly argues that the West has also failed. As such, he presents Islam as the only system that presents a true countermodernity because it is not product of Western thought. The titles of these works are instructive: *The Unique and Necessary Islamic Solution, How Imported Solutions Were Accepted by Our Umma,* and *The Suspicions of the Secularists and Westernizers for the Islamic Solution.*[67]

Qaradawi argues that the Islamic countermodernity, in the form of an Islamic state, is based upon a civil state, not a religious state. He argues that properly understanding the Islamic state as a civil state is crucial for understanding Mawdudi's concept of popular vicegerency, because acknowledging God's ultimate sovereignty on Earth does not necessarily create a theocracy. As he argues:

> A central characteristic of an Islamic state is that it is a civil state whose framework is Islam. It is not a religious state like the concept of a theocracy in Western history ... Applying Islamic law to a state does not necessarily lead to a religious state, and a religious state does not necessarily mean rule granted by the Divine to a particular class of people or person because Islam does not sanction anything of this sort.[68]

From this starting point, Qaradawi develops his conceptualization of *ḥākimiyya*. Like Mawdudi, Qaradawi argues that there are two types of *ḥākimiyya*. The first is *ḥākimiyya kawniyyah qadariyyah* (universal and determinative sovereignty). This, for Qaradawi, means that God governs all existence, "directing it with His commands and His unchanging practices, some of which we know and others remain unknown." He roots this argument in *Surat al-Ra'd*, which reveals: "Do they not see how We come to [their] land and shrink its borders? God decides [*yahkum*] - no one can reverse His decision [*hukmihi*] – and He is swift in reckoning" [13:41]. From this, Qaradawi concludes that *hakimimiyyah kawniyyah qadariyyah* "means a determinative sovereignty over the cosmos rather than a legislative sovereignty."[69]

The second kind of sovereignty that Qaradawi identifies is *tashri'iyya amriyya*, or legislative sovereignty. It provides "the authority to impose legal obligations, to command and forbid, to make things binding or a matter of choice."[70] Here, Qaradawi makes an important transition in the discourse over *ḥākimiyya*. He argues that humans do, in fact, have sovereignty on Earth. Muslims have agency to legislate and determine laws applicable to their particular needs, especially regarding areas that might not be specifically mentioned in the Qur'an. Laws that are exegetical in nature, and "laws that must inevitably arise in Muslim politics, such as navigation and flight, work and labor, health and agriculture" are legitimate so long as they "bring about good and remove evil when addressing the prevailing norms in society."[71]

True to his *wasatiyya* orientation, Qaradawi bridges the thought of Mawdudi and Qutb and their positions on *ḥākimiyya* with a more contemporary and dynamic interpretation. In formulating this position, he is reacting to the critique of those he refers to as "secularists" who question the tension between God's total sovereignty in an Islamic state and the purely rational acceptance of some degree of human agency on Earth. As Mawdudi invented the term "popular vicegerency," Qaradawi asks the reader if he might invent a term as well, namely, "divine democratic government." He argues that this "Provides the people with limited popular sovereignty" while remaining "under the authority of God."[72]

Yet, the notion of providing even limited popular sovereignty to humans is, of course, antithetical to the thought of Mawdudi and Qutb. Qaradawi is aware of this, and in defending his position he writes: "Mawdudi and Qutb said that sovereignty was God's alone. But this does not mean that God is the one who gives rulers and the 'ulama' their rights to rule ... The ruler's political power comes from the community, not God, and the community chooses its rulers, monitors them, holds them accountable, and deposes them if need be." In this, Qaradawi is describing a style of government that is rooted in a social contract between "the community" and "its rulers." Any government in which the community is the ultimate depository of God's authority on Earth is legitimately and fundamentally Islamic, argues Qaradawi, so long as the community acknowledges that "God's rule cannot be superseded." Qaradawi does not fully elaborate upon this statement, but it implies that the shari'a is the final source of law which man-made laws cannot supersede (and that all man-made laws must ultimately be in accordance with the *maqasid al-shari'a*, or the goals of the *shari'a*).[73]

Strikingly, Qaradawi adds that, properly understood, Mawdudi was arguing for a similar idea and that the notion of human agency on Earth is not, in fact, antithetical to Mawdudi's thought. Rather, he argues with a tinge of apologetics that succeeding generations have erred in interpreting Mawdudi's works. "What has happened to Mawdudi is that some people have taken parts from his works and presented them in ways that Mawdudi did not intend," he writes. "They have arranged selections from his works that belie his actual ideas and do not maintain the same conclusions as his dozens of books, letters, essays, and lectures."[74]

According to Qaradawi, then, "What can be understood from Mawdudi's works in total" is "Islamic rule in a democratic sense." As such, "The consensus of the community is the only executive authority [on Earth]" and this precludes "rule by a certain class or family with privileged rights to the religion."[75] He attempts to legitimate his claims by finding a perceived shared ground with Qutb when he argues that human agency allows for legislating according to the *shari'a* in order to prevent theocratic governance. He quotes a particular section from Qutb's *Milestones* that he interprets as Qutb arguing that human agency is acceptable in an Islamic state, and that it does not necessarily equate to theocracy. Qaradawi cites Qutb as stating:

> The Kingdom of God on Earth does not mean rulership on the ground of a privileged religious class as they see fit – as was the case for authority in the Church [in the West]. Nor can men speak on behalf of God – as was the case with the concept of Divine Rule [in the West]. They are only to institute the laws of God, and their reason for being in power is only to reflect the Will of God.[76]

The conceptualization of the community of Muslims as the ultimate depository of God's power on Earth is an important part of Political Islam. "The primary institution in Islam is the *umma* [community of Muslims]," wrote Hasan al-Turabi in describing the universal characteristics of Islamic government. "The state is only the political dimension of the collective endeavor of Muslims." Part of the collective endeavor of all Muslims, regardless of gender or class or ethnicity, is the duty to hold their rulers accountable. As Turabi puts it: "Whereas the Prophet was appointed by God, the caliph was freely elected by the people, who thereby have precedence over him as a legal authority...The caliph...or any similar holder of political power, is subject both to the *shari'a* and to the will of his electors.⁷⁷

Similarly, Qaradawi concludes that accepting God's ultimate sovereignty in an Islamic state "Does not deny that God has authorized humans with agency to legislate. Instead, it prevents humans from legislating independently of God's Will." The community becomes the ultimate depository of God's power on Earth by means of a voluntary transferal of God's sovereignty into the hands of those who will endeavor to create a system of government according to "God's Will." "Power in Islam lies in the hands of all Muslims collectively," argued Qaradawi. "They are in charge of their affairs, as stated in the Qur'an and the Sunnah of His Messenger." Furthermore, Qaradawi adds, "All legislation can come from true Muslims who legislate according to the *shari'a* for themselves," so long as this process takes into account "the public interest (*maslahah*), the warding off of evil, and the caring for the individual and communal needs of the people."⁷⁸

Political power and authority in the Muslim community

"Social and political responsibility is on no account the matter of one individual," writes the prominent Moroccan Islamist Nadia Yassine. "According to the sense of our Islamic teaching, power is always a matter of the entire community."⁷⁹ As has been demonstrated, Islamist conceptualizations of political sovereignty revolve around the concept of communal power and authority.⁸⁰ The Egyptian Islamist Fahmy Howeidy states that the trusteeship (*wilaya*) of the *umma* over itself is one of the seven "focal points" of an Islamic state. As such, the choice of leadership and the means to its selection and confirmation is the choice (*ikhtiyar*) of the *umma*. "The *umma* possesses the general leadership, and it alone has the right to choose the imam or to remove him," writes Howeidy, "that is, to end his term and impeach him as it installs him and supervises him and possess the primary right/duty in regard to him.⁸¹

Accordingly, the head of state is allowed by the community to become its "deputized trustee" (*al-naīb al-wakīl*). Political power and authority in an Islamic state thus becomes the voluntary transferal of sovereignty from the community to the ruler, whom the community agrees to be ruled by. Howeidy notes:

[The ruler] derives his authority from them [the community], and they have the duty to advise him as well as to orient him and to rectify his actions if he errs. Rather, they have the duty to remove him from the office to which he has been entrusted by their choice if they find what necessitates his removal.[82]

Qaradawi agrees with Howeidy, though he uses a somewhat simpler description than "deputized trustee." "The ruler, as viewed by Islam, is the representative of the community and thus its employee," he writes. "It is a basic right [of the community] to hold its representative accountable or to divest him of this position whenever it wishes and especially if the representative fails in his obligations."[83] Qaradawi reiterates his conviction on this matter in many of his works. In his treatise on jurisprudence of an Islamic state, he wrote:

In Islam, it is the right of the people – actually it is their duty – to advise the ruler, to straighten him if crooked, and to order him to enjoin what is right and forbid what is evil because he is only one among the Muslims. He is not greater than those who advise him and counsel him, and the ruled are not too small to advise or instruct him.[84]

Political Islamists arrive at this conclusion by divesting themselves of traditional understandings of the critical Qur'anic verse 4:59: *Ya ayyuhā alladhina 'amanū, aṭi'ū Allah wa-aṭi'u al-rasūl wa-'uli 'l-'amr minkum*. This has most often been interpreted in English to mean: "Oh, you who believe, obey God and the Prophet and those in authority among you." The phrase *uli 'l-amr minkum* (those in authority among you) has been the cause of frequent debate as Muslims throughout history have questioned exactly who is a person of authority in their society and whether that authority is meant by God to be religious or political in nature.

According to Asma Asfaruddin, in the first two centuries of Islam this phrase referred to "people of knowledge and discernment" and "military commanders" during the time of the Prophet. Its broadest connotation was one of moral authority, based on a nebulous mix of religious and legal principles, but "this locution was not understood by the first two generations of Muslims in particular to have overt political implications."[85]

By the ninth century, exegetes were interpreting the phrase in more politically relevant ways. The standard political treatises from this period (and later) restricted the phrase *uli 'l-amr minkum* to political rulers of Muslim communities. Al-Mawardi, for example, in his famous work, *The Ordinances of Government*, interpreted Qur'an 4:59 as demanding unquestioned obedience from Muslims to their rulers. This continued into the late medieval period, when jurist-scholars such as Fakhr al-Din al-Razi and Ibn Kathir argued that the phrase *uli 'l-amr minkum* referred primarily (if not exclusively) to those in possession of political authority, not religious authority. In this sense, Qur'an 4:59 was used as a religious warrant to promote despotism in the form of political quietism and obedience to all political authority.[86]

The most prominent scholar from this period, Ibn Taymiyya, diverged slightly. He interpreted Qur'an 4:59 as enjoining obedience to God and His Messenger without much treatment of the phrase *uli 'l-amr minkum*. Taymiyya's general political philosophy was important, however, for the primacy it placed on the need for rulers to consult the community. As Asfaruddin notes, he did not "underscore an assumed religiously mandated duty of practically unconditional obedience to the ruler." This important fact provides somewhat of a conundrum for the historian because contemporary Islamist doctrine, though professed to be divorced from human interpretation beyond the period of the Prophet and his companions, appears to resonate more with Taymiyya's interpretation of Qur'an 4:59 than the exegetes from the earliest Muslim generations.[87]

Regardless, scholars of all schools of thought have sought to legitimate their interpretations of this verse with many *ahadith* (pl., *hadith*). For example, Asfaruddin notes that one popular hadith used for this purpose came from the Prophet's sermon delivered at the conclusion of his last pilgrimage in 632 CE. In this sermon, the Prophet is recorded to have stated: "Obey and listen, even if an Abyssinian slave with a head like a raisin were to rule over you (*amara 'alaykum*)." Rather than interpreting this verse for what it ostensibly reveals about the Prophet's vision of political power and authority in Islam – the primacy of requirements like personal piety and moral excellence for a ruler, and that race, ethnic background, and social class were to exert no influence over who could rise to be a ruler in Muslim politics – scholars such as Ibn Kathir appropriated this hadith to "more firmly anchor the notion of practically unqualified obedience to the ruler, regardless of whether he was deemed agreeable or not, it would seem, by the general populace."[88]

Beginning with Rashid Rida, modern exegetes began expanding who was included in the phrase *uli 'l-amr minkum*. Rida provided the starting point with his interpretation that those in authority are "the people who loosen and bind," which can be interpreted as encompassing a wide group of people. Building upon this, Mawdudi echoed Rida's broad understanding and interpreted the phrase to refer to "intellectual and political leaders of the community, as well as to administrative officials, judges of the courts, tribal chiefs and regional representatives." Similarly, Sayyid Qutb continued this expansion, though he noted that any and all political authority comes directly from God, because He alone is sovereign. For Qutb, then, while the verse might seem political on the surface it ultimately confirmed the sovereignty of God over all human affairs. According to Asfaruddin, "Qutb's highly politicized understanding of the verse 4:59 with its linkage to the novel term *al-hakimiyya* represents the culmination of Mawdudi's vision of a hegemonic political Islam."[89]

Contemporary Political Islamists have diverged significantly from the Rida-Mawdudi-Qutb line of analysis. The verse has been reinvented in the Islamist discourse to legitimate ultimate political power and authority belonging to the community in a social contract-based Islamic state. As the contemporary Moroccan Islamist Nadia Yassine (1958–) describes it:

> The verse [4:59] orders us to obey "those" (plural) who hold power "among" you; on no account does it instruct us to obey "the one" who holds power "over" you. The despots of all stripes who have successively subjugated us prefer to read the verse vertically. According to the school of deceptive despotism, the verse alludes to the group of individuals who have held absolute power throughout history.[90]

Similarly, the late Egyptian scholar Fathi Osman (1928–2010) argued, "Those who are entrusted with authority by the people are always referred to in the Quran in the plural, which suggests that they form organizational bodies and are not considered as individuals." Osman interprets 4:59 as those "who are entrusted with authority from among them by them [the community]."[91] It is instructive to note once more that, though Islamists claim to represent the most pristine model of the Prophet and the *Rashidun*, their interpretation of this verse is more in line with late medieval theorists like Ibn Taymiyya than it is with the first generation of Muslims.

Regardless, Yassine, Osman, and other Islamists argue that interpreting Qur'an 4:59 in a way that does not sanction the trusteeship of the community over itself is wrong and not rooted in the model of the Prophet and his companions.

Ḥisba and *shūra*

As the Tunisian Islamist Rachid Ghannouchi states, "Political power belongs to the community (*umma*), which should adopt a form of *shūra*, which is a system of mandatory consultation."[92] The conceptualization of communal authority in an Islamic state stems from reinvented interpretations of two traditional Muslim concepts: *ḥisba* and *shūra*. Islamists have used these two concepts as the building blocks of an Islamic notion of social contract.

Ḥisba is a Qur'anic concept that stems from the phrase *al-amr bi'l- ma'rūf wa'l-nahy 'an al-munkar*, usually translated as "to demand what is right and forbid what is wrong." Found throughout the Qur'an (3:104, 110, 114; 9:112; 22:41), *ḥisba* is foremost a personal duty, *wājib 'aynī*, in that it is the obligation of every Muslim to demand what is right and forbid what is wrong in the way he lives his life. More generally, however, *ḥisba* is a collective duty, *wājib kafā'ī*, because the Qur'an implores the community of believers to demand what is good and forbid what is wrong in their society.[93] As the Qur'an commands in just one instance among many: "Believers, you are the best community among the people: you demand what is right, forbid what is wrong, and believe in God" [3:110].

The official state position of *muhtasib*, the holder of the office of *al- ḥisba*, emerged in medieval Islamic history. In terms of standing, this position fell between the offices of judge (*qadi*) and court magistrate (*walii al-mazaalim*). The *muhtasib* signified the most formal function of the concept of *ḥisba*. The individual who filled this position was "charged with enforcing public morality, overseeing the public welfare, and supervising the markets, fulfilling thereby the community's collective obligation to command the good and forbid the evil."[94] The Prophet Muhammad was the first to institutionalize the facilitation of *ḥisba* through the function of the state. Later, Muslim rulers would draw upon his example in instituting various arrangements for the state to oversee the implementation of this duty.

Historically, the implementation of *ḥisba* was "top-down," in that the state or state institutions enforced it upon society. It was not until recently – at some point in modern history – that *ḥisba* began to be interpreted in such a way as to allow the injunction to be reversed. That is, certain Muslims interpreted it in a "bottom-up" manner. This allowed individuals and the community to command good and forbid evil from the state or its government officials. "*Ḥisba* is usually taught in schools to young Muslims as something that an individual or community should strive for," notes Zainab Abu Taleb. "It is never taught as justification for the people to demand certain things from their governments."[95]

Islamists have reinvented the concept of *ḥisba* as a fundamental element of social contract-based government in an Islamic state. When combined with *shūra* in this new conceptualization, "giving advice is an obligation of every individual towards leaders and the public as well," writes Fathi Osman. "Enjoining the doing of what is right and good and forbidding the doing of what is wrong and evil is the responsibility of the state authorities as well as the people and any group of them."[96] This conceptualization is a central characteristic of Political Islam. Qaradawi provides perhaps the most succinct description of this:

> In Islam, it is the right of the people – actually it is their duty – to advise the ruler, to straighten him if crooked, and to order him to enjoin what is right and forbid what is evil. He is only one among the Muslims; he is not greater than those who advise him and counsel him, and the ruled are not too small to advise or instruct him. [97]

Similarly, Ismail Abu Shannab, declared that the ruler "does not derive his authority except from representing the community which has ... the right to watch him and forbid him from getting beyond the orders of his brief."[98] As such, the *umma* is held to be culpable (*mukallaf*) and responsible (*masūl*) unto itself. "From the standpoint of this discourse," writes Howeidy, "a society can be classified as a guarantor of its interests, mobilizing all its vital sectors for rectification and reform through its observance of commanding the right and forbidding the wrong."[99]

The conceptualization of the community as such must be understood in the context of *shūra*. *Shūra* is mentioned in the Qur'an twice. The first verse, *Surat al-Imran*, obliges the Prophet Muhammad, as exemplar of all Muslims, to consult with his followers: "So pardon them and ask forgiveness of them, and consult them in the conduct of affairs" [3:159]. The second, *Surat al-Shūra*, reveals that those persons most blessed by God are those who conduct their affairs by mutual consultation: "Far better and more lasting is what God will give to those ... who conduct their affairs by mutual consultation" [42:38]. Islamists interpret *shūra* as being equally binding and obligatory for the community and the ruler. As Mawdudi characterizes it: "The function of the Head of the State shall not be autocratic but consultative (*shūra'i*)."[100]

To be certain, *shūra* has been interpreted in different ways politically throughout Islamic history and has performed functions of varying degrees of importance to all Muslim governments. Yet when placed alongside *ḥisba*, Islamists have reinvented the concept not just to embody a Qur'anic injunction that orders rulers to consult the ruled, but a grand political philosophy in general that is founded upon a social contract. The Egyptian Islamist Muhammad Salim el-Awa writes in his treatise *On the Political System of the Islamic State*, "The right of *shūra* itself and the obligation of individual members of the *umma* to enjoin right and forbid wrong [*ḥisba*] constitute evidence of the right of the *umma* to question the head of state. Had it not been the right of the *umma* to watch over the head of state, he would not be obliged to consult it."[101]

Whether *shūra* is binding or obligatory is a question that arises throughout this discourse. Islamists conclude that *shūra* is binding and not merely for informative purposes.[102] Demonstrating the transition in Islamic thought of Political Islam emerging from Islamic Modernism, el-Awa cites Muhammad ʿAbduh in answering this question. Theoretically speaking, what happens if a ruler neglects his duty to consult his constituents? El-Awa cites ʿAbduh has having answered that *ḥisba* "Establishes a mandate that there must exist among the people a strong and united group who call for goodness and for enjoining the right and forbidding the wrong, which is a general mandate to be observed by both rulers and the ruled. Hence, there is no right greater than justice and no wrong worse than tyranny."[103]

In this line of analysis, Islamists conceptualize *ḥisba* as constituting evidence that *shūra* is obligatory and binding. Qaradawi refutes those scholars who conclude that *shūra* "is only for informational purposes rather than something binding." He questions how, given the history of absolute despotism in the Muslim community, anyone could be of the opinion that *shūra* is not binding upon a ruler. In fact, any ruler who "consults but then does as he and his retinue please" is *haram*, forbidden, because *shūra* is a basic stipulation in the Qur'an. And, as the Qur'an reveals, Muslims are bound by their stipulations: "Fulfill any pledge you make in God's name and do not break oaths after you have sworn them, for you have made God your surety" [16:91].[104]

Of course, when the Qur'anic verses regarding *shūra* were revealed, it might very well have been possible for the Prophet to consult with the entire Muslim community at Medina, given its rather small size at the time. As the Muslim community grew throughout history, it became traditional for the ruler to consult not the entire community - a politically infeasible act - but rather "the People who Loosen and Bind," *ahl al-hall wa al-aqd*. Regarding whether *shūra* remains relevant as obligatory in a large Islamic state, Qaradawi writes, "How can those referred to in our tradition as the People who Loosen and Bind be characterized as such when, in fact, they do not 'loosen' or 'bind' anything?"[105]

Mawdudi was among the first intellectuals to argue that the traditional concept of *ahl al-hall wa al-aqd* can be interpreted as providing basis for a modern legislature composed of "such learned men who have the ability and the capacity to interpret Qur'anic injunctions and who, in giving decisions, would not take liberties with the spirit or the letter of the *shari'a*." Mawdudi concluded that the purpose of this legislature is to make rules and regulations according to the *shari'a* and in mutual consultation with the head of state. Furthermore, in the event that more than one interpretation of a component of the *shari'a* arises, this body will decide by mutual consultation, which "should be placed on the Statute Book." Finally, it is the duty of the legislature to formulate laws "wherever and in whatever matters even basic guidance is not available from the Qur'an, or the Sunnah, or the conventions of the Righteous Caliphs."[106]

Islamists also argue that *shūra* is binding, especially when combined with *ḥisba*, because it is part of a Muslim's obligation to seek social justice. As Howeidy notes, this is of considerable import for the concept of an Islamic state because "Allah threatens those who remain silent about injustice with punishment if they acquiesce to it." One aspect of this struggle for social justice in an Islamic state, as it relates to concepts of political power and authority, is the necessity for members of the community to question their rulers (*musa'ala al-hukkam*). Howeidy writes that this matter is not merely a duty of the *umma* to inform a ruler; rather, "it is a legal obligation of the *shari'a* where the *umma* is guilty of sin and is taken to account before Allah if it is negligent in carrying it out." [107]

Howeidy's statement demonstrates a reinvention of the Qur'anic concepts of *shūra* and *ḥisba* in Muslim politics of profound significance. "If we consider the ranks of those asserting that *al-shūra* is a genuine value in Islamic society, we would find that it covers a much wider area than the limits of the political system," he concluded.[108] As such, *shūra* becomes more than government officials mutually consulting upon important matters, or traders in the suq consulting each other on prices. It is even more than a method of choosing a ruler, as was the initial case after the Prophet's death in Medina. Rather, it becomes an all encompassing political and moral philosophy for establishing social justice, the embodiment of the *maqasid al-shari'a*.

Furthermore, Islamists assert that the primary reason for the decline of Muslim societies throughout the past several centuries of world history is that Muslims allowed tyrannical, despotic rule by neglecting *shūra*. "The first and foremost thing which afflicted the Islamic *umma* in its history is the neglect of the principle of *al-shūra*," wrote Howeidy. Howeidy argues that the disastrous neglect of *shūra* allowed for despotism to overtake Muslims and divert them from living in a true Islamic society of freedom and egalitarianism. He writes:

> Nothing has afflicted Islam and its *umma* and *da'wah* (call) in the Modern era except the crimes of tyrannical rule taking control over people by the sword of the arrogant and their gold. Nothing has disabled the *shari'a* or imposed secularism and necessitated the alienation of people except hegemony and draconian rule and the use of iron and fire. Nothing has struck the Islamic movement and *da'wah* or punished those engaged in these and its sons and exiled them and turned them into refugees except the tremendous burden of tyrannical rule.[109]

The female Moroccan Islamist Nadia Yassine shares similar conviction. In her work *Full Sails Ahead*, Yassine reflects upon the example of the caliph Omar consulting with his constituents, and contrasts this against the lack of *shūra* she sees in contemporary Muslim politics. She writes that many Muslims today would be surprised by actual *shūra*, "since most of us have been worn down like pebbles by a thousand-year flow of the stupefying jurisprudence that assassinated *shūra* at the very dawn of Islam and has since deadened our reasoning." Yassine argues that reinstituting *shūra* to a place of primacy in Muslim politics is crucial for bringing about social justice, especially in an Islamic state. She writes, "Social justice becomes not a political or humanitarian conviction, but a sacred duty and a spiritual ascent."[110]

Fahmy Howeidy argues a similar position. *Shūra* is not merely a political function but the basis of an entire political philosophy. "Islam specified *al-shūra* as a basis among bases of Islamic life and made it incumbent upon the ruler to seek council and incumbent upon the *umma* to advise," he writes, "even to the extent that it made advice (*al-nasihah*) tantamount to religion in its entirety."[111]

Fathi Osman extends the function of *shūra* in an Islamic society even further. "*Shūra* is not limited to the political field," he writes. "It has to be developed starting with the family base to be a general way of life in all areas...The family and the schools have essential roles in developing *shūra* as a way of life."[112] Similarly, *ḥisba* becomes a "mandatory obligation" as part of the all-encompassing political philosophy of social contract. Howeidy writes that "the best jihad [is] a word of truth spoken to the deviant sultan." He continues to write that:

> The meaning of this is that it made resisting internal excess and corruption weightier with Allah than resistance against external invasion because the first is often times a cause of the second. Indeed, the ruler in the view of Islam is a trustee of the *umma* and an employee of it; and it is an original right/duty to take him to account or to remove him from the trusteeship and especially if he breaks its obligations.[113]

The conceptual justification for the right of the community to question its rulers comes from the social contract formed by *shūra* and *ḥisba*. As el-Awa asserts, "The right of *shūra* itself and the obligation of individual members of the *umma* to enjoin right and forbid wrong [*ḥisba*] constitutes evidence of the right of the *umma* to question the head of state. Islamists augment this position by interpreting different Qur'anic verses as sanctioning the right of the community to question its rulers and as depicting rule not in accordance with God's design to be worthy of blame. As el-Awa states, "The right of the *umma* to call the head of state to account is also indicated by the Qur'anic verses which depict some deeds of some rulers as blameworthy."[114] In fact, Islamists argue that it is not simply the *right* of the community to do so; rather, it is a religious imperative. Howeidy argues that it is a matter of necessity (*musa'ala al-hukkam*) for Muslims to question rulers in an Islamic state: "The matter is not merely a duty of the *umma* to inform him [the ruler] and then back down from him, but it is a legal obligation of the *shari'a* where the *umma* is guilty of sin and is taken to account before Allah if it is negligent in carrying it out."[115]

To support this position, Islamists rely on innovative interpretations of the Qur'anic message. Howeidy cites as supportive evidence for his position *Surat Hud,* which commands: "Do not incline towards those who do wrong as hellfire will touch you" [11:113]. He also cites *Surat al-Kahf:* "These villages, We destroyed them when they committed wrong and we made their destruction a pledge" [18:59].[116] El-Awa cites a verse from *Surat as-Sad*: "Therefore judge rightly between people, and do not follow an opinion which would entice you from the way of God. Those who stray away from the way of God will have severe punishment since they forgot the Day of Reckoning" [38:26]. In a verse that praises Muslims for practicing *hisba* in managing their affairs, *Surat al-Ma'idah* reveals that, "They [Christians and Jews] used not to forbid one another from committing any of the evils they were committing" [5:79]. Similarly, Islamists legitimate their religion-based opposition to certain rulers they deem as having distorted the faith with *Surat al-Baqarah*: "There is [a kind of] man whose views on the life of this world may please you, he even calls on God to witness what is in his heart, yet he is the bitterest of opponents. When he leaves, he sets out to spread corruption in the land, destroying crops and livestock – God does not like corruption" [2:204-205].[117]

In addition to these Qur'anic verses, contemporary Islamists record numerous *ahadith* to support their vision of a social contract-based Islamic state. As el-Awa notes, many *ahadith* "establish the basis of obedience to rulers in their doing right; thus the sayings imply the obligation of disobedience in wrongdoing or sin. The sayings also establish the principle of permissibility of questioning rulers about their deeds." El-Awa recounts one quite popular hadith that records the Prophet as saying to his followers, "You are all guardians and you are all responsible for your wards." Also cited by el-Awa is: "Any slave [of God] to whom Allah entrusts a group of subjects and who dies cheating his subjects, Allah will deny him the Garden [Heaven]."[118] Similarly, Qaradawi writes that, "The first Caliph of Islam stated in his first speech as such: 'Obey me so long as I obey God, but if I disobey God, you have no obligation to obey me.'" Another hadith that Qaradawi recounts admonishes the people to be vigilant in their private and public affairs: "If the people see something that is unjust, and do not take it upon themselves to correct it, then God's punishment will be upon them."[119]

Bayʿa and 'shūracracy'

Though contemporary Political Islamists insist upon the primacy of *shūra* and *ḥisba* in the function of an Islamic state, they acknowledge that neither the Qurʾan nor the sunna stipulate any particular form of government for implementing them. "Islam in the Qurʾan and sunna does not define a particular system of government," says el-Awa. Rather, "It defines the Islamic values that the *umma* must hold to and to which the rulers must be referred." For Islamists, one of the most critical "general principles" and "universal concerns" in their conceptualization of government is that, as el-Awa argues, "The ruler should be chosen by the will of a free people, as happened in the choice of the four Rightly-Guided Caliphs. But there is no specific way of arriving at this choice and every age invents its own methods."[120]

Contrary to popular opinion, Political Islam is not antithetical to democracy. The Islamist discourse over democracy demonstrates the dynamic themes of transition and reinvention in modern Islamic thought, especially of the Islamist variant. Granted, Mawdudi and Qutb wrote decades ago on the incompatibility of Islam and democracy. Yet, contemporary Political Islamists have put forth innovative and practical interpretations of how to implement democracy in Muslim politics and especially in an Islamic state. This discourse over the relationship between Islamism and democracy has appropriated some legitimate critique. Some non-Islamist Muslims, like the eminent Muslim intellectual Aziz al-Azmeh, point out that though Islamists have sought to dismiss Western modernity, the fact remains that, "Political Islam itself routinely resorts to notions borrowed from the modern ... ideologies of European origin that pervade contemporary Arab culture and politics."[121]

It is precisely this critique that demonstrates the innovative nature of contemporary Islamist thought. Islamists would refute al-Azmeh by arguing that democracy is not, in fact, of European origin nor is it a modern ideology. Rather, as Fahmy Howeidy argues and as was first written by ʿAbbas Mahmud al-ʿAqqad in his 1952 book *Democracy in Islam*, "The concept of democracy was engendered by Islam for the first time in the history of the world."[122]

In this conceptualization of democracy as a political tool or framework rather than a culture particular to the West, Islamists argue that it is, in fact, the most legitimate form of government for an Islamic state. Furthermore, they argue that the word itself is of little significance if it is used to describe an essentially Islamic concept. Howeidy demonstrates this:

> It is important for me to affirm that I am not among those who are enamoured with using words of foreign origin such as 'democracy' and so forth in order to express Islamic concepts. However, if the term and its use have become widespread among people, then our ears will not be deaf to it ... It will not prejudice or harm us that the term has come from others, as judgment does not turn on names and titles, but rather on what is *named* and *content*.[123]

The use of the word 'democracy' by Islamists in a Muslim framework is part of their project to provide an Islamic countermodernity to the dominant Western model. Islamists use the word 'democracy' because it is the closest word in contemporary usage to describe certain functions of an Islamic state. They argue that this does not detract from the unique world-system that is the Islamic system. Howeidy quotes Muhammad Diya' al-Din al-Rayyis to demonstrate that even if Islamists use the word 'democracy' it should not be construed as their adopting a foreign system or culture. As al-Rayyis wrote:

> The Islamic state [is] a unique system particular to Islam. The assertion that it correlates to any other known system is not correct; and thus, there ought to be posited for it a special terminology – which describes it according to a term representative of its true nature. And as long as the like of such a term is not clear or has not yet been found, it is sufficient now to indicate it according to its comprehensive characteristic – that it is an 'Islamic system.'[124]

Democracy, then, becomes simply a word adopted by Islamists to denote the long-refined concepts in Islamic history of a political system based upon *shūra*. Rachid Ghannouchi writes that democracy is "a set of mechanisms to guarantee freedom of thought and assembly, and peaceful competition for governmental authority through the ballot box." Furthermore, he notes that the refusal of some factions within Political Islam to embrace democracy as a tool to implement an Islamic state is detrimental to the Islamist cause. "We have no modern experience in Islamic activity that can replace [the word] democracy," he writes. "The Islamization of democracy is the closest thing to implementing *shūra*."[125]

The general political philosophy that emerges from this discourse, as Qaradawi describes it, is "Islamic rule in a democratic sense."[126] Democracy is conceptualized as a political tool with a conveniently accessible name for advancing the political program of an Islamic system. To use Qaradawi as just one example, his willingness to use the term 'democracy' (and its cognate in Arabic, *demokratiyya*) is merely an expression of his conviction to speak to people "in the language of the age."[127] More importantly, though, Islamists argue that all the contemporary facets of democracy (as it is known today)[128] characterized the Islamic system long before the word came into common usage in the West. Fahmy Howeidy describes this, with a hint of critique toward his secular-nationalist counterparts:

> The Muslim who calls for democracy does so on the basis that it constitutes a form of rule embodying the political principals of Islam in the choice of the ruler, the specification of *al-shūra* and advice, commanding what is right and forbidding what is wrong, resisting deviance and rejecting rebellion (against Allah) – especially if it gets to the degree of 'blatant unbelief.'[129]

For Islamists, and indeed many Muslims in general, one of the greatest points of contention regarding Muslim politics and democracy has been the ostensible prerequisite of secularism.[130] Mawdudi was speaking from fact when he stated: "Islam, speaking from the point of view of political philosophy, is the very antithesis of secular Western democracy."[131] Indeed, even non-Islamist Muslims concede that secularism in its Western sense – and especially the argument that secularism is a prerequisite to democracy – is unacceptable from the viewpoint of Islam.[132] Therefore, Islamists have reinvented the meaning behind the concept of secularism.

Yousuf Qaradawi provides an interesting example of this. In his writings, Qaradawi presents secularism not as an ideology or method that removes religion from affairs of state and public life. Rather, it is reinvented as a certain construct that prevents a particular person or persons from claiming privileged access to the faith.

In Qaradawi's conceptualization, an Islamic state is at once secular and Islamic: it is Islamic because its basic underlying framework in all things – social, economic, political, moral – is Islam, and it is secular because the nature of Islam as he interprets it does not allow for "rule granted by the Divine to a particular class of people or person."[133]

Rachid Ghannouchi provides a similar understanding of secularism. For Ghannouchi, secularism is not a protection of the state from religion, but a protection of religion from the state. An Islamic state is therefore a secular state, not a "religious state," because it allows for the free practice of religion. In a lecture regarding secularism in Islam given on March 2, 2012 at the Center for the Study of Islam and Democracy, Ghannouchi described the Islamist conceptualization of secularism thus:

> While the problematic in the West revolved around ways of liberating the state from religion and led to destructive wars, in our context the problem is one of liberating religion from the state and preventing it from dominating religion, and keeping the latter in the societal realm, open to all Muslims to read the Qur'an and understand it in the manner that they deem appropriate, and that there is no harm in the plurality that is combined with tolerance. But should Muslims be in need of laws, the democratic mechanism is the best embodiment of the *shūra* value in Islam.[134]

The conceptualization of secularism represented by Qaradawi and Ghannouchi is a reaction to the anxieties of many Sunni Muslims (both Islamists and non-Islamists) that that an Islamic state would follow the model of Iran and Khomeini's *vilayat-i faqih*, or rule by clerics.[135] Therefore, a common theme throughout Sunni Islamist writings is that "Islamic rule in a democratic sense" will not follow the Iranian model of *vilayat al-faqih*. Islamists also argue that an Islamic state will not be a theocracy, in the sense of the Christian historical experience. As Osman writes, "The religious dimension in the Islamic ideology or plan, of individual and social, local and global reform, does not mean the establishment of a theocracy." He continues:

> There is no clergy in Islam; any intelligent human being who knows the language and the style can understand and interpret God's message and no supernatural or metaphysi-

cal power can be required or claimed for such a work. God's message has been preserved and made known publicly through centuries; and no human being can add to it or detract from it.[136]

Mawdudi provided another refutation of the idea that an Islamic state is theocratic. While he conceded that an apt name for an Islamic state might be the "Kingdom of God," he qualified this by stating that his theoretical state has no correlation with the Western experience of theocracy. As he wrote:

Islamic theocracy is something altogether different from the theocracy of which Europe has had a bitter experience wherein a priestly class, sharply marked off from the rest of the population, exercises unchecked domination and enforces laws of its own making in the name of God, thus virtually imposing its own divinity and godhood upon the common people. Such a system of government is satanic rather than divine. Contrary to this, the theocracy built up by Islam is not ruled by any particular religious class but by the whole community of Muslims including the rank and file. The entire Muslim population runs the state in accordance with the Book of God and the practice of His Prophet.[137]

In refuting the equation of an Islamic state with a Christian-style theocracy or the Islamic Republic of Iran, Islamists seek to differentiate 'Islam' and 'religion' as two separate concepts. "There is ... a lot of confusion about what is Islamic and what is religious," writes Qaradawi. "Many think that all that is Islamic is also religious, but the fact is that Islam is broader and larger than the word 'religion.'" In supporting this, Qaradawi notes that jurists and the 'ulama' consider 'religion' to be only one of five or six components of the *maqasid al-shari'a*. "It is incorrect to think that the Islamic state that I am calling for is a religious state," wrote Qaradawi. "An Islamic state is a civil state founded upon choices, the oath of allegiance (*bay'a*), consultation (*shūra*) and the accountability of the ruler to the community." He continued: "This state provides each person with the right to advise the ruler – to command what is right and forbid what is evil [*hisba*].[138]

In stating that one of the central components of an Islamic state is *bay'a*, Qaradawi is drawing upon a long-refined pre-Islamic Arab tradition. This tradition evolved to maintain a voluntary and egalitarian nature of political power and authority in all human associations, including those between rulers and ruled. The *bay'a* is a voluntary oath of allegiance from one party, who agrees to cede power and authority, to another, who agrees to maintain it in an accountable and reciprocal manner. Though Islamists argue that in an Islamic state "the primary area for *shūra* is in choosing the head of state," *bay'a* also plays a critical role in the selection of rulers.[139] *Bay'a* thus complements the social contract formed by *shūra* and *ḥisba* in creating "Islamic rule in a democratic sense." According to Fathi Osman, this is not merely theoretical speculation:

> According to the Islamic historical precedents, there is a real binding contract – not a fictitious one – between the ruler and the ruled. The mutual pledge, which was called *"bay'a,"* holds the ruler responsible for assuring the supremacy of God's law (*shari'a*) and justice, securing human dignity, serving the public interest, and fulfilling the entire duties of the position, while it holds the people responsible for supporting the ruler, obeying his decisions that comply with God's law, and fulfilling their obligations.[140]

The question naturally arises of how rulers in an Islamic state can be chosen democratically by the people. *Shūra* is the obvious answer for Islamists. Fathi Osman, for example, writes that, "Everyone has the right and obligation to participate in deciding who will be their leaders and representatives by *shūra*, and the elected bodies must reach their decisions by *shūra*." He continues to note, "Any procedure can be followed according to its own merits and to the given circumstances, and Islam accepts that which is in the interest of the people."[141] Of course, one of the facets of contemporary democratic procedure, especially in large polities, is that of political parties. Traditionally held to be antithetical to Islam, the evolution of the Islamist discourse over party politics in a democratic setting demonstrates the dynamic and innovative nature of Political Islam.

In the early part of the twentieth century, Hasan al-Banna represented traditional fundamentalist-style thinking when he declared: "There should be no party politics (*hizbiyya*) in Islam." As Qaradawi writes, al-Banna's position was the standard one for early Islamists, who generally believed that party politics was antithetical to Islam and dangerous for the unity of the *umma*. This position stemmed from the belief that, "Islam requires unity and precludes factionalism and differences." It was traditionally held that political parties would cause *fitna*, or strife and upheaval.[142]

Mawdudi maintained al-Banna's position. "We should get rid of the party-system," he wrote. "It pollutes the Government with a false sense of loyalties, and it carries within it the possibility that once a group of self-seeking people comes into power, it may maneuver party-politics, at the public expense itself, in such a way as to continue in the saddle *ad infinitum*."[143]

Significantly, contemporary Islamists have broken from this position and embraced party politics as beneficial to an Islamic state. Yousuf Qaradawi, for example, argues that, "There is no impediment to the existence of more than one political party in an Islamic state." Furthermore, he adds that a multiplicity of political parties is necessary in an Islamic state to safeguard the community's status as the depository of God's power and to allow Muslims to speak truth to power. He acknowledges that "diversity of political parties" is a reality and even a necessity "in this day and age." Party politics is necessary because it "represents a safety mechanism against the tyranny of an individual or governance by a particular class and their domination over other people and the loss of the people's right to tell them 'No!'"[144]

Qaradawi notes that political parties must "recognize Islam" and not "antagonize its doctrine or laws."[145] Turabi agrees that there are some theoretical problems with the multi-party political system from an Islamic viewpoint. "The majority-minority pattern in politics is not an ideal one in Islam," he writes. Instead of a majority winning out, Turabi argues, rather, that people should be provided with the political tools to "deliberate openly and argue and consult to ultimately reach a consensus and not simply assert or submit to a majority opinion."[146]

In speaking of consensus, Turabi is referring to *ijmāʿ*, a critical component of Islamic jurisprudence. Basically, *ijmāʿ* connotes the consensus of the Muslim community and it stems from the hadith of the Prophet when he declared: "My community shall never agree upon an error."[147] It usually refers to consensus of the *fuqaha*, or Muslim jurists, though Political Islamists like Turabi have extended its meaning to the community. As such, *ijmāʿ* plays a crucial function in the grand vision of a social contract-based Islamic state. Turabi writes, "As reflected in Islamic jurisprudence...save for the express provision of the *shariʿa*, the consensus (*ijmāʾ*) of the community is paramount. A process of consultation that leads ultimately to *ijmāʿ* is mandatory." Turabi concludes that so long as this remains paramount, there is no legal bar to the development of different parties or to the freedom of opinion and debate in an Islamic state. As he writes:

> While there may be a multiparty system, an Islamic government should function more as a consensus-oriented rather than a minority-majority system with political parties rigidly confronting each other over decisions. Parties should approach the decision-making process with an open mind and, after a consensus, adopt a mutually agreeable policy.[148]

Fathi Osman also discusses the concept of *ijmāʿ* and majority decisions in Muslim politics. He points out that the Qurʾan differentiates between a decision being considered sound because it was the majority opinion and a decision being considered sound because it was arrived at by consensus. The Qurʾan reminds Muslims that a majority of human beings may not always be right, despite having a majority of opinion [2:243; 6:116; 7:187; 11:17; 17:89; 37:71]. Regardless, Osman concludes that mistakes are inevitable in human affairs, and majority decisions are more reliable and less prone to error than decisions arrived at by an "individual or a minority among them." Osman interprets *ḥisba* as demanding the right of assembly and allowing for different political parties. Qurʾan 3:104 reveals: "And let there be from among you a community (*umma*) that calls to good and enjoins the doing of what is right and forbids the doing of what is wrong." Osman interprets this verse to mean that "*umma*" does not always necessarily refer to the entire community of Muslims; rather, it can be "just a group of people." Accordingly, he writes, "Muslims can form several Islamic political parties: all of them are committed to Islam, but each with its own concepts or methods of political activity, or with different programs of reform when they rule."[149]

El-Awa subsumes the issue of party politics within the larger issue of freedom of opinion and the God-given right to differ. "Islamic political thought needs to take a renewed stance on political diversity," he writes, "to make people aware that those calling for political reform are basing their view on Islam, not standing against political diversity, or supporting dictators, or paving the way for a new/old despotism dressed up as religion and protected by it." He cites from the Qurʾan *Surat Hud* to legitimate his views on diversity of thought in Islam: "If thy Lord had willed, He verily would have made mankind one nation, yet they cease not differing, save him on whom thy Lord hath mercy; and for that He did create them" [11:118-119]. For el-Awa, then, the acceptance of political parties is merely a reflection of the acceptance of human diversity as a purposeful creation of God. In his words:

> The acceptance of human diversity leads inevitably to the acceptance of the right to differ, and the consequence of the right to differ is the right of different people to gather together in groups and communities (various parties and groupings), which each express the views of people who agree on a particular issue or issues in opposition to those who differ from them on one or all points.[150]

Despite concerted attempts by Islamists to demonstrate the correlation between their political philosophy and democracy, the Islamic state is still presented as a countermodernity to the Western model, founded upon the perception of the failure of the West in obtaining social justice for the people of God. The use of the democratic label does not detract from the authenticity of the Islamic system because, as Howeidy says, "The essence of democracy is decisively in agreement with the essence of Islam." In fact, Islamists argue that using democracy as a tool to establish an Islamic state is an Islamic obligation. If the establishment of an Islamic state is deemed an obligation to fulfill, as it is by Islamists, then they interpret the *shari'a* as demanding that any thing that is necessary to fulfill that obligation is, itself, obligatory. Furthermore, "in the case of the demands of the legal intents of the *shari'a*, if there is a means specified to achieve these, then such a means takes the legal force of intent." This reinvented interpretation of the *shari'a* thus demands that Muslims use democracy to fulfill their obligation of establishing an Islamic state. Despite an embrace of democracy as an electoral tool, the Islamic state is not presented as being derived from a Western model because "Islam preceded democracy in decreeing the principles upon which its essence persists."[151] Muhammad Diya' al-Din al-Rayyis characterizes this as such:

> The Islamic state, then, is according to this form, a unique system particular to Islam. The assertion that it correlates to any other known system is not correct; and thus, there ought to be posited for it a special terminology – which describes it according to a term representative of its true na-

ture. And as long as the like of such a term is not clear or has not yet been found, it is sufficient now to indicate it according to its comprehensive characteristic – that it is an 'Islamic system.'[152]

Perhaps the most legitimate attempt at inventing a word to describe the unique 'Islamic system' mentioned by al-Rayyis is the concept of *shūracracy* or *shūrakratiyya* (the latter a combination of *shūra* and the Arabic transliteration of 'democracy,' *demokratiyya*). The German convert to Islam Murad Wilfried Hoffman notes that the Algerian Islamist Shaykh Mahfoudh Nahnah was the first to use these words.[153] Despite the problems with naming the 'Islamic system' that underlies an Islamic state, it is without doubt that this state is based upon a social contract between rulers and ruled and relies upon democracy as an electoral tool for instituting that social contract.

In fact, it might be more feasible and accurate to describe this social contract as a dual contract, as the Dutch scholar Jeroen Gunning does in the case of Hamas's political philosophy. For Islamists, the human invention of a social contract between rulers and ruled is merely an expression of God's will and the divine contract that each Muslim enters into with Him. It is cast as a function of *tawhid* and *hakimiyyat-Allah*: the inseparable unity of God's sovereignty in all things. As Mawdudi described:

> [Islamic society] is the result of a deliberate choice and effort; it is the outcome of a "contract" that takes place between human beings and their Creator. Those who enter into this contract undertake to recognize God as their sovereign, His guidance as supreme, and His injunctions as absolute law. They also undertake to accept, without question or doubt, His classification of good and evil, right and wrong, the permissible and the prohibited. In short, the Islamic society agrees to limit its volition to the extent prescribed by the All-Knowing God.[154]

The concept of the dual contract resolves the paradox in the concept of *ḥākimiyya*, or God's sovereignty on Earth. As Jeroen Gunning notes, neither the social contract between rulers and ruled nor the divine contract between human and God is sufficient by itself in the Islamic system. A divine contract without a social contract negates people's sovereignty because it negates the ability of each human to serve as God's vicegerent on earth. Furthermore, a divine contract by itself does not solve who is to rule in God's stead, or how to interpret His laws in different circumstances and contexts. However, without a social contract, despotic rulers predominate, as has been pointed out by Islamists countless times. Yet, a social contract without the divine contract negates God's sovereignty on Earth and does not guarantee that the government governs according to God's laws.[155]

In conceptualizing the concept of a dual contract, Islamists draw upon the respect with which Islamic tradition regards contractual associations. The Qur'an admonishes believers to be true to their contracts and obligations. As *Surat Ibrahim* reveals:

> Do you not see how God sets forth as a parable that a good word is like a good tree, whose root is firm and its branches are in the sky? ... And a foul word is like a foul tree, which has been uprooted from the surface of the earth, having no stable base ... God blesses those who believe with the firm word of the present life, and in the life to come; but he leads wrongdoers astray [14:24-27].

Furthermore, contracts are interpreted as methods of association that are sanctioned by the Divine because the Qur'an reveals that man accedes to a contract with God. In *Surat al-Baqarah* the Qur'an warns that, "Those who break the promise of God (*'ahd Allah*) after its confirmation, sever what God ordered to be joined, and make mischief in the land – those are the losers" [2:27]. The English interpretation of "its confirmation" refers to the Arabic word *mithaq*, which literally means contract, thus revealing the relationship (promise) between man and God as a divine contract.

Those individuals who break the contract with God suffer consequences that are described throughout the Qur'an. *Surat al-Imran* reveals that he who righteously fulfills his contract with God will be rewarded, because that is what God wants. Conversely, those "who sell the divine contract (*'ahd Allah*) and their own oaths for a small price will have no share in the life to come; God will not speak to them or guide them or judge them on the Day of Resurrection. A painful punishment is in store for them!" [3:76-77]. This verse is particularly significant because it reveals that those who break their own oaths – social contracts – are deviating from God's will and thus also breaking the divine contract.

Ultimately, the concept of the dual contract emerged in Islamist thought from the desire to achieve the *maqasid al-shari'a,* or the end-goals of God's laws, which is social justice in Islamic society. The social contract between rulers and ruled is put in place to ensure that the ruler governs according to *al-masalih al-mursalah,* or the public interest.[156] The divine contract stipulates that any person in a position of political power and authority who does not govern in such a way is deviating from God's will, and will thus be punished. Muhammad Qutb, the younger brother of Sayyid Qutb, described this as such: "[The] entrusted ruler has to act in accordance with *al-masalih al-mursalah,* so that he does not disregard the end goals of the shari'a (*maqasid al-shari'a*)."[157] With this conceptual framework of contractual political philosophy, Political Islam emerges as a dynamic and creative function "of the extent to which state performance in Muslim societies falls short of the principles of Islamic social justice."[158] Political Islam must be understood as a popular movement seeking change in opposition to the status quo. That the movement relies upon religious mobilization and a religious discourse should be viewed as a response to the failure of the existing secular governments to deliver the most basic tenets of sound, equitable, and accountable governance to their citizens.

PART FOUR

Arabia and the Prophet at Medina

They refused to be servants of kings,
And never were ruled by any...

- 'Abid ibn al-Abras of Asad

For all practicing Muslims the historical period surrounding the Prophet Muhammad at Medina stands "splendidly alone" as the ideal model of human endeavor. In the words of Hasan Turabi, for example, this historical example is the "eternal model that Muslims are bound to adopt as a perfect standard for all time."[1] Turabi's declaration is especially true for Islamists, who present their reform projects as the most authentic representation of the Prophet's model. Islamists attempt to legitimate their entire political philosophy and reformist vision by linking them to examples from this historical period. "It is an article of faith with every Muslim that the age of the Holy Prophet and the rightly guided Caliphs is the blissful and glorious period of our history and a perpetual source of inspiration to us," wrote Mawdudi. "It is the ideal which all our efforts are directed to approximate to.[2]

The model of this historical period gained new significance for many Muslims in the post World War One political landscape as European powers divided the *umma* into territorially defined nation-states. Many Muslims in this period felt alienated from their vision of their past and besieged by the realities of contemporary circumstances. This sentiment was augmented by brutally repressive domestic regimes that continually failed to deliver even the most basic services. Political Islam emerged from this context as a "search for authenticity, a search for 'roots'...as a necessary aspect of contending with the Muslim situation in the contemporary world."[3]

As part of this search for authenticity and 'roots,' Islamists recast the Medinan period not as a distant, reified vision of the past – a model only to strive toward – but as a comprehensive blueprint for life that was to be realized again in the present. "Truly this period is not the product of an unrepeated miracle; it was the product of the human effort exerted by early Muslims," wrote Sayyid Qutb. "It is attainable again when a similar effort is put forth."[4] With this conceptualization, Islamists present the historical period surrounding the Prophet at Medina as an easily accessible and familiar package containing within it systems and practices that are relevant to solving the problems facing Muslims in contemporary times.

Arab tribal society and communal authority

As has been described, a common theme in Islamist thought is opposition to absolutism and the conviction that man's natural state on Earth is free. While this conviction has foundation in the Qur'anic message, it also has foundation in pre-Islamic Arab thought and practice. Even before the revelation of Islam, Arab society was "strikingly egalitarian" and "displayed a high level of social homogeneity" among a people who "disliked structures of authority."[5] Freedom of the individual was central to the pre-Islamic Arab world-view. Islamists have interpreted Islam, as a faith embodying the values of fairness and equality to all believers, as enshrining this Arab world-view. Sayyid Qutb confirmed this when he wrote:

> Islam grew up in an independent country owing allegiance to no empire and to no king, in a form of society never again achieved. It had to embody this society in itself, had to order, encourage, and promote it. It had to order and regulate this society, adopting from the beginning its principles and its spirit along with its methods of life and work.[6]

In many ways, pre-Islamic Arab society was radically different from its neighboring societies in Egypt, the Fertile Crescent, and Iran. Social identity and political structures were founded on perceived ties of kinship that formed the basis of tribal units. These kinship ties and tribal units were bonded together by contractual associations.[7] This method of societal organization was developed to maintain an egalitarian socio-political ethos, but was also a consequence of the particular geography of the Arabian Peninsula.

The medieval Muslim historian Ibn Khaldun described this ethos or world-view as one characterized by *asabiyya*, or group feeling, a natural response of the Arabs for self-preservation in a harsh environment. He explained that "group feeling" was necessary because it "gives protection and makes possible mutual defense, the pressing of claims, and every other kind of social activity." Furthermore, he argued that the tribe was specifically adapted to its environment: "Only tribes held together by group feeling [*asabiyya*] can survive in the desert...The desert is a place of hardship and starvation, but to them [Arabs] it has become familiar and accustomed."[8]

Travelers to the region and historians have described the life of the Arabs in the desert in different ways; however, as in Ibn Khaldun's *Muqaddimah*, descriptions of hardship are common. Edward Gibbon, in his classic work of history *The Decline and Fall of the Roman Empire*, describes the landscape of the Arabian Peninsula as such:

> [In] Arabia, a boundless level of sand is intersected by sharp and naked mountains, and the face of the desert, without shade or shelter, is scorched by the direct and intense rays of a tropical sun. Instead of refreshing breezes, the winds... diffuse a noxious and even deadly vapour; the hillocks of sand which they alternately raise and scatter are compared to the billows of the ocean; and whole caravans, whole armies, have been lost and buried in the whirlwind.[9]

Though the tribal unit might have been specially adapted to the particularities of the Arabian Peninsula, it is a common historical misconception that Islam is a "religion of the desert" or a "religion of nomadic simplicity." As historian Jonathan Berkey points out, not all of Arabia was desert and not all Arabs were bedouin. For example, *Felix Arabia*, "fruitful" or "happy" Arabia, which formed the southwest quadrant of the Arabian Peninsula (present day Yemen), was an area of significant rainfall, rich soil, and lush vegetation. The noted historian of early Islam Fred Donner wrote that, although the very name 'Arabia' reminds people today, as was also the case in antiquity, of a vast desert occupied by nomads and bedouins, it is unlikely that nomadic peoples have ever formed more than a small fraction of its population.[10]

In fact, pre-Islamic Arab society revolved around thriving, cosmopolitan trading cities. While Qutb contended that Islam grew up in an independent country, in actual fact it grew up in Mecca, a bustling city of traders and businessmen, and Muhammad's most powerful followers were each sophisticated, upper class Meccans. Although tradition holds that Muhammad was uneducated and illiterate, after marrying Khadija, one of the wealthiest and most successful inhabitants of Mecca, he became quite wealthy. While the overall societal ethos of Arabia was egalitarian, then, in historical reality there were social classes and the majority of Arabs lived in or around trading cities where life was stratified.[11]

Despite the great diversity in economic and cultural patterning of Arabian life, however, historians of this period often remark upon the striking uniformity to Arabian social organization. "For everywhere, it appears, Arabian society on the eve of Islam was tribal," wrote Fred Donner.[12] Contractual associations were a fundamental aspect of tribal society because they resolved the apparent paradox between the stratification of urban Arabia and the Arabs' fierce sense of independence. As Gibbon characterized it: "[The Arabs'] spirit is free, their steps are unconfined, the desert is open, and the tribes and families are held together by a mutual and voluntary compact." Political and social structures based upon voluntary contracts maintained a world-view that did not legitimate absolute power of any one man over others. Indeed, as Gibbon observed, the degree to which the Arabs reveled in their independence "has been the theme of praise among strangers and natives" alike. "If the Arabian princes abuse their power," he wrote, "they are quickly punished by the desertion of their subjects, who had been accustomed to a mild and parental jurisdiction."[13]

Political power and authority in Arabia was, in fact, mild in its depth. A quote by the Assyrian King Sargon II demonstrates this: "The distant Arabs dwelling in the desert...know neither overseers nor officials."[14] Usually, the shaykh, or chief, was the person entrusted with political authority, and his authority was meant to maintain the mutual and voluntary contracts between tribes and between individuals. This authority, however, was never absolute. As Oxford historian Robert Hoyland notes, a tribal shaykh filled the role of spokesman or guide for the tribe; he was never a director. To demonstrate this, Hoyland records in his book *Arabia and the Arabs* an ancient lament on the death of Shaykh Kulayb of the powerful northeast Arabian *Taghlib* tribe:

> Who now will help the indigent when they cry out?
> And who will stain the tips of supple spears with blood?
> Who will cast lots for the slaughter camel

When the morning wind cuts through the knotted ropes?
Who will come forward with blood monies and gather them?
And who will succor us when calamities befall?[15]

This passage confirms Gibbon's characterization of power and authority as mild and parental in nature; it demonstrates a people aghast at losing a guide, not an overseer. The contemporary Egyptian Islamist Mohammad el-Awa maintains this narrative in his writings on the nature of political power and authority in an Islamic state. He writes that in Arabia, tribal shaykhs were first and foremost individuals within a tribe. They were considered equal in rights and duties so much so that the shaykh "constituted a mere theoretical authority whose objective was to preserve the unity among the sons of his tribe."[16] As this evidence suggests, political power in Arabia was manifested through the voluntary transferal of power from the tribe to the shaykh by means of a contract. Authority in the sense of individuals or tribe submitting completely to the absolute power of another did not exist.

Granted, there are examples of kings who reigned during this time. However, even they were not absolute sovereigns. Hoyland describes the role of an Arabian king as initiating and sponsoring major public works, enforcing the rulings of various legislative assemblies, and serving as commander-in-chief during times of war. Ultimate authority lay with various arrangements of consultative bodies that granted the king his power, and of which the king was but a single member. "So though inferior to none," concludes Hoyland of kings in this time, "they were not considered far above all."[17]

The kingship was rooted in the pre-Islamic Arab egalitarian world-view of communal power and authority. A king's authority was derived from the will of the people whom he represented and whose freedom he was responsible for respecting. Hoyland recounts "a slightly bizarre account" of this from the ancient historian Agarthicides of Cnidus (*c.* 200-131 BC) that confirms the limited power of kings:

> The king of all the tribe holds his office from the people. Though it is prized, it is very hazardous. It is prized because the king is in command of many and he does whatever he wills in accordance with his judgements; it is hazardous because, although he has received the whole charge, he is not able thenceforth to leave the palace. Otherwise he is stoned

by everyone in accordance with an ancient oracle, and thus his pre-eminence is deleterious.[18]

Elsewhere, in the Kingdom of Saba (modern day Yemen) for example, accession to the throne "required the consent of 'the Sabaeans, the *qayls* and the army.'" Laws were regularly drafted in the name of the king plus a group of other functionaries. Further limiting the power of the king, there was no state taxation system. Tithes, common in pre-Islamic Arabia and maintained in Islam in the form of *zakat*, or alms giving, went to temples, not to the king, who was never considered to be a divine being or a person with a divine right to rule. An ancient Greek writer describing the nature of the kingship among the Nabataeans (a kingdom in northern Arabia) confirmed this:

> The king is so democratic (*demotikos*) that, in addition to serving himself, he sometimes even serves the rest himself in his turn. He often renders an account of his kingship in the popular assembly; and sometimes his mode of life is examined...The king has as chief administrator one of his companions, who is called 'brother.'[19]

Furthermore, a king could not create or negotiate tribal law on his own. Tribal law could only be created or updated when a *shūra* council received the approval of all members of the community, or the appointed representatives of the community. *Ijmā'* was thus a central characteristic of pre-Islamic law making and guarded against absolute rule. The renowned Arabian poet Zuhayr described the *shūra* councils that decided legislation as such:

> Among them [the Arabs] are assemblies of fine men, councils from which follow decisive words and deeds ... when you come to them, you will find them round their tents in session, at which impetuous action is often obviated by their prudent members.[20]

The political system between and among tribes in pre-Islamic Arabia was one based upon *shūra* and *ijmā*. This was a system based not on submission to any one man but on *bay'a*, an oath of allegiance and contractual association between equal counterparts. The purpose of this system was to preserve the independent and egalitarian nature of society. "In the more simple state of the Arabs the nation is free, wrote Gibbon, "because each of her sons disdains a base submission to the will of a master...the love of independence prompts him to exercise the habits of self-command."[21]

Before the revelation of Islam, a system of voluntary contractual associations governed every aspect of society. Herodotus, the famous historian of ancient Greece who is often labeled the father of history, wrote, "The Arabs keep such pledges more religiously than almost any other people."[22] The pledges that Herodotus refers to were quite literally contracts that were bound by the comingling of blood between the contracting parties, while "at the same time applying blood to the [gods] so as to make [them] a party to the covenant also."[23] The oath was thus a dual contract: a social contract between the consenting parties and a divine contract between the parties and their gods. Herodotus described the process as such:

> They plight faith with the forms following. When two men would swear a[n oath], they stand on each side of a third: he with a sharp stone makes a cut on the inside of the hand of each near the middle finger, and, taking a piece from their dress, dips it in the blood of each, and moistens therewith seven stones lying in the midst, calling the while on Bacchus [Dionysus] and Urania [Aphrodite]. After this, the man who makes the pledge commends the stranger (or the citizen, if citizen he be) to all his friends, and they deem themselves bound to stand to the engagement.[24]

Travelers to the region who witnessed the bearing of these oaths by Arabs frequently remarked upon the fidelity to which such arrangements were held. In the editor's notes to Herodotus, the late George Rawlinson, a scholar of ancient history at Oxford, noted one such traveler who stated, "The Arabs have been commended by the ancients for the fidelity of their attachments, and they are still scrupulously exact to their words."[25] Furthermore, Robert Hoyland explains the degree to which contractual associations were entrenched in Arab culture by noting that such practices are described in pre-Islamic Arab poetry nearly 1,000 years after Herodotus' writing.[26]

Though Islamists regard all of history before the revelation of Islam as *jahaliyyah*, the age of ignorance for humankind, scholars agree that many features of pre-Islamic Arabia survived the radical social transformation brought by Islam. Indeed, Arab tribal identity continued to shape the political and social history of the early Muslims. As the scholar of early Islam R.B. Serjeant wrote, "So long as conditions in the Arabian Peninsula did not greatly change, society and language did not alter much either, and in many areas Islam had but slightly modified the culture as it had been in the days of the Jahiliyyah."[27] Concepts such as *shūra, ijmā,* and *bay'a,* each a long-refined pre-Islamic concept, became especially enshrined by God's revelations to Muhammad. Marshall Hodgson, in a passage that has been exclusively drawn upon by contemporary Islamists, described this best. Of the *shari'a* law that was revealed by God to Muslims, he wrote:

> It was highly egalitarian, and therefore, perhaps, what may be called contractualistic. A very wide range of relations were left to contracts between responsible individuals – including, in theory, even the whole range of politics. In principle, no man was properly a ruler till he had been accepted in covenant by the representatives of the Muslim community; and even then...public duties were potentially the obligation of every Muslim if no one Muslim was fulfilling them...The directive offices of society were never filled on the basis of fixed heredity, but normally by designation and/or consultation...Remarkably little was left, in the *sharia* law, to ascribed status...Even the marriage law, in which ascribed status played a relatively large role, reflected this egalitarian contractualism.[28]

Hodgson's description of the *shari'a* as 'contractualistic' and 'egalitarian' is reflective of a general mistrust of absolutism or monarchy in the revelations of the Qur'an. *Surat al-Naml,* for example, reveals the Queen of Sheba (Saba), one of the most powerful kingdoms in pre-Islamic Arabia, as saying before her constituents: "Oh, my dignitaries, give me your counsel in this, my affair. I will make no decision until you bear witness to me" [27:32]. The Queen also spoke of monarchy in a disparaging fashion when she stated: "When kings enter a city, they ruin it and reduce its proud inhabitants to subjection. Thus they will always do" [27:34]. *Surat al-Baqarah* reveals the ancient Israelites as skeptical and hesitant to accept a kingship – even a divinely ordered one – over them. "God has ordered Saul to be your King," the Qur'an reveals, to which the Israelites replied, "How can he hold kingship over us while we have a greater right to kingship than he, for he is not erudite enough?" [2:246-248]. The skepticism with which the idea of kingship was regarded is confirmed in *Surat al-Ma'idah,* which reveals that each person is a king unto himself: "And when Moses said to his people, 'Oh, my people, remember God's grace for you when He raised Prophets among you and made you kings and gave you what He had not given to any other nation'" [5:20].

The Prophet at Medina

The most demonstrative example of the "egalitarian contractualism" as embodied in the *shari'a* law was the establishment of the first Muslim community by Muhammad at Medina. The pre-Islamic concepts of *bay'a, shūra,* and *ijmā'* provided the conceptual foundation for this community. As the scholar of Islam Ovamir Anjum observes, Muhammad established Medina as a city-state based on a political philosophy that gave "agency, responsibility, and a set of goals to the entire community."[29]

Muhammad's vision of contractual and communal authority must be understood in the context of his *hijra* from Mecca. The word *hijra* is often translated into English as "flight." However, as the late scholar of Islam W. Montgomery Watt noted, the Arabic verb from which *hijra* is formed is *hajara.* Properly understood, this word means "to cut someone off from friendly association" or "to avoid association with." Thus, Watt concluded, "*Hijra* properly does not mean 'flight'...but connotes primarily the breaking of the ties of kinship and association."[30] The Prophet's departure from Mecca, then, must be understood as the breaking of his contractual association with the Meccans.

The Prophet was prompted to flee Mecca after nearly thirteen years of repression by polytheist Arabs there. Ibn Ishaq, one of the first of Muhammad's biographers, describes that dissent in Mecca began as soon as Muhammad began preaching the monotheism (*tawhid*) of Islam, which was offensive to the pagan Arabs. He wrote:

> The apostle continued on his way, publishing God's religion and calling men thereto. In consequence his relations with Quraysh [the dominant tribe in Mecca] deteriorated and men withdrew from him in enmity. They were always talking about him and inciting one another against him... Then the Quraysh incited people against the companions of the apostle who had become Muslims. Every tribe fell upon

the Muslims among them, beating them and seducing them from their religion...They stirred up against him [Muhammad] foolish men who called him a liar, insulted him, and accused him of being a poet, a sorcerer, a diviner, and of being possessed.[31]

Muhammad's offenses ultimately became too much for the Meccans and they set out to plot his murder. According to Ibn Ishaq, a group of Meccans decided that:

Each clan should provide a young, powerful, well-born, aristocratic warrior; that each of these should be provided with a sharp sword; then that each of them should strike a blow at him [Muhammad] and kill him. Thus they would be relieved of him, and responsibility for his blood would lie on all the clans.[32]

Ishaq wrote that the angel Gabriel came to Muhammad around nightfall and said to him, "Do not sleep tonight on the bed on which you usually sleep." Upon hearing this, Muhammad decided to flee, under the cover of darkness, with his most trusted ally, Abu Bakr. While Muhammad and Abu Bakr fled Mecca, another close companion, 'Ali, deceived the Meccans who were watching his home and waiting to murder him. "Before much of the night had passed they assembled at his door waiting for him to go to sleep so that they might fall upon him," described Ishaq. "When the apostle saw what they were doing he told 'Ali to lie on his bed and to wrap himself in his green Hadrami mantle [scarf]; for no harm would befall him. He himself used to sleep in this mantle."[33]

With 'Ali's help, Muhammad went to the home of Abu Bakr, "and the two of them left by a window in the back of the latter's house and made for a cave on Thaur, a mountain below Mecca." Ishaq recounts that the two men remained in the cave for three days, before departing for Medina.

A range of peoples greeted Muhammad upon his arrival there. The population of Medina consisted of polytheist Arab and Jewish tribes living under a fragile political truce, a consequence of many years of intertribal conflicts. The scholar of early Islam Patricia Crone described this:

It is well known that Medina on the eve of Islam was torn by feuds. Ibn Ishaq does not tell the full story of these feuds, but he refers to them on several occasions, and they play a crucial role in his account of how Muhammad came to be accepted there: the Yathribis [Medinans] who decide to throw in their lot with him explain that their people is divided by hatred and rancor to an unusual degree, and they express the hope that 'perhaps God will unite them through you.'[34]

There is some debate among scholars of early Islam regarding the particularities of the power structures among the tribes at Medina around the time of the Prophet's arrival. The German scholar of Islamic studies Marco Scholler notes that the Jewish tribes were the dominant military power there.[35] However, R.B. Serjeant notes that recently before the Prophet's arrival, the Jewish tribes had lost power and influence and fallen under the protection of Arab tribes.[36] Regardless of which tribes were dominant at Medina when Muhammad arrived there, what is clear is that he and his followers would have been clearly outmatched. Ibn Hashim, the editor of Ibn Ishaq's writings, described the political environment that greeted Muhammad:

> We have left our people [the tribes of Aws and Khazraj] in such a state of enmity and war as exists in no other people. It might be that God will unite them through you. We shall come to them and invite them to join your affair and propose to them that to which we consented, namely this religion. If God unites them around it [Islam], nobody will be stronger than you [Muhammad].[37]

Ibn Hashim's description portrays Muhammad's efforts to establish a system that would allow the people to voluntarily consent to a political system that maintained their freedom to worship and practice as they wished, and that maintained their traditional identities. The famous early Muslim historian Muhammad ibn 'Umar al-Waqidi describes this, in a translation by Serjeant:

> The Apostle of Allah came to Medina and its inhabitants were a mixed lot, consisting of the Muslims whom the confederation/brotherhood (*da'wah*) of Islam was uniting (*tajma'u-hum*), part being people of mail coats and forts, and

part allies (*halif*) in a state of union with the two tribes, the Aws and Khazraj. The Apostle of Allah wished, when he arrived at Medina, to establish peace/concord between them, all of them/as a collective group (*jami'-an*), and to make peace (*muwada'ah*) with them. A man would be a Muslim and his father a polytheist (*Mushrik*).[38]

One of Muhammad's first acts in Medina was conducting a census of its residents. The Turkish scholar Ali Bulaç notes that from the census, Muhammad determined that 10,000 persons lived in Medina. Of these, 1,500 were Muslims, 4,000 were Jews, and 4,500 were polytheist Arabs. Tradition holds that Muhammad marked distinct physical boundaries of Medina, and in so doing declared that, "his aim was not to establish an absolute rule over Medina" but rather to create "possible ways of coexisting through the realization of a pluralist social project based on religious and legal autonomy."[39]

It is generally regarded that one of the first political acts in establishing the city-state at Medina was the second *bay'a* of *al-'Aqaba*, which actually was confirmed before Muhammad's migration to Medina. This contract affirmed mutual protection between the leading Medinan tribes and Muhammad and his followers, thus providing necessary assurances for the besieged Muslims of Mecca to fully migrate to Medina. "Then Mus'ab returned to Mecca and the Muslim Ansar [supporters] came to the fair there with the pilgrims of their people who were polytheists," recorded Ibn Ishaq. "They met the apostle at al-'Aqaba in the middle of the days of Tashriq, when God intended to honour them and to help His apostle and to strengthen Islam and to humiliate heathenism and its devotees."[40] Gibbon recounts the story of this as preserved by Ibn Ishaq and Ibn Hisham:

> Seventy-three men and two women of Medina held a solemn conference with Mahomet, his kinsmen, and his disciples; and pledged themselves to each other by a mutual oath of fidelity. They promised in the name of the city that, if he should be banished, they would receive him as a confederate, obey him as a leader, and defend him... 'All things,' [said the Prophet] 'are now common between us; your blood is as my blood, your ruin as my ruin.'...They reiterated the oath of allegiance and fidelity. Their treaty was ratified by the people.[41]

The document that eventually emerged for posterity is the Constitution of Medina; however, strictly speaking it is not actually a constitution. According to Ibn Ishaq, "The apostle wrote a document concerning the emigrants and the helpers in which he made a friendly agreement with the Jews and established them in their religion and their property, and stated the reciprocal obligations."[42] The "Constitution of Medina" as it is presently known is actually a collection of eight distinct documents issued on various occasions over the first seven years or so of Muhammad's Medinan period. Regardless, these documents established a governing system at Medina to which each tribe pledged its voluntary consent, and which maintained each tribe's right to practice its particular faith and worship freely. The text of the document, as preserved by Ibn Ishaq, begins, in Arabic: *hadha kitab min Muhammad al-nabi bayna l-mu'minina wa-l-muslimina min quraysh wa-yathrib wa-man tabi'ahum fa-lahiqa bihim* (This is a compact from Muhammad the Prophet between the *Mu'minun* and Muslims of Quraysh and Yathrib and those who join them as clients, attach themselves to them and fight the holy war with them).[43]

The language of the document demonstrates its contractual and pluralistic ethos. As Michael Lecker concludes in his analysis of the document, the Arabic describes it as a *kitab*, which, in this particular setting, is best interpreted as a compact or contract between the Prophet and the contracting tribes at Medina. Furthermore, it denotes those who join – namely, "the believers and Muslims of Quraysh and Yathrib" – to be clients voluntarily acceding to a pact, demonstrating a philosophy of political power and authority not based on domination and subordination but on voluntary consent and allegiance.[44]

The document then lists each contracting tribe one by one, for example: *"al-muhajirun min quraysh 'ala riba'atihim..."* ("The Muhajirun from Quraysh keep to their tribal organization and leadership") and *"wa banu 'awf 'ala riba'atihim"* ("The Banu 'awf keep to their tribal organization and leadership.") The phrase *'ala riba'atihim* is repeated nine times throughout the document, and denotes that each tribe was allowed to maintain its particular indigenous tribal organization and practices and religious and legal autonomy.[45] Consultation as a means of obtaining consensus throughout the community was thus paramount in establishing Muhammad's political system at Medina. As Ali Bulaç points out, "Information from [Malik ibn] Anas [Companion of the Prophet (710-796)] and other sources indicate that the Document took shape as a result of negotiations and as a product of social consensus." The so-called Constitution of Medina outlined a social and political project based on the active participation of groups who voluntarily consented to grant power to their ruler, in this case, Muhammad.[46]

Many Islamists have drawn upon the model of Muhammad at Medina to inform their contemporary political philosophy, especially regarding the establishment of an Islamic state. Nadia Yassine, for example, argues that based on this model, an Islamic state in the contemporary world can only be one that is "participatory, egalitarian, committed to freedom, and expressive of God's mercy."[47] Like others, Yassine uses the fundamental primacy of *shūra* in the political system at Medina as evidence for the argument that the continued decline of the *umma* throughout modern history has been a consequence of "the transfer of power from the *shūra* to the *fardiya*, literally, 'the power of the individual.'" Yassine cites the work of the Yemeni scholar Zayd bnu ʿAli al-Wazir, who wrote that:

> The first thing we learn from the text [of the Constitution of Medina] is that the *umma* governs itself through institutions that differ from the models of power known until then that were based on despotism and absolutism...The Constitution emphasizes the fact that the *umma* governs itself by means of communitarian institutions...It mentions four relational frameworks: Muslims among themselves, Muslims and Jews, Muslims and pagans, and finally a much broader framework we may describe as one of general structures.[48]

For many Muslims, the concept of the four frameworks that al-Wazir illustrates is evidence for an indigenously Islamic concept of secularism. "The only model for this purpose," wrote the late Indian Muslim reformist Ashgar Ali Engineer, "can be the Mithaq-i-Madina and this Covenant, as pointed out above, did not make any distinction between people of one religion and the other in matters of political rights."[49] Yet, for many contemporary Islamists, what most demonstrates the Prophet's conviction that an Islamic state must be founded upon communal power, consultation, and contractual authority is that he left no instructions regarding what the Medinan community should do after his death. As Yassine writes, "He crowned his support for the principle of *shūra* by his ultimate silence as to his successor, leaving the community free to choose its rulers."[50]

Conception of the Caliphate

Islamists interpret the process by which the Caliphate was conceived after the death of Muhammad as establishing the precedent that a ruler's power derives only from the community's voluntary oath of allegiance to him.⁵¹ As Muhammad el-Awa puts it, "Choosing a ruler was the cornerstone in the organization of the Islamic state when it was first established...this is exactly how the four guided Caliphs were chosen."⁵² Similarly, Fathi Osman explicitly mentions the primacy of *bay'a* in the establishment of the Caliphate and describes it in terms of social contract. He writes:

> The first four caliphs were chosen in different ways, but in the end they went to the public in the mosque to obtain their approval in the form of *bay'a*...a mutual pledge from the ruler to follow *shari'a* and earn the public's approval and support through his services, and from the people to support the ruler and advise him.⁵³

Because there was no divine instruction on how to choose a ruler after the Prophet's death, his closest companions and the Medinan community improvised and used the long-refined Arab concepts of *shūra, ijmā', and bay'a* to elect a successor to Muhammad and thus establish the Islamic Caliphate. Close scrutiny of Ibn Ishaq's account reveals the improvisatory nature of the decisions made by the companions after Muhammad's death. The Arabic word he uses is *falta*. According to the late Arabic linguist Alfred Guillaume, the exact meaning of this word in English is elusive, though he translates it as either "hasty mistake" or "unpremeditated affair." Regardless of how one interprets *falta* in English, Ibn Ishaq's use of the word demonstrates that the Prophet's closest companions had no instruction or precedent from which to draw upon in choosing his successor, thus demonstrating why they reverted to long-refined Arab traditions. As Ibn Ishaq described it:

> Don't let a man deceive himself by saying that the acceptance of Abu Bakr was an unpremeditated affair which was ratified. Admittedly it was that, but God averted the evil of it. There is none among you to whom people would devote themselves as they did to Abu Bakr. He who accepts a man as ruler without consulting the Muslims, such acceptance

has no validity for either of them: they are in danger of being killed.[54]

The Caliphate was thus established the day after the Prophet's death in the year 11/632, when Abu Bakr received the voluntary consent of the Medinan community to serve as *khalifat rasūl Allah*, or the successor to the messenger (prophet) of God. Ibn Ishaq's description reveals the respect with which the companions regarded concepts such as consultation and accountability to the people. For the first generation of Muslims, this act established the voluntary oath of allegiance as "the explicit and formal vehicle by which one man committed himself to another."[55]

Abu Bakr's first speech as Caliph demonstrates the contractual authority the people had entrusted him with. Ibn Ishaq recorded him as having stated:

> I have been given authority over you but I am not the best of you. If I do well, help me, and if I do ill, then put me right. Truth consists in loyalty and falsehood in treachery...Obey me so long as I obey God and His apostle, and if I disobey them you owe me no obedience.[56]

Countless contemporary Islamists draw upon this tradition as evidence for the social contract in Islam. El-Awa cites Abu Bakr's first speech as evidence for the right of the *umma* to call the head of state to account and demand accountability. According to el-Awa, this hadith among others "establish the basis of obedience to rulers in their doing right; thus the sayings imply the obligation of disobedience in wrongdoing or sin."[57] Similarly, Qaradawi writes that, as evidenced by Abu Bakr's speech, "Among the rights of the Muslims is to show him [the ruler] the right way when he errs, to set him straight when he deviates."[58]

Abu Bakr's first speech (*khutba*) set a precedent that was acted upon well after his death. Numerous rebellions occurred in the first generations of the Muslim community when the community sought to rescind their social contract with the ruler. The era of the third caliph, 'Uthman, is particularly instructive. Contemporary Islamists draw upon this time as containing examples that demonstrate precedent for the deposition of an unjust ruler in an Islamic state. As Ashghar Ali Engineer describes it, "The people who had experienced the conduct of the Prophet were so sensitive to the doctrine of accountability that there was a great uprising when the regime of the third Caliph deviated from this doctrine for various reasons."[59] There were indeed many different reasons for the uprising against 'Uthman, including new factions competing for power in the wake of early Arab conquests, the rise in power of Meccan economic elite, and increasing influence of tribe and clan heads. As the late scholar on the historiography of early Islamic history Martin Hinds notes, it was reportedly in 34 [AH], probably at the time of the *hajj*, that discontented provincials from Egypt, Kufa and Basra first came together and discussed the possibility of joint opposition to 'Uthman.[60] Gibbon provided an eloquent description of this:

> From Cufa, from Bassora, from Egypt, from the tribes of the desert, they rose in arms, encamped about a league from Medina, and dispatched a haughty mandate to their sovereign, requiring him to execute justice or to descend from the throne.[61]

The reasons for this "haughty mandate" dispatched to 'Uthman were many, but each was basically rooted in dissatisfaction with the ways 'Uthman diverged from the political tradition of the Prophet and the first two caliphs, Abu Bakr and Omar. Hinds notes that the opposition accused 'Uthman of not governing by *shūra*, or in accordance with the Qur'an or the sunna of Muhammad. 'Uthman was also accused of consolidating his power and impeding upon the community's role as depository of God's sovereignty on earth. Among the other reasons, Hinds notes that, "'Uthman was criticized for favouring his family, on whom he counted for support and from whom he was able to recruit governors upon whom he could rely; for his dismissal and rough treatment of *sahaba* and his deportation of others, all of whom had obstructed his organizational efforts; and for his standardized recension of the Qur'an, which was intended to supersede varying recensions in the provinces."[62] Nepotism, used by 'Uthman as a tool for consolidating his own authority, was especially offensive to the Arabs and their ethos of tribal meritocracy steeped in the concepts of *shūra* and *ijmāʿ*.

'Uthman's dismissive or contemptuous attitude toward communal power and authority is evident from his reported remark "They hope to rule" (*amaluhum al-imra*), and "They desire the passing away of the caliphate [i.e. 'Uthman's]" (*yarumuna 'l-khilafata an tazula*).[63] Dissatisfaction with cronyism and nepotism in 'Uthman's government ultimately led the opposition to demand that the Caliph dismiss his powerful governor in Kufa, al-Walid ibn 'Uqbah. Contemporary Islamists frequently draw upon this example. El-Awa, for example, says that one of the most significant reasons behind the call for al-Walid's ouster was that he regularly consumed wine, even during prayer. Despite ostensibly providing proof to the contrary, 'Uthman accepted the opposition's request, punished al-Walid and removed him from his post as provincial governor. This did not entirely appease the opposition, however, and they soon demanded the ouster of his successor, Sa'id ibn al-'Aas; they even went to far as to prevent his entry into Kufa upon his arrival from Medina. 'Uthman acceded to this demand as well, and replaced al-'Aas with Abu Musa al-Ash'ari, who had already been relived of his post as governor of Basra because of the demands of the people there.[64]

The significance of 'Uthman acceding to these demands for dismissal of his provincial governors is not just that it demonstrates the primacy of accountability and consultation for the early Muslim community. Of even greater significance is that these concepts were so deeply rooted in the Muslim community that its dissatisfaction with the offenses of 'Uthman and his growing strongman rule ultimately led to his murder. As Engineer described it, "The Prophet of Islam and his Companions had sensitized the Muslims to such an extent in respect of accountability and transparency in governance that any deviation from it was strongly protested."[65]

Even beyond the period of the first four caliphs (called the *Rashidun* or "Rightly Guided Ones" by Sunni Muslims) there are numerous examples of dissatisfaction with the divergence of Muslim governments from the model of the Prophet at Medina. Engineer, for example, stated that, "The Umayyad and the Abbasid empires which came into existence after what is called *khilafat-e-rashidah* (i.e. the rightly guided period of khilafat, Islamic state) never followed [the model of] the Islamic state which came into existence after the death of the Prophet."[66] As has already been noted, many Islamists attribute the disavowal of the concept of *shūra* by Muslim governments after the Medinan period to the continued decline of the *umma* throughout history. Though despotism became the dominant characteristic of Muslim government beginning with the Umayyad dynasty, there are instances from this period that demonstrate the Muslim community rising up to seek the deposition of a ruler or governing official.

The rebellion of the army under the Caliph al-Muqtadar in 317/929 is one such example. In his book *Loyalty and Leadership in an Early Islamic Society*, Roy Mottahadeh provides a letter written by the Caliph to his troops who were rebelling against his rule and seeking his deposition. Mottahadeh notes that the first part of the letter was written by the Caliph to placate his troops and urge them to end their rebellion and accept his rule. In the next part of the letter, the Caliph wrote:

> Most of your benefits are from me, but it would not be my way to reproach you with any favor that I have conferred, and that I regarded at the time – and still regard – as small compared with your merits; rather, it suits me to fertilize and increase them...I long to bring you to the utmost limit of your aspirations...I claim from you that oath of allegiance [*bay'a*] which you have affirmed time after time. Whoever has sworn allegiance to me has sworn allegiance to God, so that whosoever violates that oath, violates the covenant with God ['*ahd Allah*]. I also claim gratitude for benefits and favors you enjoy, benefits and gifts from me that I hope you will acknowledge and consider binding.[67]

The Caliph's letter is instructive because it demonstrates his conceptualization of the nature of his power and authority. The letter not only identifies his source of authority as having been derived from the contractual allegiance (*bay'a*) of the people who entrusted him with his power; it also demonstrates that, should the ruler not fulfill his duties to those people (or if those people do not fulfill their obligation to demand accountability), they are then breaking their divine contract with God. Furthermore, the letter demonstrates the Caliph as providing the people with "benefits and favors" and "gifts" to fulfill his obligation to rule before them according to God's will. To break the social contract between ruler and ruled, in other words, is to "perjure oneself before God."[68]

Contemporary Islamists draw upon this narrative in framing their movement of renewal and reform as the only one capable of reviving the strength of the *umma*. Years living under despotic rulers, they argue, allowed Muslims to forget this narrative of their own history. "The most devastating ignorance is doubtless that of one's history," writes Nadia Yassine in introducing a part of her book, *Full Sails Ahead*, on the Constitution of Medina. "The lack of knowledge about oneself and one's history is even more caustic when it is maintained by a world order in which national and international tsarism combines to perpetuate the moral and physical massacre of the [Muslim] nations."[69] Other Islamists are more direct and radical in their reading of their own history. "Islamic history must be rewritten according to new principles and a new methodology," declared Sayyid Qutb.[70]

One aspect of the Islamist conceptualization of this new methodology is the disregard of much of history itself. The period after the Prophet at Medina and the *Rashidun* is cast as anomalous, bordering on the *jahiliyya* of pre-Islamic history. The Medinan example is cast as the only true rendering of pure Islam, and is the primary source of historical inspiration for Islamists. "The callers to Islam in every country and in every period should give thought to one particular aspect of the history of Islam," wrote Qutb in *Milestones*, "and they should ponder over it deeply." He continued:

> At one time this Message created a generation – the generation of the Companions of the Prophet, may God be pleased with them – without comparison in the history of Islam, even in the entire history of man. After this, no other generation of this caliber was ever again to be found. This is an obvious and open truth of history, and we ought to ponder over it deeply so that we may reach its secret.[71]

For Qutb, as with other Islamists, the secret to the success of this first generation of Muslims was that their political, moral, and social framework for organizing themselves was "pure in heart, pure in mind, pure in understanding" that all aspects of human experience "was to be based on the method prescribed by God Who gave the Qur'an, purified from the influence of all other sources." Implicit in this interpretation of history is the perceived failure of the West and its world view and all other things not explicitly found in the "one source of guidance...the Book of God." The Prophet and his first followers were successful because God and His Prophet taught them that, "This group should dedicate itself purely to the Book of God and arrange its lives solely according to its teachings." Qutb continues to frame the interpretation of all things not directly revealed by God as failures in contrast to the purity of the Qur'anic message:

> This generation, then, drank solely from this spring and thus attained a unique distinction in history. In later times it happened that other sources mingled with it. Other sources

used by later generations included Greek philosophy and logic, ancient Persian legends and their ideas, Jewish scriptures and traditions, Christian theology, and, in addition to these, fragments of other religions and civilizations. These mingled with the commentaries on the Qur'an and with scholastic theology, as they were mingled with jurisprudence and its principles. Later generations after this generation obtained their training from this mixed source, and hence the like of this generation never arose again.[72]

Islamists use this discriminatory reading of the history of Islam to legitimate their project as the most pristine and most closely aligned with the political practice of the Prophet Muhammad at Medina. This reading of history is used not only as an attempt to legitimate a political philosophy suitable to contemporary issues before a Muslim audience, but also to be framed as the most suitable countermodernity to the perceived failure of the Western model of modernity.

Part Five

Conclusion

> From all this, we should not conclude...that politics and religion have for us the same objective, but that when nations are formed the one serves as instrument to the other.
>
> Jean-Jacques Rousseau
> *The Social Contract*

Political Islam and the invention of tradition

In 1989, the political scientist Francis Fukuyama wrote an essay titled "The End of History?" in which he described "the end point of mankind's ideological evolution and the universalization of Western liberal democracy as the final form of human government." The West was triumphant, and modernity had manifested itself throughout the world because of "the total exhaustion of viable systematic alternatives to Western liberalism."[1] Three years later, Fukuyama wrote the book *The End of History and the Last Man*, which was based on his 1989 essay. In this book he wrote:

> While nearly a billion people are culturally Islamic – one-fifth of the world's population – they cannot challenge liberal democracy on its own territory on the level of ideas.[2]

Political Islam is precisely such a challenge to Western liberal democracy on the level of ideas. The numerous transitions in thought and reinventions of concepts and symbols that have been described throughout this book led to the emergence, in the second half of the twentieth century, of Political Islam as an ideological package challenging the *status quo*.

Political Islam emerged as a function of the long-refined themes in Islamic history of *tajdid* and *islah*, renewal and reform. Renewal and reform of the *umma* gained newfound significance in the modern era as Western soldiers and sailors carried the world-view of modernity throughout the Muslim world. This unprecedented physical penetration of Muslim lands spawned four modes of reform, each of which operated as a function of changing Muslim perceptions of the West and modernity.

The Tanzimat mode of renewal and reform sought to adapt already existing institutions to Western norms, and occurred during a time of favorable Muslim perceptions of the West and modernity. The modernist mode, emerging toward the end of the 19th century, sought to create a new conceptual framework for the discourse of *tajdid* and *islah*, and occurred during a period of increasing discernment toward the West and modernity. The Modernists argued that each of the most vaunted aspects of modernity – such as reason, rational thought, and scientific discovery – were fundamentally Islamic. Intellectuals in each of these modes explained the uneven and asymmetric development and modernization of Muslim society as a function of *taqlid*. The basic reformist project was, therefore, the modernization of Islam itself.

The events surrounding the First World War changed the discourse surrounding renewal and reform. The basic unit of analysis in Islamic thought, historically the *umma*, was reinvented to be the *dawla*. This Arabic word was reinvented in this time to connote the European concept of 'state' as it was imposed throughout Muslim lands. With this transition, two new reformist modes emerged: the secular-nationalist mode and the fundamentalist-style mode. The secular-nationalist mode of reform was dominant for most of the twentieth century, as epitomized by Nasirism in Egypt, Baathism in Syria and Iraq, the proliferation of leftist groups in Palestine, and Sukarno in Indonesia. A confluence of different global events changed this.

The establishment and continued success of the state of Israel, as well as the savagery of two world wars, continued recessions and depressions in the global capitalist economy, and the Arabs' newfound power from a virtual monopoly over world oil supplies led many intellectuals to begin casting the West and modernity as having failed. The concept of the failure of the West allowed for reformers in the fundamentalist-style mode to dismiss the basic conceptual framework of Western thought, which freed them to base their analysis not on the secular nation-state, but on the new concept of the 'Islamic state.'

With the emergence of the fundamentalist-style mode, the nature of reform transitioned from modernizing Islam to the Islamization of modernity, or the creation of an authentically Islamic countermodernity. The West was no longer viewed as an ally or guide, as it was for early reformers such as Khayr al-Din and al-Tahtawi. Rather, certain intellectuals within this mode, such as Hassan al-Banna, Mawdudi, and Qutb, argued that any and all answers to the issues facing the Muslim community could be found in Islam. Islam was cast as a total and comprehensive system containing a complete blueprint for matters facing the individual, society, and the state. The melding of religion and life, *dīn,* with the state, *dawla,* was a turning point in the history of Islam and the nature of Islamic thought. Contrary to popular understanding today, the conceptualization of Islam as both religion and state is a modern phenomenon.

Political Islam is a function of this conceptualization. It emerged in the 1970s and 1980s as a distinct ideological program that condemns the present situation of Muslims and the world-systems that created it. As Deina Abdelkader concluded in her study *Social Justice in Islam,* the rise of Islamic activism in opposition to existing institutions must be understood "as a cultural expression of grievances and of Muslim peoples' understanding of rulership and justice." Therefore, not only is the program of Political Islam a consequence of the concept of the failure of the West and modernity, but it is also "a function of the extent to which state performance in Muslim societies falls short of the principles of Islamic social justice."[3] The continued failure of Muslim states to deliver even the most basic components of sound governance to their citizens is, then, equally important to the program of Political Islam as the failure of the West.

Political Islam, however, cannot properly be understood as defensive in nature, or as seeking a return to some distant, reified past, embodied by an Islamic state run entirely according to the *shari'a,* because no such past has ever existed in the history of Islam. The eminent scholar of Islamic law and history Wael Hallaq states this simply: "There never was an Islamic state."[4] Along the lines of what Thomas Hobbes famously wrote, Political Islamists are using the past to create a future, or calling the past the future. As such, Islamists are unique and dynamic in their thinking, and their basic reformist vision rests upon a series of reinvented understandings of traditional Muslim concepts and symbols. The concept of *shūra*, for example, would be familiar to any Muslim from any period of history; it is, after all, a concept enshrined in the Qur'an. Yet, contemporary Islamists have taken this concept and extrapolated it to embody an overarching, grand philosophy of an Islamic system of politics in the democratic sense.

Similarly, the concept of *bay'a*, a pre-Islamic Arab tribal practice, has been reinvented to embody the concept of freedom of choice in electoral politics. *Ijmā'*, long understood to represent the consensus of Muslim legal jurists and scholars on religious rulings, has been reinvented to represent the primacy of public opinion in the governance of an Islamic state. Therefore, as Khurshid Ahmad describes the movement of which he is a prominent actor, "The contemporary Islamic upsurge deserves to be seen as a *positive* and *creative* response to the challenge of modernity."[5] Despite being fundamentalist *in style*, Islamists do not seek a return to the past, but rather the creation of a countermodernity as the basis of a new future for Muslim peoples.

From the perspective of world history, there is little unique about the "Islamic upsurge" that Ahmad describes. Indeed, Political Islam - and the fundamentalist-style mode of reform of which it is but one part – is a consequence of the changing ways in which humans interact with modernity in the contemporary world. One of the results of this is the resurgence of religions and religiously identified persons and movements throughout the world in shaping public life. It was long held by scholars that modernization and development would relegate religions to the sidelines of public life. Indeed, this was a central aspect of Fukuyama's declaration that mankind had reached the end of its ideological evolution.

The resurgence of religions throughout the world in shaping public life has turned the secularization paradigm upside down.[6] In the early 1990s, the scholar of religions José Cassanova wrote in his matchless study, *Public Religions in the Modern World*, that:

> Religions throughout the world are entering the public sphere and the arena of political contestation not only to defend their traditional turf, as they have done in the past, but also to participate in the very struggles to define and set the modern boundaries between the private and public spheres, between system and life-world, between legality and morality, between individual and society, between

family, civil society, and state, between nations, states, civilizations, and the world system.⁷

Casanova's depiction of a struggle between perceived 'traditions' and 'modernity' provides the best context for understanding the global religious resurgence, particularly in the Islamic context. The religious resurgence is an effort by peoples to use their faith as a guiding principle for meeting the challenges of the present. In the Islamic context, religious activism is a "popular vehicle for change" seeking to provide an indigenous and organic challenge to the perceived intellectual imperialism of the West.⁸ Rather than the long-held supposition that reason or rational thought would be the guiding elements of modernity, religion and religious interpretations have assumed a prominent role in political activism throughout the world.

In 1996 the leading sociologist of religion Peter Berger gave a keynote lecture at a conference on religion and public life. "The assumption that we live in a secularized world is false," he declared. "The world today ... is as furiously religious as it ever was, and in some places more so than ever." Professor Berger went on to conclude that the entire body of literature based on the assumption that secularization is a necessary part of modernization was "essentially mistaken."⁹

Within this conceptual framework, other scholars, such as Nader Hashemi, have demonstrated that democratic political development does not require (and never has required) the marginalization or privatization of religion. In fact, it goes against nearly every example in world history to require a state be secular *before* it can be democratic. This remains especially true for societies where religion is a marker of identity, Hashemi points out, because in such societies "the road to liberal democracy, whatever other twists and turns it makes, cannot avoid passing through the gates of religious politics."¹⁰

The global religious resurgence, even in Western democratic societies, has led to many different debates regarding the nature of modernity in the contemporary world. John Voll has argued that, beyond the debate over secularization and modernization, "the rise to prominence of movements of religious resurgence may reflect an even broader phenomenon of the nature of social movements of opposition and militancy and of advocacy of radical social change."¹¹

The changing nature of social movements in the modern era

reflects a transition in the area of contestation. Accordingly, scholars have developed what has been labeled "new social movement theory." For example, in 1981 Jürgen Habermas, a noted proponent of this theory, wrote: "New conflicts [in the world] no longer arise in areas of material reproduction. ... Rather, the new conflicts arise in areas of cultural production, social integration and socialization. ... In short, the new conflicts are not sparked by *problems of distribution*, but concern the *grammar of forms of life*."[12]

In new social movements, contestations over the grammar of forms of life no longer rely upon what Ronald Inglehart described as "materialist values." Rather, the religious resurgence is indicative of a broader shift to "postmaterialist" value priorities. The emergence of new value priorities, then, is an important factor in understanding the proliferation of movements that identify themselves by a religious heritage.[13] Therefore, the contemporary global religious resurgence is a function of the broader context of changing value priorities, and the emergence of contentious politics and new social movements based on postmaterialist values.

The discourse of new social movements has occurred alongside a debate over the changing character of modernity. Some scholars have argued that modernity, as it was usually understood in the Weber-Durkheim-Marx line of analysis, has ended and that humans now live in an age of postmodernity. The French intellectual Jean-Francois Lyotard was the first to articulate this. In 1979 he wrote *La condition postmoderne: rapport sur le savoir* (*The Postmodern Condition: A Report on Knowledge*), in which he argued that the metanarratives underlying the classic conceptualization of modernity were no longer applicable.[14]

Other scholars, such as Jürgen Habermas or Anthony Giddens, rejected the concept of postmodernism.[15] In his definitive collection of essays *The Consequences of Modernity*, Giddens argued: "Rather than entering a period of post-modernity, we are moving into one in which the consequences of modernity are becoming more radicalized and universalized than ever before." Despite the universalization of modernity, he argued, the different ways that various peoples interacted with modernity could be characterized by the themes of "security versus danger" and "trust versus risk."[16]

The uneven and asymmetric development and modernization of the *umma* in the modern era follows Giddens's pattern of "traditional cultures." In this pattern, risk and danger are the defining characteristics of the challenge of modernity to a particular group of peoples. "In traditional cultures," wrote Giddens, "the past is honored and symbols are valued because they contain and perpetuate the experience of generations." He continued:

> Tradition is a mode of integrating the reflexive monitoring of action with the time-space organization of the community. It is a means of handling time and space, which inserts any particular activity or experience within the continuity of the past, present, and future, these in turn being structured by recurrent social practices. Tradition is not wholly static, because *it has to be reinvented by each new generation* as it takes over its cultural inheritance from those preceding it. Tradition does not so much resist change as pertain to a context in which there are few separated temporal and spatial markers in terms of which change can have any meaningful form.[17]

As Giddens argued, movements that develop as a consequence of interactions with modernity generally follow four different modes: pragmatic acceptance, sustained optimism, cynical pessimism, and radical engagement.[18] These four modes can be applied to understanding the changing nature of the way Sunni Muslim reformers have interacted with modernity. Early reformers operating in the Tanzimat mode were pragmatic in their acceptance of modernity as a successful model to be emulated in whole; they sought to modernize and Westernize existing Ottoman institutions while looking to the West as a guide and ally - a harbinger of all the good things that modernity could bring. The optimism of this mode of reform was sustained into the movement of Islamic Modernism and the modernist mode of renewal and reform. Figures like al-Afghani and ʿAbduh were optimistic that modernity was symbiotic with Islam and traditional Muslim values, and they sought to create a new conceptual framework of reform that reflected this symbiosis.

In the first half of the twentieth century, the events surrounding the two world wars as well as the faltering of the modern capitalist world economy led many Muslim reformers to interpret the West and modernity with cynicism and pessimism. The epitome of Arab nationalism, Jamal ʿAbd al-Nasir of Egypt, cast himself as a cynic toward all things Western; he was the face of resistance to Western hegemony. The fundamentalist-style mode of reform and Political Islam represents both cynical pessimism toward modernity and radical engagement with it. Though Islamists do, in fact, borrow conceptual labels from the West, such as '*demokratiyya*,' they regard with cynical pessimism their Western origins. Instead, they argue that concepts such as the social contract, democracy, and electoral politics are fundamentally Islamic in origin and tradition.

The somewhat nebulous combination of cynical pessimism and radical engagement with the functions of modernity has added a new element to the debate over the nature of the modern world. For example, the late Israeli sociologist Shmuel Eisenstadt refuted postmodernism and argued that modernity remained, but had become displaced from the geo-temporal Weberian conceptualization and could be expressed through different cultural, social, and historical lenses. He argued that "classical" theories of modernization assumed that the cultural program of modernity, as it developed in Western Europe, would "ultimately take over in all modernizing and modern societies." Eisenstadt's concept of "multiple modernities" acknowledges that, since the conclusion of the Second World War, "Many of the [reform or modernizing] movements that developed in non-Western societies articulated strong anti-Western or even antimodern themes, yet all were distinctively modern."[19]

While Political Islam is distinctively modern and does seek the modernization and reformation of society, it is not modernist in that it does not espouse the ideology of modernity. Eisenstadt's theory of "multiple modernities" cannot, therefore, be used to properly understand the ideology, function, or emergence of Political Islam because it is a rejection of modernity itself. Other scholars operating in similar frameworks have written on the concept of "alternative modernities." Dilip Parameshwar Gaonkar begins his edited volume, *Alternative Modernities,* by stating: "To think in terms of 'alternative modernities' is to admit that modernity is inescapable and to desist from speculations about the end of modernity."[20]

Though Political Islam is certainly a *function* of modernity, just as fundamentalism is a function of modernity, it is not a *derivative* of it. It has developed not as a modernity among many modernities, something better represented by the reform projects of intellectuals associated with the secular-nationalist mode of reform, but as a derivative of the concept of the failure of modernity and a rejection of it. It is a positive and creative approach to creating a new toolbox of concepts and symbols that are perceived as being Islamic in character and tradition and the basis of an Islamic countermodernity.

Political Islam is one facet of the evolving crystallization of a civilizational narrative for Muslim peoples rooted in what are presented as indigenous discourses and dynamics.[21] It is reflective of the evolving ways in which Muslims, Christians, and Jews interact with the contemporary world in an era characterized by an increasing reliance upon religion in shaping public life. Religiously informed political thought has emerged throughout the world often as an enabling factor for change, not as merely a defensive mechanism resisting change and seeking a return to the past. As the anthropologist Richard Antoun points out:

> The use of familiar aspects of a culture provides a commonly understood terminology and has the advantage of appealing to formerly inculcated emotions and attitudes. Movement leaders or ideologues will generally either change the emphasis in the traditional ideologies or modify them to make them more appropriate to the new set of circumstances.[22]

The leaders of the major movements of Islamic reform in the modern Middle East have both changed the emphasis of traditional ideologies and modified them. In the modern era, Muslims have found themselves living in a world that is not situated as a consequence of their own history or traditions. As Wael Hallaq observed, "Just as the modern West drew and continues to draw on its last five centuries of experiences and traditions ... Muslims nowadays are challenging this traditional narrative and are increasingly developing their own history – as a discursive moral practice – in such a way as to provide a source of their own."[23] In developing this history, Islamic reformers have reinvented the understandings of traditional concepts such as *ḥisba, shūra, ijmāʿ*, and *bayʿa* to create the concept of an Islamic state, in strict accordance with the *shariʿa*, and governed by a social contract between rulers and ruled. In a radical interpretation of history, the leaders of the Islamist movement present this as the most pristine of Islamic traditions. Yet, as has been noted by Wael Hallaq, such a state has never existed in the history of Islam. In fact, the renowned anthropologist of Islam Talal Asad states: "It is clear that there has never been any Muslim society in which the religious law of Islam has governed more than a fragment of social life."[24]

In the final analysis, Political Islam and its project to establish an Islamic state is best understood as a distinct countermodernity drawing upon a package of invented traditions. The concept of 'invented traditions' was first articulated by the eminent historians

Eric Hobsbawm and Terence Ranger. In the introduction to *The Invention of Tradition* Hobsbawm wrote:

> 'Invented tradition' is taken to mean a set of practices, normally governed by overtly or tacitly accepted rules and of a ritual or symbolic nature, which seek to inculcate certain values and norms of behavior by repetition, which automatically implies continuity with the past. In fact, where possible, they normally attempt to establish continuity with a suitable historic past.[25]

Tradition refers not to a particular body of beliefs and practices or creed, but to the way those beliefs and practices are organized and acted upon in relation to particular temporal circumstances. As the Prophet's closest companions invented the tradition of the caliphate in the 7th century, contemporary Islamists have invented the tradition of Islamic rule in a democratic sense in an Islamic state founded upon a social contract. These invented traditions, rooted in a dynamic reading of the history of Islam, are used to create a new civilizational narrative for Muslims. This phenomenon is a reflection as much of some Muslims' opposition to a Western-dominated modernity as it is of the inherent weakness and general failure of domestic Muslim governments, nearly all of which have been secular and Western-oriented. The existence of the tradition of Political Islam, and its continued ability to garner massive followings throughout the Middle East, requires scholars, analysts, policy makers and students to understand the movement as its participants and leaders understand themselves, and to escape dogmatic, superficial modes of thinking.

In the beginning of the twenty-first century, Islamic activism is only one function of important changes in the way states and societies function. As the intellectuals John Micklethwait and Adrian Wooldridge argue in an important new book, *The Fourth Revolution: The Global Race to Reinvent the State*, the long-held position that a Western-style liberal democracy based in a nation-state embodies the best system of governance for humans is being challenged in dramatic ways throughout the world. There is ongoing, as they argue, a global race to reinvent the state.

For many, Western government no longer serves as an example to be emulated. As Micklethwait and Wooldridge note, "For all its frustrations with government, the emerging world is beginning to produce some striking new ideas, eroding the West's competitive advantage in the process." For example, as Micklethwait and Wooldridge point out, while the United States political system was gridlocked in a stalemate over Obamacare, China extended pension coverage in two years to more than 240 million rural people. Similarly, staunchly authoritarian Singapore offers its citizens significantly better overall access to health care and opportunities for education. Using health care as just one example of governance, the future of this industry lies, at least in part, in India's efforts to apply mass-production techniques in hospitals, and Brazil's innovative practice of conditional cash transfers likely offers a glimpse of the future of state-based entitlements. "At the very least," wrote Micklethwait and Wooldridge in an article for the *Wall Street Journal*, "the West no longer has a monopoly on ideas."[26]

Islamic activism is one important component of this global intellectual challenge to long-held suppositions regarding governance. Many of the world's nearly two billion Muslims are turning to religion to seek answers to basic inadequacies of secular, Western-style governance in their societies. The old styles of thinking about the present - of debates between secularism and religiosity, of modernity and postmodernity, of alternative modernities or global modernity - are no longer suitable for properly explaining the dramatic new realities of the present. Indeed, as the prominent German sociologist Ulrich Beck cogently observed, with this major historical transformation "An entire political and social lexicon has become obsolete in one stroke, and must now be rewritten."[27]

One of the basic principles of this new lexicon must be the understanding that religious mobilization is a precursor to democratization. A question that remains for Islamic activists, then, is not whether or to what extent Islam will shape public life, but whether Islam is better expressed as a function of society or as a normative function of the state. Regardless of which direction this debate goes, the role of religion is and will remain a decisive force shaping the world stage and its players.

Afterword

by Deina Abdelkader

Nicholas Roberts's important treatment of history and modern Islamic political thought presented here provides a necessary perspective and incredibly well informed analysis of the contemporary religiously-informed political movement of some Muslim activists to establish an "Islamic state." Given that this book was published in the midst of media hysteria, daft government rhetoric, and, most of all, the actions of the "Islamic State" (or ISIS), it is important to clarify that the "Islamic State" of Abu Bakr al-Baghdadi, save the name alone, is in no way similar to the grassroots, mainstream religious and political activism of the intellectuals discussed in Roberts's *Political Islam and the Invention of Tradition.* Roberts's work demonstrates the need to lower the volume of a minority of radicals and, instead, to listen more carefully to the issues that pertain to the majority of Muslims.

In many Western societies, it is common to hear of the plague of "oriental despotism," "the clash of Islam and the West," "bloody borders" and even that Muslims have done little to think of issues relating to representative, accountable government systems. As Roberts clearly demonstrates, however, there is a rich history of Muslim intellectuals who have sought to devise a system of representative and accountable governance that is indigenous in character and tradition. Many important Muslim intellectuals have wrestled with the ideas of governance and social justice throughout the modern era, and the more contemporary events of the "Arab Spring," rather than being random, are more properly viewed as a consequence of this intellectual history. The seriousness of the project of Political Islam, with its focus on social justice and legitimate government, is, however, never captured in the Western news cycles.

It is important to clarify that going back to the prophetic tradition is one of the sources of Islamic law. While groups such as al-Qaʿida or ISIS provide one fringe interpretation of this tradition, Robert's has put forth a nuanced narrative that represents with remarkable clarity the views of the majority. Islamic law (Shariʿa) plays a crucial role in affecting the decisions and opinions of justice in Muslim societies. Political Islam and the movement to establish an Islamic state based upon a social contract between rulers and ruled is born from the desire of Muslims to seek social justice in Islam.

All Muslims recognize shariʿa as the set of rules and mores decreed by the Qurʾan and the sunna. Even though some Muslims might argue for secularism and a separation between the modern Western concepts of "church" and "state," they would still recognize Shariʿa as an embodiment of Islamic codes and regulations. Islamic activists are neither the sole nor the principle proponents of the importance of Shariʿa. It is, therefore, necessary to briefly explore the importance of sharia and fiqh in Muslim public life.

Shariʿa, and more specifically Fiqh, are upheld by Muslim scholars as a "pure" form of Muslim thought. Al-Fasi, for example, maintains that even though Roman, Greek, Persian, and Indian civilizations have affected Muslim culture in significant ways, Muslim legal thought has retained its uniqueness. Therefore, according to al-Fasi, in order to restructure Muslim thought and utilize Shariʿa in Muslim courts of law, the study of Fiqh, its sources and goals, are indispensable necessities.[1]

With very few exceptions, Islamic activists have invoked Shariʿa as the body of legal principles to which Muslims should adhere. The late Sayyid Qutb, as elaborated by Mr. Roberts, is a widely read Islamic activist, who described the Shariʿa as an extensive body of knowledge that has a preset general framework that branches off into details and applications, thus safeguarding the human being regardless of place and time.[2]

Qutb writes of the importance of Fiqh as "the theoretical space allowing for change, however, within the constraints of a general framework of the Shariʿa." According to Qutb, the Shariʿa is a constant body of rules that do not change, since they dictate God's word, derived from the Qurʾan and sunna. Fiqh, however, is promulgated by the people, thus making it more flexible and inclusive of the changes and needs that take place in society.[3]

Qutb's *History: Thought and Discourse* stresses certain rights which are part and parcel of the *maqasid,* or the preservation of the goals of shariʿa. As he wrote:

> Every person is entitled to food, drink, clothes, transportation, housing, marriage, because those are necessities that preserve and provide the basics of life. Likewise, every person is entitled to medical care and treatment and education, to work and be trained.[4]

Within this conceptual framework of the necessity of shariʿa in guiding Muslim public life, many intellectuals have gone to great lengths to analyze the rise of violent extremism in their own societies. Al-Qaradawi, for example, has explained that Islamic extremism has been studied through different perspectives. As he writes:

> One has to recognize that one factor or the other does not cause extremism, i.e., it is not fair to reflect a partial explanation by stressing one factor or the other like many theorists have done. There are theorists who have focused on psychological factors that relate every human action to particular psychological elements; then there is the psychological explanation that takes the Durkheimian view that man is a puppet that is moved by society, i.e., it relates everything to society and its effect on the individual. Another explanation is historical materialism, which relates everything to economics: to them, economics creates history. Last but not least are the few who understand that extremism is not related to one cause or the other, i.e. that the phenomenon needs a balanced combination of all factors. Those factors could be religious, psychological, ideological, or all of the above.[5]

The reason for extremism, Qaradawi continues to write, could also be related to the corruption of the rulers, their tyranny, and their selfish desires and their neglect of the people's rights. Those rulers are the leaders who follow the corrupt at home and ally themselves with the perceived opponents of Islam abroad. Thus a gap between Qurʾan and rulership was created, religion and state therefore became two parallel phenomena that do not intersect at any point.[6]

Al-Hudaybi, who, like Qaradawi, comes from the Muslim Brotherhood, writes of issues stressed in the Qur'an that relate to governance and rulership:

> Shari'a is a flexible body of law, the Qur'an stresses the importance of educating men and women about the Islamic Shari'a, the Qur'an emphasizes the rights of all the poor, whereby they are provided with shelter, clothes and food, and the Qur'an stresses the necessity of respecting other religions: the freedom of its believers, the protection of their lives and their property.[7]

In al Hudaybi's writing we find that the first grievance relates to equality among the rulers and ruled; therefore, it is a grievance that relates to human rights. The second grievance relates to the failure to reinstate the Shari'a as the supreme law of the land. The third grievance is related to education, thus stressing the cultural issue. The fourth grievance relates to economic inequality, and the fifth point expresses al Hudaybi's concern with protecting believers of other faiths.

As Roberts demonstrates, *ḥisba* and *shūra* are key principles historically in the Islamic tradition. As with these two concepts, it is also important to note that Islamic law depends on two primary sources and two secondary sources. The primary are the Qur'an and sunna (the sayings and actions of the Prophet). The secondary sources are Ijmā' and Qiyas, respectively, the consensus of Muslim legal scholars and the exercise of reason. Jurisprudential thought (fiqh) was created in Islam mainly to deal with issues that are doubtful in the primary sources (sgl: Dhanni, pl: Dhanniyat), rather than what is clearly mentioned and talked about in the Texts and thus is clearly emphasized: absolute (Qat'yi /Qat'iyat (pl)).

As Roberts clarifies, Islam is not "antithetical" to democracy, simply because the issue of governance under Islamic law is left to human interpretation, i.e. as discussed earlier, it is part of what legalists refer to as: dhanni (doubtful, or in need of human interpretation). Thus governance is an issue that was left to the people to decide. The people decide as long as it does not conflict with the threshold that certain rights are not violated. The five goals of Islamic law (maqasid) are meant to protect human rights, dignity, and freedom of belief. This is a legal principle that was written about by the originators of the five legal schools: Maliki, Hanafi,

Shafi'i, Hanbali, and Ja'fari, and later expanded on by Al-Shatibi (d 1388).

The majority of Muslims do not hold views that are antithetical to democracy. The literature proves that Islamic scholars have been struggling with primarily three issues:

1) The lack of political space/freedom in their respective countries to discuss the ideal Islamic government, whether one talks about repressive regimes or indigenous "conservative liberals."[8]
2) The influence of the "Enlightenment complex," i.e. the "enlightenment" influence in academic circles and their belief that "modernity" or "democratization" are unilateral projects that have to pass through the rite of excising faith from public life.
3) The dramatization of 'vilayet-i-faqih', whereby any Islamic government/project is de-legitimized by simply referring to the Iranian experience and to the evils of theocratic rule, disregarding the clear calls by Islamic governments to have a civil government that represents the people.

Two contemporary cases that testify to this de-legitimization process are Tunisia's Nahda and Egypt's Muslim Brotherhood after they were successfully elected by the people in a process that was as close as they will get to free elections in the history of those two nations.

Academic research, such as this book, with regard to issues of social justice and governance in the Muslim world, is especially necessary at time when the religion is utilized to serve political purposes by al-Qaʾida, ISIS and other such organizations. It is important to define and clearly delineate the beliefs and actions of such violent extremist groups not only to inform Western audiences, but also to save Islam from ISIS's violation of its basic tenets.

Nicholas Roberts's writing runs counter to generalizations that are still strongly part of how many Westerners view the Other: the Muslim. The impressions left by a number of beheadings by ISIS terrorize many, and these barbaric actions lead many non-Muslims to question the legitimacy of the concept of falsely stereotyping Muslims as violent extremists who are antithetical to the general world order. It also leads to overgeneralizations that are used in academic and non-academic circles. The idea that there is a clash of civilizations was revived after 9/11 and with the actions of ISIS.

Roberts reminds us of the history and ideas that are most important to the majority of Muslims today.

Deina Abdelkader
University of Massachusetts Lowell

Glossary of Non-English Terms

ʿadl : justice, upright and just.
ahkam (pl. of hukm) : laws, values and ordinances.
amr (pl. awamir, umur) : command, matter, affair.
bayʿa : contract or oath of allegiance.
caliph : Westernized spelling of *khalifah*. In Islamic history, the caliphs were the successors of the Prophet as leaders of the Muslim community.
dawla: in its most modern usage, a word used to denote the European concept of "state."
dīn: an Arabic word that, in its most modern usage, is generally accepted to mean "religion."
faqih (pl. fuqahāʾ) : jurist, one who is learned in *fiqh*.
fiqh : the process of inferring Islamic law from the Qurʾan and the hadith. The *fuqahāʾ* are the legal scholars who perform such a task.
fard : obligatory, obligation.
fard ʿayn : personal obligation.
fard kafaʾi : collective obligation.
grand vizier : this title was commonly given to the highest administrative official in a premodern Islamic political system. The grand vizier of the Ottoman Empire was one of the most powerful figures in the state.
hadith (pl. ahadith) : the words spoken by the Prophet that were reported by his companions. The *hadith* is an integral part of Islamic law that is second in importance after the Qurʾan. These accounts were collected in medieval times and are used to supplement the text of the Qurʾan.
hijra : the Prophet's migration from Mecca to Medina, signifying the beginning of the Islamic calendar.
ḥisba : literally means computation or checking, but commonly used in reference to what is known as *al-amr biʾl-maʿrūf waʾl-nahy ʿan*

al-munkar, that is, 'promotion of good and prevention of evil.'

hukm (*pl. akham*) as in *hukm shar'i* : law, value, or ruling of shari'a.

ijmā' : the consent of legal scholars concerning a certain issue. It is considered to be one of the sources of Islamic law.

ijtihād : lit. 'exertion', and technically the effort a jurist makes in order to deduce the law, which is not self-evident, from its sources. A person who uses *ijtihād* is called a *mujtahid*.

islah : Arabic word for "repair" or "reform."

imam : There are three different meanings for this title: (1) the leader of a group of praying Muslims; (2) a general title for any Muslim leader with some religious authority; (3) in Shi'i Islam, the title of the rightful, divinely guided ruler. In the Shi'i tradition, there is a line of succession to the imamate from the Prophet Muhammad through his cousin and son-in-law, 'Ali.

istihsan : its origin is *hasin*. To deem something good, juristic preference; a legal principle invoked as a general guideline in Muslim legal thought.

istislah : consideration of public interest; a legal principle that applies public good or public welfare as a guideline for legislating Islamic law.

khalifah : see *caliph*.

khilafah : in theological terms, humanity is the follower and caretaker of the Earth, after God. Therefore, each individual is *khalifat Allah fi al-Ard* (God's vicegerent or deputy on Earth).

mamluk : literally meaning "owned," this term is applied to military slaves who were a ruling oligarchy in many parts of the Islamic world in premodern times.

maqasid (*pl. of maqsud*) as in *maqasid al- shari'a* : goals and objectives of Islamic law; that is, the spirit of the law and its guiding principles.

maslahah : considerations of public interest; public welfare or the common good, sought by practicing *istislah* according to Islamic law. In Islamic legal thought, the public good is qualified according to the Qur'an and the sunna.

maslahah mursalah : the *maslahah* that has nothing for or against it according to the Qur'an, sunna, and ijmā'.

mujaddid : Arabic word meaning "renewer." A widely accepted hadith reports that the Prophet Muhammad said that God would send a *mujaddid* (renewer) at the beginning of each century to strengthen the faith of the Muslims. Frequently, fundamentalist-style reformers were thought of as *mujaddids*. The process of this type of renewal is called *tajdid*.

nahy : prohibition.

qadi : judge.

Qur'an: the holy book of Islam. Record of the revelations Muslims believe were sent to mankind through the messenger of God, Muhammad. The Qur'an is thus the hart of the Islamic faith and the foundation for Islamic law and social order. Commonly written as Koran.

rashidun : the period of the first four caliphs of Islam. Sunni Muslims believe that the community of Muslims at this time can provide a model for Muslim life.

salaf : the pious ancestors who lived at the time of Muhammad and the Rashidun caliphs are the *salaf*. They are believed by Sunni Muslims to have had special insight into the requirements of the faith because of their close association with the Prophet Muhammad. As a result, fundamentalist-style reformers and others frequently call for a return to the attitude or the ways of the *salaf*. In the twentieth century, reformers in the tradition of Muhammad 'Abduh have been called the Salafiyyah because they called for a return to the principles followed by the *salaf*.

al- shari'a (pl. shara'i') : the canonical revealed Islamic law that is found in the Qur'an, the sunna, the consensus of legal scholars, and from their use of analogical reasoning.

shaykh : also written in English as *sheikh*, this term can apply to a tribal leader, a religious teacher, or a ruler.

Shi'ism : a major tradition within Islam. It has its origins in the faction (*shi'ah*) within the community who believed that 'Ali was the rightful successor to the Prophet Muhammad.

shūra : consultation.

sirah : the biography of the Prophet, i.e., the entirety of the Prophet Muhammad's acts and sayings.

sultan : a ruler in later medieval Islamic states. Although the sultans had legitimate authority, they were primarily military commanders and therefore are not the same as caliphs, who led the early Muslim community as direct successors to the Prophet Muhammad.

sunna : accepted custom or practice. The sunna of the Prophet Muhammad is defined by the *ahadith* and is an authoritative model for Islamic behavior.

Sunni : Sunni Islam is the tradition that accepts the legitimacy of the caliphs who actually succeeded the Prophet, in contrast to Shi'ism. The majority of the Muslims in the world are Sunni.

tajdid : See *mujaddid*.

Tanzimat : literally, this means "reorganization." The term is applied to the program of modernizing reforms within the Ottoman Empire in the middle years of the twentieth century.

taqlid : imitation, following the views and opinions of others. The opposite of *ijtihād*.

tawhid : literally, "union or unity." In Islamic thought this is the term applied to the oneness of God and implies the absolute and single sovereignty of God in the universe. In modern Islamic thought, *tawhid* is stressed as the basis for unity of religion and politics and religion and economics.

'*ulama*' (*s.* '*ālim*) : Religious scholars (see *fuqahā*').

uli al-amr : persons in authority and in charge of community affairs.

umma : Arabic for "community," and refers to the total community of believing Muslims throughout the world.

wahy : divine revelation.

wājib : obligatory, often synonymous with *fard*.

wājib 'ayni : personal obligation.

wājib kafa'i : collective obligation of the entire community.

Notes

Foreword

1. Peter L. Berger, "The Desecularization of the World: A Global Overview," in *The Desecularization of the World: Resurgent Religion and World Politics*, ed. Peter L. Berger. Washington: Ethics & Public Policy Center, 1999, 2.
2. Scott M. Thomas, "A Globalized God: Religion's Growing Influence in International Politics," *Foreign Affairs* (November/December 2010). www.foreignaffairs.com/articles/66804/scott-m-thomas/a-globalized-god. Accessed 1 October 2014.
3. F. Gregory Gause, III, "Why Middle East Studies Missed the Arab Spring," *Foreign Affairs* 90, No. 4 (July/August 2011): 81.
4. Gause, "Why Middle East Studies Missed the Arab Spring," 88-89.
5. Fouad Ajami, "The Arab Spring at One," *Foreign Affairs* 91, No. 2 (March/April 2012): 56.

Introduction

1. Bernard Lewis, "Communism and Islam," in *The Middle East in Transition*, ed. Walter Z. Laqueur, (New York: Frederick A. Praeger, 1958), 318–319.
2. Ahmad A. Galwash, *The Religion of Islam: A Standard Book*, 5th ed. (Cairo: Imprimerie Misr, 1958), 1:105. 8
3. Ahmad Shawqi al-Fanjari, *al-Hurriyat al-siyasiyyah fi al-Islam* (1973) as quoted in Hamid Enayat, *Modern Islamic Political Thought* (Austin, TX: University of Texas Press, 1982), 131.For a contextualization of this note and notes 1 and 2, as well as sources and the contested concepts of both "Islam" and "democracy," see John O. Voll, "Islam and Democracy: Is Modernization a Barrier?" in *Modernization, Democracy, and Islam*, eds. Shireen T. Hunter and Huma Malik (Westport, CT: Praeger Publishers, 2005), 82–97.

Part One

1. Stephen Hay, ed., *Sources of Indian Tradition: Modern India and Pakistan*, vol. 2, 2nd ed. (New York: Columbia University Press, 1988), 10.
2. William H. McNeill, *The Rise of the West: A History of the Human Community* (Chicago: University of Chicago Press, 1991), 565; Ibrahim M. Abu-Rabi', *Contemporary Arab Thought: Studies in Post-1967 Arab Intellectual History* (London: Pluto Press, 2004), xv; Paul Kennedy, *The Rise and Fall of the Great Powers* (New York: Vintage Books, 1989), 3.
3. Hay, *Sources*, 13.
4. Nazih Ayubi, *Over-stating the Arab State: Politics and Society in the Middle East* (London: I.B. Tauris, 2009), 86.
5. Kennedy, *Rise and Fall*, 3.
6. Ibid., 3-4, 9-13.
7. Marshall G.S. Hodgson, *Rethinking World History: Essays on Europe, Islam, and World History*, ed. Edmund Burke, III (Cambridge: Cambridge University Press, 1993), 97, 100-101.
8. Albert Hourani, *A History of the Arab Peoples*, new ed., (Cambridge, MA: Belknap Press, 2010), 259; David B. Ralston, *Importing the European Army: The Introduction of European Military Techniques and Institutions into the Extra-European World, 1600-1914* (Chicago: University of Chicago Press, 1996), 47; Bernard Lewis, *The Emergence of Modern Turkey*, 3rd ed. (New York: Oxford University Press, 2002), 37.

    For a general overview of Ottoman decline, see Lewis's *Emergence of Modern Turkey*, 21-128. Recent scholarship problematizes the traditional periodization of the Ottoman decline paradigm, arguing instead for a new paradigm, centered on the idea of "transformation" rather than decline, that emphasizes the flexibility and vitality of Ottoman society and economy in the seventeenth and eighteenth centuries. This scholarship aligns well with Hourani's conclusions, in that the most significant period of decline did not begin until the latter part of the eighteenth century. See, for example, Gabor Agoston, "Military Transformation in the Ottoman Empire and Russia, 1500-1800" in *Kritika: Explorations in Russian and Eurasion History* 12, no.2 (2011): 287.

    See also Cemal Kafadar, "The Question of Ottoman Decline," *Harvard Middle Eastern and Islamic Review* 4, 1-2 (1997-98): 30-75; Jane Hathaway, "Problems of Periodization in Ottoman History: The Fifteenth through the Eighteenth Centuries," *Turkish Studies Association Bulletin* 20, 2 (1996): 25-31; Linda Darling, "Another Look at Periodization in Ottoman History," *Turkish Studies Association Bulletin* 26, 2 (2002): 19-28.
9. Marshall Hodgson, *The Venture of Islam: Conscience and History in a World Civilization*, vol. 3 (Chicago: University of Chicago Press, 1977), 177-178.

10. The core premise of 'the Eastern Question' was a point of concern as much for the Ottomans as it was for the Russians or the Europeans, thus it can and should be considered from several different perspectives. For a recent treatment of this issue, see Lucien J. Frary and Mara Kozelsky, eds., *Russian-Ottoman Borderlands: The Eastern Question Reconsidered* (Madison: University of Wisconsin Press, 2014).

    For more on the 'Eastern Question' from a European perspective see J.A.R. Marriott, *The Eastern Question: An Historical Study of European Diplomacy* (Oxford: Clarendon Press, 1917).

    For a Russian perspective see Barbara Jelavich, *Russia's Balkan Entanglements, 1806-1914* (Cambridge: Cambridge University Press, 2004). 'The Eastern Question' was of course especially problematic for the Russians because the Russian Empire was so multi-ethnic, including large numbers of Muslim Russians who, to varying degrees, looked to the Ottoman Sultan for spiritual guidance. See Andreas Kappeler, *The Russian Empire: A Multi-Ethnic History* (New York: Routledge, 2001).

    For the Ottoman perspective see Candan Badem, *The Ottoman Crimean War* (Leiden: Brill Academic Publishers, 2012); M.S. Anderson, *The Eastern Question, 1774-1923: A study in international relations* (New York: St. Martin's Press, 1966).

    Alfred Rieber argues for placing the concept within a far broader world historical narrative in *The Struggle for the Eurasian Borderlands: From the Rise of Early Modern Empires to the End of the First World War* (Cambridge: Cambridge University Press, 2014).
11. *Encyclopedia Britannica,* 11th ed., s.v. "Eastern Question." As quoted in David M. Goldfrank, *The Origins of the Crimean War* (New York: Longman Publishing, 1994), 1, 40.
12. Goldfrank, *Origins,* 1-2, 10; McNeill, *Rise of the West,* 566.

    For Russian military reform under Nicholas I see John Shelton Curtiss, *The Russian Army under Nicholas I* (Durham, NC: Duke University Press, 1965). For a full analysis of Russia's long struggle to reform its military according to Western models see David R. Stone, *A Military History of Russia: From Ivan the Terrible to the War in Chechnya* (London: Praeger Security International, 2006); William C. Fuller, Jr., *Strategy and Power in Russia, 1600-1914* (New York: Free Press, 1992); Frederick W. Kagan and Robin Higham, eds., *The Military History of Tsarist Russia* (Basingstoke, UK: Macmillan Palgrave, 2002).

    Kagan and Higham's collection of essays should be read concurrently with David Goldfrank's review of them. See David M. Goldfrank, review of *The Military History of Tsarist Russia,* eds. F.W. Kagan and R. Hingham, *The Historical Journal* 47 (2004): 195-196.

    For a helpful introductory work on the relative question of 'sickness' in the Russian context see Dietrich Geyer, *The Russian Revolution: Historical Problems and Perspectives*, trans. Bruce Little (Oxford: Berg Publishers, 1983).

Contrary to many, John P. LeDonne argues that Russia had been part of the "Great Powers" as long as the "Great Powers" existed. See *The Grand Strategy of the Russian Empire, 1650-1831* (New York: Oxford University Press, 2003).

13. Hourani, *A History*, 259; Charles Tilly, "Reflections on the History of European State Making," in Charles Tilly, ed., *The Formation of National States in Western Europe* (Princeton: Princeton University Press, 1975), 42; John Obert Voll, *Islam: Continuity and Change in the Modern World*, 2nd ed. (Syracuse: Syracuse University Press, 1994), 31. This periodization, while conceptually helpful, is of course somewhat arbitrary and thus open for debate. Bernard Lewis, for example, writes that the failure of the Ottomans to take Vienna more than one hundred years earlier, in 1529, was a decisive event demonstrating Ottoman military backwardness. See Lewis, *Emergence*, 25.
14. Hourani, *A History*, 259.
15. Goldfrank, *Origins*, 10-11; Paul Bairoch, "International Industrialization Levels from 1750 to 1980," *Journal of European Economic History* 11 (1982): 270-287; Kennedy, *Rise and Fall*, 148-149.

    Bairoch's findings are not without refutation, though even the most articulate refutation deals with methodological starting points, not final conclusions. See Agnus Maddison, "A Comparison of Levels of GDP Per Capita in Developed and Developing Countries, 1700-1980," *Journal of Economic History* 43 (1983): 27-41.
16. Ibrahim M. Abu-Rabi', *Contemporary Arab Thought*, 10, 159.
17. Malek Bennabi, *Islam in History and Society*, trans. Asma Rashid (Kuala Lumpur, Berita Publishing, 1991), 52-55, 59.
18. Abdallah Laroui, *The Crisis of the Arab Intellectual: Traditionalism or Historicism?*, trans. Diarmid Cammell (Berkeley: University of California Press, 1976), 154.
19. Roxanne L. Euben and Muhammad Qasim Zaman, eds., *Princeton Readings in Islamist Thought: Texts and Contexts from al-Banna to Bin Laden*, eds. Roxanne L. Euben and Muhammad Qasim Zaman (Princeton: Princeton University Press, 2009), 107-108.
20. Abu'l-Hasan 'Ali Nadwi, "Muslim Decadence and Revival," in *Princeton Readings*, 122-125.
21. John O. Voll, "Renewal and Reform in Islamic History: *Tajdid* and *Islah*," in *Voices of Resurgent Islam*, ed. John L. Esposito (New York: Oxford University Press, 1983), 32. See also John Obert Voll, "The Revivalist Heritage," in *The Contemporary Islamic Revival: A Critical Survey and Bibliography*, Yvonne Yazbeck Haddad, John Obert Voll, and John L. Esposito (New York: Greenwood Press, 1991), 23-36.
22. Abu-Rabi', *Contemporary Arab Thought*, 11.

23. L. Carl Brown, *Religion and State: The Muslim Approach to Politics* (New York: Columbia University Press, 2000), 22, 56, 60, 82.
24. Albert Hourani, introduction to *The Modern Middle East*, Albert Hourani, Philip Khoury and Mary C. Wilson, eds., 2nd ed. (New York: I.B. Tauris, 2004), 3.
25. Ottoman reform in the modern era was first and foremost a military matter, and this began under Selim III. See Ralston, *Importing*, 49-51; Lewis, *Emergence*, 38-39, 55-64.
26. Hodgson, *Venture*, vol. 3, 205-206; John L. Esposito, *Islam and Politics*, 4th ed. (Syracuse: Syracuse University Press, 1998), 43.
27. Immanuel Wallerstein, *World Systems Analysis: An Introduction* (Durham: Duke University Press, 2004), 57-58.
28. Some scholars take issue with the label "Islamic resurgence" because it might imply that Islam, to some extent, had been sidelined from public life. However, the phenomenon of renewal and reform since 1798 has been labeled the modern or contemporary "Islamic resurgence" by Muslims who have most directly shaped it. See, for example, Khurshid Ahmad, "The Nature of Islamic Resurgence," in *Voices of Resurgent Islam*, 220.
29. Hodgson, *Venture*, vol. 3, 196; Abdullah al-Ahsan, *Ummah or Nation? Identity Crisis in Contemporary Muslim Society* (Leicester: The Islamic Foundation, 1992), 4.
    The exception to this statement is Turkey, which self-imposed the secular nation-state of socio-political organization.
30. Wilfred Cantwell Smith, *Islam in Modern History* (Princeton: Princeton University Press, 1957), 41.
31. For the best discussion of the themes in the revivalist literature see Yvonne Yazbeck Haddad, "The Revivalist Literature and the Literature on Revival: An Introduction," in *Contemporary Islamic Revival*, 3-22.
32. Mansoor Moaddel, *Islamic Modernism, Nationalism, and Fundamentalism: Episode and Discourse* (Chicago: University of Chicago Press, 2005), 24. Similarly, Islamic scholar Ibrahim M. Abu-Rabi' writes that the emergence of Political Islam is the consequence of "a distinctive intellectual formation that must be located within the larger context of Arab intellectual history that has been weltering with all sorts of discourses, both secular and religious." See Ibrahim M. Abu-Rabi', *The Intellectual Origins of Islamic Resurgence in the Modern Arab World* (Albany: State University of New York Press, 1996), 2.
33. Abu-Rabi', *Contemporary Arab Thought*, 128; John O. Voll, "Islamic Renewal and the 'Failure of the West,'" in *Decolonization: Perspectives from Now and Then*, ed. Prasenjit Duara (New York: Routledge, 2004), 200.
34. Voll, "Islamic Renewal," in *Decolonization*, 200.
35. Matar, *Europe Through Arab Eyes*, 9.
36. Hay, ed., *Sources of Indian Tradition*, 10.

37. Ibrahim Abu Lughod, "Retreat from the secular path? Islamic dilemmas of Arab politics," *The Review of Politics* 28 (1966), 475. Also cited in Voll, "Islamic Renewal," in *Decolonization*, 206. See also Hourani, *A History*, 263.
38. See Sayyid Jamal al-Din al-Afghani, "Lecture on Teaching and Answer to Renan," in *Modernist Islam: A Sourcebook, 1840-1940*, ed. Charles Kurzman (New York: Oxford University Press, 2002), 103-110.
39. Charles Kurzman, "The Modernist Islamic Movement," in *Modernist Islam*, 4.
40. Ibid; Voll, "Islamic Renewal," in *Decolonization*, 202.
41. Haddad, "Revivalist Literature and Literature on Revival," in *Contemporary Islamic Revival*, 7.
42. Voll, "Islamic Renewal," in *Decolonization*, 203.
43. Daniel Yergin, "The Oil Weapon," in *The Prize: The Epic Quest for Oil, Money and Power* (New York: Free Press, 2009), 570; Daniel Pipes, "'This World is Political!' The Islamic revival of the seventies," *Orbis* 24 (1) (spring), 22; Voll, "Islamic Renewal," in *Decolonization*, 203, 205.
44. John O. Voll, "Political Islam and the State," in *The Oxford Handbook of Islam and Politics*, ed. John L. Esposito and Emad el-Din Shahin (New York: Oxford University Press, 2013), 59.
45. Nazih Ayubi, *Political Islam: Religion and Politics in the Arab World* (London: Routledge, 1991), 51.
46. Eric Hobsbawm and Terence Ranger, eds., reissue ed., *The Invention of Tradition* (Cambridge: Cambridge University Press, 2012), 2.
47. Ayubi, *Political Islam*, 51.
48. Gilles Kepel, "Islamism Reconsidered: A Running Dialogue with Modernity," *Harvard International Review* 22, no. 2 (Summer 2000), 22, 24; Olivier Roy, *The Failure of Political Islam*, trans. Carol Volk (Cambridge: Harvard University Press, 1994), ix.
49. Aziz al-Azmeh, *Islams and Modernities*, 3rd ed. (London: Verso, 2009), 67-68.
50. Rachel M. Scott, *The Challenge of Political Islam: Non-Muslims and the Egyptian State* (Stanford: Stanford University Press, 2010), 96. For Kamal Habib's original statement in Arabic see Kamal al-Sa'id Habib, *al-Harakat al-Islamiyya min al-Muwajaha ila al-Muraja'a* (Cairo: Maktabat Madbuli, 2002), 141. Yvonne Haddad describes the first use of the word *ta'adudiyya* as having occurred in the mid-1980s in "Islamists and the Challenge of Pluralism," Occasional papers (Washington, DC: Center for Contemporary Arab Studies, Georgetown University, 1995), 3.
51. Albert Hourani, *Arabic Thought in the Liberal Age, 1798-1939*, revised edn. (Cambridge: Cambridge University Press, 1983), 144, 344.
52. Hodgson, *Venture*, vol. 1, 45-69; John O. Voll, paper presented at the World History Association Meeting, 26 June 2009, 1.
53. Al-Azmeh, *Islams and Modernities*, 1.

54. Bruce Lawrence, "Reinterpreting the Rise of the West," in *Defenders of God: The Fundamentalist Revolt Against the Modern Age* (Columbia, SC: University of South Carolina Press, 1989), 43-58; Hodgson, *Venture*, vol. 3, 202-203.
55. Fouad Ajami, *The Arab Predicament: Arab Political Thought and Practice Since 1967* (New York: Cambridge University Press, 1992), 204.
56. Matar, *Europe Through Arab Eyes*, 29.
57. Lewis, *Emergence*, 1.
58. Max Weber, *The Protestant Ethic and the Spirit of Capitalism*, ed. and trans. Stephen Kalberg, rev. ed. (New York: Oxford University Press, 2011); Max Weber, "The Development of the Capitalist Frame of Mind," in *Protestant Ethic*, 255; Max Weber, "The 'Rationalism' of Western Civilization," in *Max Weber: Readings and Commentary on Modernity*, ed. and trans. Stephen Kalberg (Oxford: Blackwell Publishing, 2005), 53-68.
59. Immanuel Kant, "An Answer to the Question: 'What is Enlightenment?'" in *Kant: Political Writings*, ed. Hans Reiss, trans. H.B. Nisbet, 2nd ed. (Cambridge: Cambridge University Press, 1991), 54-60.
60. Michel Foucault, "What is Enlightenment?" in *The Foucault Reader*, ed. Paul Rabinow (New York: Vintage Books, 2010), 39.
61. Ibid., 39, 42.
62. Edmund Burke III, introduction to *Rethinking World History: Essays on Europe, Islam, and World History*, Marshall G.S. Hodgson (New York: Cambridge University Press, 1993), xx.
63. Hodgson, *Venture*, vol. 3, 176-177. The description of the GWT as a "momentous, glacial-like shift" is from Lawrence, *Defenders*, 47.
64. Hodgson, *Venture*, vol. 3, 178-179; Richard T. Antoun, *Understanding Fundamentalisms: Christian, Islamic, and Jewish Movements* (Lanham, MD: Rowman & Littlefield Publishers, 2008), 11.
65. Hodgson, *Venture*, vol. 3, 180; Lawrence, *Defenders*, 47-48.
66. Hodgson, *Venture*, vol. 1, 52-53.
67. Ibid., vol. 3, 190.
68. The classic articulation of the notion of impermeable, distinct world civilizations is Samuel Huntington, *The Clash of Civilizations and the Remaking of World Order* (New York: Simon & Schuster, 1996). Huntington's claims have been fiercely critiqued and largely discredited. See, for example, Edward Said, "The Clash of Ignorance," *The Nation*, October 4, 2001 and Roy P. Mottahedeh, "The Clash of civilizations: an Islamicist's Critique," *Harvard Near Eastern and Islamic Review*, 2:2 (Fall 1995), 1-26.

    There are several fine works that challenge the Western-centric view of world history. See John M. Hobson, *The Eastern Origins of Western Civilization* (Cambridge: Cambridge University Press, 2004); C.A. Bayly, *The Birth of The Modern World, 1780-1914* (Oxford: Blackwell Publishing, 2004); Robert B. Marks, *The Origins of the Modern World*, 2nd ed. (Lanham, MD: Rowman and Littlefield Publishers, 2007).

69. Hodgson, *Venture,* vol. 3, 197-198. Hodgson defines the label *Afro-Eurasian Oikoumene* in vol. 1, 109-110.
70. Hodgson, *Venture,* vol. 3, 200, 202.
71. Lawrence, *Defenders,* 27.
72. Malise Ruthven, *Fundamentalism: The Search for Meaning* (Oxford: Oxford University Press, 2009), v, 5.
73. For more on the original concept of fundamentalism in its Protestant setting see Barry Hankins, ed., *Evangelicalism and Fundamentalism: A Documentary Reader* (New York: New York University Press, 2003). See also George Marsden, *Understanding Fundamentalism and Evangelicalism* (Grand Rapids, MI: Wm. B. Eerdmans Publishing, 1991).

    For the most complete study of fundamentalism in general, see Martin E. Marty and R. Scott Appleby, eds. *The Fundamentalism Project.* 5 vols. Chicago: University of Chicago Press, 1987-1995.

    For works that extend the concept of fundamentalism beyond its original Protestant setting to explain modern world religio-political events see Gabriel A. Almond, Scott Appleby, and Emmanuel Sivan, *Strong Religion: The Rise of Fundamentalisms Around the World* (Chicago: University of Chicago Press, 2003); Richard T. Antoun, *Understanding Fundamentalism: Christian, Islamic, and Jewish Movements,* 2nd ed. (Lanham, MD: Rowman and Littlefield Publishers, 2008); Gilles Kepel, *The Revenge of God: The Resurgence of Islam, Christianity and Judaism in the Modern World,* trans. Alan Braley (University Park: Pennsylvania State University Press, 1994); Karen Armstrong, *The Battle for God: A History of Fundamentalism* (New York: Random House Publishing, 2011).

    To be certain, 'fundamentalism' should not be mistaken for religious violence. See Bruce Hoffman, "'Holy Terror': The Implications of Terrorism Motivated by a Religious Imperative," (Santa Monica, CA: RAND Corporation, 1993); David C. Rapoport, "Fear and Trembling: Terrorism in Three Religious Traditions," *The American Political Science Review* 78 (1984), 658-677; Mark Juergensmeyer, *Terror in the Mind of God: The Global Rise of Religious Violence,* 3rd ed. (Berkeley: University of California Press, 2003) and *The New Cold War? Religious Nationalism Confronts the Secular State* (Berkeley: University of California Press, 1993); Charles Kimball, *When Religion Becomes Evil* (New York: Harper Collins, 2008) and *When Religion Becomes Lethal* (San Francisco: Jossey-Bass, 2011).
74. Lawrence, *Defenders,* 96.
75. Ibid., 2.
76. Voll, "Islamic Renewal," in *Decolonization,* 212.
77. Ibrahim M. Abu-Rabi', ed., *The Contemporary Arab Reader on Political Islam* (New York: Pluto Press, 2010), vii, and xxiii, note four.

Part Two

1. Geoffrey Parker, *The Military Revolution: Military innovation and the rise of the West, 1500-1800,* 2nd ed. (New York: Cambridge University Press, 1996), 83. See also Jeremy Black, *Naval Power: A History of Warfare and the Sea from 1500* (New York: Palgrave Macmillan, 2009).

    Parker's thesis that radical changes in military strategy and tactics led to major changes in European government structure and political philosophy, ultimately allowing for the emergence of European global hegemony, expands upon and is originally indebted to Michael Roberts, "The Military Revolution, 1560-1660" in *Essays in Swedish History* (London: Weidenfeld and Nicolson, 1967), 195-225.

    Some historians take issue with placing the revolution within Roberts's dates. See Jeremy Black, *A Military Revolution? Military Change and European Society, 1550-1800* (London: Humanities Press, 1991); Brian M. Downing, *The Military Revolution and Political Change: Origins of Democracy and Autocracy in Early Modern Europe* (Princeton: Princeton University Press, 1992).

    For the best treatment of the general debate regarding Parker's and Roberts's argument, see Clifford Rogers, ed., *The Military Revolution Debate: Readings on the Military Transformation of Early Modern Europe* (Boulder, CO: Westview Press, 1995). See also William R. Thompson, "The Military Superiority Thesis and the Ascendancy of Western Eurasia in the World System" in *Journal of World History* 10, no. 1 (Spring, 1999): 143-178.

    Finally, some scholars take issue with the lack of consideration for the Ottoman Empire in the "military revolution" concept as a whole. W.H. McNeill argues that the Ottomans were an important actor in the age of "gunpowder empires" in *The Age of Gunpowder Empires, 1450-1800* (Washington: American Historical Association, 1989). Gabor Agoston argues that the Ottomans did share in the military revolution until around the mid to late eighteenth century in "Military Transformation in the Ottoman Empire and Russia, 1500-1800" in *Kritika: Explorations in Russian and Eurasian History* 12, no.2 (2011): 281-319 and *Guns for the Sultan: Military Power and the Weapons Industry in the Ottoman Empire* (New York: Cambridge University Press, 2008).
2. *Napoleon in Egypt: al-Jabarti's Chronicle of the French Occupation, 1798,* ed. Robert L. Tignor, trans. Shmuel Moreh, expanded ed. (Princeton: Markus Wiener Publishers, 2006), 22-23.
3. *Al-Jabarti's Chronicle,* 24-27.
4. Afaf Lutfi al-Sayyid Marsot, *Egypt in the reign of Muhammad Ali* (New York: Cambridge University Press, 1988), 20; P.J. Vatikiotis, *The History of Egypt,* 2nd ed. (Baltimore: Johns Hopkins University Press), 38-41.

5. F. Robert Hunter, *Egypt Under the Khedives, 1805-1879* (Cairo: The American University in Cairo Press, 1999), 13; Hodgson, *Venture of Islam*, vol. 3, 217; Vatikiotis, *History*, 49-50.

   For more on the Tanzimat see Bernard Lewis, *The Emergence of Modern Turkey*, 3rd ed. (New York: Oxford University Press, 2002); Stanford J. Shaw and Ezel Kural Shaw, *History of the Ottoman Empire and Modern Turkey*, vol. 2 (Cambridge: Cambridge University Press, 1977); Carter Vaughn Findley, *Bureaucratic Reform in the Ottoman Empire: The Sublime Porte, 1789-1922* (Princeton: Princeton University Press, 1980) and "The Tanzimat" in *Turkey, Islam, Nationalism, and Modernity* (New Haven: Yale University Press, 2010), 76-132; Roderic H. Davison, *Reform in the Ottoman Empire, 1856-1876* (Princeton: Princeton University Press, 1963). Though Davison's work focuses primarily on the third quarter of the nineteenth century it includes a fine analysis of pre-1856 reform as well. For an analysis of the intellectual origins of the Tanzimat see Uriel Heyd, "The Ottoman 'ulama and westernization in the time of Selim III and Mahmud II" in *Studies in Islamic History and Civilization*, ed. Uriel Heyd (Jerusalem: Magnes Press, 1961), 63-96.
6. Roger Owen, *The Middle East in the World Economy, 1800-1914* (New York: I.B. Tauris, 2002), 57-58. See also Ayubi, *Over-stating*, 87.
7. Vatikiotis, *History*, 46; Daniel L. Newman, "The 'Egyptian' Mission to Europe," in *An Imam in Paris: Account of a Stay in France by an Egyptian Cleric (1826-1831)* [*Takhlis al-Ibriz fi Talkhis Bariz aw al-Diwan al-Nafis bi-iwan Baris*], Rifaa Rafi al-Tahtawi, ed. and trans. by Daniel L. Newman (London: Saqi Books, 2004), 16.
8. Newman, *Imam in Paris*, 27. Hunter, *Egypt*, 17. To be clear, Selim III had begun sending Ottoman citizens abroad to Europe to establish Ottoman embassies in the major European capitals well before Muhammad 'Ali's program. The goal of this, as part of a broader package of reforms, was to bring Turkey in line with common European practice. See Lewis, *Muslim Discovery of Europe*, 132.
9. Vatikiotis, *History*, 58.
10. Rifa'ah Badawi Rafi' al-Tahtawi, *Takhlis al-ibriz fi talkhis Bariz* (Cairo: Dar al-Kutub, 2005), 158-162; Al-Tahtawi, *An Imam in Paris*, 288-302.
11. Albert Hourani, *Arabic Thought in the Liberal Age, 1789-1939* (Cambridge: Cambridge University Press, 1983), 69-70.
12. See Muhammad 'Imarah, ed., *al-A'mal al-kamilah li-Rifa'ah Rafi' al-Tahtawi* (Cairo: Dar al-Shuruq, 2010), 351-516. See also Rifa'ah Rafi' al-Tahtawi, *al-Murshid al-amin lil-banat wa-al-banin*, ed. 'Imad Badr al-Din Abu Ghazi (Cairo: Majlis al-A'la lil-Thaqafah, 2002); Rifa'a Rafi' al-Tahtawi, "The Extraction of Gold, or an Overview of Paris and The Honest Guide for Girls and Boys," in *Modernist Islam*, 31-39; Rifa'a Badawi Rafi' al-Tahtawi, "Fatherland and Patriotism," in *Islam in Transition: Muslim Perspectives*, eds. John J. Donohue and John L. Esposito, 2nd ed. (New York: Oxford University Press, 2007), 9-12.

13. Lewis, *Islam and the West* (New York: Oxford University Press, 1993), 136, 167 – 168.
14. Hourani, *Arabic Thought*, 79; C. Ernest Dawn, "From Ottomanism to Arabism: The Origin of an Ideology," in *Modern Middle East*, 376.
15. Al-Tahtawi, *Manahij*, as cited in Hourani, *Arabic Thought*, 79.
16. Al-Tahtawi, "Overview of Paris and Honest Guide," in *Modernist Islam*, 33-34; Lewis, *Islam and the West*, 171 – 172; Hourani, *Arabic Thought*, 79.
17. Al-Tahtawi, "Overview of Paris and Honest Guide," in *Modernist Islam*, 34.
18. Ibid., 37.
19. Hunter, *Egypt*, 29, 31.
20. Vatikiotis, *History*, 117; Hourani, *Arabic Thought*, 76; Jamal Mohammed Ahmed, *The Intellectual Origins of Egyptian Nationalism* (London: Oxford University Press, 1960), 12.
21. Khayr al-Din, "The Surest Path," in *Modernist Islam*, 40-42.
    For the original Arabic see Khayr al-Din al-Tunisi, *Aqwam al-masalik fi ma'rifat ahwal al-Mamali*, vol. 1, ed. Monsef al-Shannufi (Tunis: Bayt al-Hikmah, 2000), 98-100. For an English translation see Khayr al-Din, *The Surest Path*, trans. Leon Carl Brown (Cambridge: Harvard Center for Middle Eastern Studies, 1967). See also Hourani, *Arabic Thought*, 88.
22. Hourani, *Arabic Thought*, 88-89.
23. Al-Din, "Surest Path," in *Modernist Islam*, 44.
24. Al-Din, *Aqwam*, 142, 146; Hourani, *Arabic Thought*, 89, 92; al-Din, "Surest Path," in *Modernist Islam*, 45.
25. Hourani, *Arabic Thought*, 81, 95.
26. Hodgson, *Venture*, vol. 3, 240.
27. Jamal al-Din al-Afghani, "Lecture on Teaching and Learning," in *An Islamic Response to Imperialism: Political and Religious Writings of Sayyid Jamal ad-Din "al-Afghani,"* trans. Nikkie R. Keddie (Berkeley: University of California Press, 1968), 102; Nikkie R. Keddie, *Sayyid Jamal ad-Din "al-Afghani"* (Berkeley: University of California Press, 1972), 130.
28. Voll, "Alternative Modernities," 2. For the debate between al-Afghani and Khan, see Jamal al-Din al-Afghani, "The Materialists in India," in Keddie, *Islamic Response*, 177; Voll, *Islam*, 112-114.
29. Nikkie Keddie notes, for example, that the Turkish reformer Namik Kemal had been appealing for Pan-Islamic unity over a decade before Afghani first began to. See Keddie, *Sayyid Jamal*, 129-130. Similarly, L. Carl Brown notes, referring to al-Afghani, that, "Pan-Islam was not, however, the creation of one man." See Brown, *Religion and State*, 107.
30. Hourani, *Arabic Thought*, 114-115. Hourani is quoting Guizot's original French.
31. Jamal al-Din al-Afghani, "Refutation of the Materialists," in *Islamic Response*, 141.
32. Ibid., 173.

33. Sayyid Jamal al-Din al-Afghani, "An Islamic Response to Imperialism," in *Islam in Transition,* 13-15.
34. Ibid.
35. Keddie, *Islamic Response,* 3.
36. Jamal al-Din al-Afghani, "Answer of Jamal ad-Din to Renan: *Journal des Debats,* May 18, 1883", in *Islamic Response,* 187. See also Moaddel, *Islamic Modernism, Nationalism, and Fundamentalism,* 86-87.
37. Stanford J. Shaw and Ezel Kural Shaw, *History of the Ottoman Empire and Modern Turkey,* vol. 2 (Cambridge: Cambridge University Press, 1977), 212; Voll, *Islam,* 90-91. See also Hodgson, "Despotism in Modern Style: 'Abdulhamid and pan-Islamism," in *Venture of Islam,* vol. 3, 253-256. See also Carter Vaughn Findley, "The Reign of Abdulhamid," in *Turkey, Islam, Nationalism, and Modernity,* 133-191.
38. L.M. Kenny, "Al-Afghani on Types of Despotic Government," *Journal of the American Oriental Society* 86, no.1 (1966), 20-21.
39. L.M. Kenny, "Al-Afghani," 22-23, 27.
40. Keddie, *Islamic Response,* 65.

    Some scholars critique al-Afghani for perceived categorization, reification and contradiction, yet none of this takes away from the extent to which his thought – although perhaps contradictory at times – influenced Muslims of his time and subsequent reformist movements. See Nikki R. Keddie, "Sayyid Jamal ad-Din's Ideas: A Summary of Afghani's Aims and Methods" in *Islamic Response,* 36-97; Moadell, *Islamic Modernism, Nationalism, and Fundamentalism,* 89.
41. Keddie, *Sayyid Jamal,* 220. See also Hourani, *Arabic Thought,* 109-110.
42. Jamal al-Din al-Afghani and Muhammad ʿAbduh, *al-Urwa al-Wuthqa* (Beirut: Dar al-Kitab al-'Arabi, 1980), 79-88. See also Keddie, *Sayyid Jamal,* 223.
43. Al-Afghani and ʿAbduh, *al-Urwa al-Wuthqa,* 99-106, 140-146; Hourani, *Arabic Thought,* 158.
44. Hourani, *Arabic Thought,* 136-137, 139.
45. Abdou Filali-Ansari, introduction to *Islam and the Foundations of Political Power,* by Ali Abdel Raziq, trans. Maryam Loutfi, ed. Abdou Filali-Ansari (Edinburgh: Edinburgh University Press, 2012), 4; el Omari, Racha. "Muʿtazilah." In *The Oxford Encyclopedia of the Islamic World. Oxford Islamic Studies Online,* http://www.oxfordislamicstudies.com/article/opr/t236/e1073 (accessed 26-Mar-2013).
46. Hourani, *Arabic Thought,* 142, 144.
47. Translation from C. Ernest Dawn, "From Ottomanism to Arabism: The Origin of an Ideology," in *Modern Middle East,* 382. Dawn is quoting from Muhammad Rashid Rida, *Taʾrikh al-Ustadh al-Imam al-Shaykh Muhammad ʿAbduh,* 2nd ed. (Cairo: al-Manar, 1926), vol. 2, 506.
48. Hourani, *Arabic Thought,* 140-141. Hourani is quoting Muhammad Rashid Rida, *Taʾrikh al-Ustadh al-Imam al-Shaykh Muhammad ʿAbduh,* vol. 1, pt. 1 (Cairo: Dar al-Fadilah, 2003), 11.

49. Muhammad ʿAbduh, *The Theology of Unity*, trans. Ishaq Musaʿad and Kenneth Cragg (Kuala Lampur: Islamic Book Trust, 2004), 38-39.
50. Ibid., 126-127.
51. Ibid., 30-31.
52. Ibid., 127.
53. Voll, *Islam*, 84-85, 109.
54. Ibid., 158, 162.

   Islamic Modernism and the modernist mode of renewal and reform continued well into the twentieth century. Some of the most important works from this movement after ʿAbduh's death are Qasim Amin, *The Liberation of Women and The New Woman*, trans. Samiha Sidhom Peterson (Cairo: American University of Cairo Press, 2000); Mohammad Iqbal, *The Reconstruction of Religious Thought* (Dubai: Kitab al-Islamiyyah, n.d.); Fazlur Rahman, *Islam & Modernity: Transformation of an Intellectual Tradition* (Chicago: University of Chicago Press, 1982); Amina Wadud, *Qur'an and Woman: Rereading the Sacred Text from a Woman's Perspective* (New York: Oxford University Press, 1999).

   Many other important Modernists from throughout the Muslim world are less accessible in English. Charles Kurzman's anthology remains irreplaceable in this regard. See his *Modernist Islam: 1840-1940* (New York: Oxford University Press, 2002). In this anthology note the works by Mahmud Tarzi of Afghanistan; Namik Kemal and Ziya Golkap of Turkey; 'Abd al-Rahman al-Kawakibi of Syria; Ismail Bey Gasprinskii of the Crimea; Sayyid Ahmad Khan of North India; Ameer 'Ali of Bengal; Achmad Dachlan of Java; and Sheykh Ahmad Surkati of Sudan-Java.

55. Voll, *Islam*, 152. For more on the contemporary Muslim debate regarding nation-states and Islam see Abdullah al-Ahsan, *Ummah or Nation? Identity Crisis in Contemporary Muslim Society* (Leicester: The Islamic Foundation, 1992); Tamam al-Barghouti, *The Umma and the Dawla: The Nation State and the Arab Middle East* (Ann Arbor, MI: Pluto Press, 2008); James P. Piscatori, *Islam in a World of Nation-States* (Cambridge: Cambridge University Press, 1986). E.I.J. Rosenthal has distinguished three general attitudes toward the problem of state and society in modern Islamic thought: an 'Islamic state'; a 'Muslim state'; and a 'secular state' in *Islam in the Modern National State* (Cambridge: Cambridge University Press, 1965).
56. For the work that provides the standard European definition of 'state' (and 'nation-state') and government see S.E. Finer, *The History of Government*, 3 vols. (Oxford: Oxford University Press, 1992). See in particular volume three: *Empires, Monarchies and the Modern State* (1997).

   Some might argue that certain countries - namely Egypt, Yemen, and Morocco - have historical precedence for being considered a state. This argument can only account for a partial exception of a 'state' at best and certainly not a 'nation-state.' For this as well as a discussion of the difference concepts associated with 'state' in European political thought in the context of Arab history and Islamic thought see Ayubi, *Over-stating the Arab State*, in particular "The Middle East and the State Debate: a Conceptual Framework," 1-37.

57. Arskal Salim, *Challenging the Secular State: The Islamization of Law in Modern Indonesia* (Honolulu: University of Hawai'i Press, 2008), 16.
58. Ayubi, *Over-stating*, 3,7,15,21-22. See also Akhavi, Shahrough. "Dawla." In *The Oxford Encyclopedia of the Islamic World. Oxford Islamic Studies Online*, http://www.oxfordislamicstudies.com/article/opr/t236/e0183 (accessed 03-Feb-2014).

    The classic work explaining the natural rise and fall of governments from a Muslim viewpoint is 'Abd al-Rahman Ibn Khaldun, *The Muqaddimah*, trans. Franz Rosenthal, 3 vols (New York: Pantheon Books, 1958).

    For the formation of concepts of state and government in Islam in pre-modern history see Robert Irwin, ed., *The New Cambridge History of Islam*, vol. 4 (Cambridge: Cambridge University Press, 2010); Ann K.S. Lambton, *State and Government in Medieval Islam* (Oxford: Oxford University Press, 1981); Erwin I.J. Rosenthal *Political Thought in Medieval Islam: an Introductory Outline* (Cambridge: Cambridge University Press, 1958); W. Montgomery Watt, *Islamic Political Thought: the Basic Concepts*, Islamic Surveys no. 6 (Edinburgh: Edinburgh University Press, 1968).

    See also the following by Patricia Crone, *God's Caliph: Religious Authority in the First Centuries of Islam* (Cambridge: Cambridge University Press, 2003); *God's Rule: Government and Islam, Six Centuries of Medieval Islamic Political Thought* (New York: Columbia University Press, 2005); *Medieval Islamic Political Thought* (Edinburgh: Edinburgh University Press, 2004). See also Bernard Lewis, *The Political Language of Islam* (Chicago: University of Chicago Press, 1988).
59. Ali ibn Muhammad al-Mawardi, *al-Ahkam al-sultaniyah wa-al-wilayat al-diniyah*, eds. 'Ali ibn Muhammad ibn Habib al-Basri al-Mawardi and Muhammad Fahmi al-Sirjani (Cairo: al-Maktabah al-Tawfiqiyah, 1978). For English see Wafaa H. Wahba, trans., *The ordinances of government: a translation of Al-Ahkam al-Sultaniyya w' al-Wilayat al-Diniyya of al-Mawardi* (London: Garnet Publishing Limited, 1996).
60. Voll, *Islam*, 154.
61. Bahgat Korany, "Alien and Besieged Yet Here to Stay: the Contradictions of the Arab Territorial State," in *The Foundations of the Arab State*, ed. Ghassan Salame (New York: Routledge, 1987), 47.
62. Al-Ahsan, *Ummah or Nation?*, 4.
63. Enayat, "The Crisis over the Caliphate," in *Modern Islamic Political Thought* (Austin: University of Texas Press, 1982), 52-68.

64. Lewis, *Emergence of Modern Turkey*, 207; Hodgson, *Venture*, vol. 3, 276-277.

For more on the Young Turks before and after the 1908 revolution see M. Sukru Hanioglu, *Preparation for a Revolution: The Young Turks, 1902-1908* (New York: Oxford University Press, 2001) and *The Young Turks in Opposition* (New York: Oxford University Press, 1995). For a coverage of the Young Turks that focuses more on their ideology see Hasan Kayali, *Arabs and Young Turks: Ottomanism, Arabism, and Islamism in the Ottoman Empire, 1908-1918* (Berkeley: University Of California Press, 1997).

Note that some scholars, namely C. Ernest Dawn, conclude that secular-nationalism had been growing in Arab ranks long before the movement of the Young Turks: "The Arab nationalists were not reacting to Young Turk innovations." See C. Ernest Dawn, "The Origins of Arab Nationalism," in *The Origins of Arab Nationalism*, ed. Rashid Khalidi et al (Chicago: University of Chicago Press, 21. Regardless of particular ancestral identification, however, Arab nationalists throughout the twentieth century were acting in the mode of engagement most prominently characterized first by the Young Turks.

65. Hodgson, *Venture*, vol. 3, 266-267.

The oft-cited cliché that Islam knows no separation between "church and state" is not rooted in historical reality; historical analysis demonstrates that among Muslims there never has been a single, accepted relationship between religion and state. This is the subject of Brown, *Religion and State,* in which he concludes that, "Muslim history has been marked by a de facto separation of state and religious community" (80). This is also a central theme in Ayubi, *Political Islam* (pp. 3-4, 22, 123, 230). See also Scott, *Challenge of Political Islam,* 13-16.

In contemporary times, Modernists, secularists, and Islamists interpret the historical narrative regarding the relationship between religion and state in different ways. For a Modernist interpretation, see Asma Afsaruddin, *The First Muslims: History and Memory* (Oxford: Oneworld, 2007). Secularist and Islamist interpretations are discussed in the present work.

For general analysis of the matter, see Ira Lapidus, "The Separation of State and Religion in the Development of Early Islamic Society," *International Journal of Middle East Studies* 6, no. 4 (1975). See also Bernard Lewis, *The Political Language of Islam* (Chicago: University of Chicago Press, 1988).

66. ʿAli ʿAbd al-Raziq, *al-Islam wa-usul al-hukm: bahth fi al-Khilafah w-al-hukumah fi al-Islam*, 3rd ed., (Cairo: Matbaʿat Misr, 1925).

For an English translation see Ali Abdel Razek, *Islam and the Founda-*

tions of Political Power, trans. Maryam Loutfi, ed. Abdou Filali-Ansary (Edinburgh: Edinburgh University Press, 2012).
67. Hourani, *Arabic Thought*, 184-192; Charles Kurzman, ed., *Liberal Islam: A Sourcebook* (New York: Oxford University Press, 1998), 29; Ali Abdel Razek, *Islam*, 81.
68. ʿAli ʿAbd al-Raziq, "The Caliphate and the Bases of Power," in *Islam in Transition*, 28; Ali Abdel Razek, *Islam*, 81.
69. Filali-Ansary, introduction to *Islam and the Foundations of Political Power*, 13.

For more on responses to al-Raziq's work see Mohammad ʿAmara, *al-Islam wa Usul al-Hukm: dirassa wa wathaʿiq* (Beirut: al-Muʿassassa al-ʿArabiya li al-Dirasat wa al-Nahr, 1972); Abdou Filali-Ansary, preface and introduction to *Islam and the Foundations of Political Power* by Ali Abdel Razek, trans. Maryam Loutfi (Edinburgh: Edinburgh University Press, 2012), xi-xii, 1-17.

For critiques by al-Raziq's contemporaries see Muhammad al-Khidr Hussein, *Naqd Kitab al-Islam wa usul al-Hukm* [A Critique of the Book *Islam and the Foundations of Political Power*], (Cairo: 1925); Muhammad Bakhit al-Matʿi, *Haqiqat al-Islam wa Usul al-Hukm* [The Truth about Islam and the Foundations of Political Power], (Cairo, 1926).

For a later but classic critique placed squarely in the faults of falling to Western secular liberalism see Muhammad ʿImarah, *al-Islam wa Usul al-Hukm li ʿAli ʿAbd al-Raziq* [On ʿAli ʿAbd al-Raziq's *Islam and the Foundations of Political Power*], (Beirut: 1972).

For a fine contextual treatment and summary of al-Raziq's main arguments and major criticisms of them see Leonard Binder, "ʿAli ʿAbd al-Raziq and Islamic Liberalism: The Rejected Alternative," in *Islamic Liberalism: A Critique of Development Ideologies* (Chicago: University of Chicago Press, 1988), 128-169.
70. Dawn, "Origins of Arab Nationalism," in *Origins of Arab Nationalism*, 4-5; Hodgson, *Venture*, vol. 3, 239; Voll, *Islam*, 92, 152-158.
71. Brown, *Religion and State*, 111-112; Rashid Khalidi, "The Origins of Arab Nationalism: Introduction," in *Origins of Arab Nationalism*, vii. Hourani discusses these important events in three sections of *Arabic Thought*, "Egyptian Nationalism," 193-221; "Christian Secularists," 245-259; and "Arab Nationalism," 260-323. Note that despite common ties of Christianity, however, Bustani and others "resented the perceived patronizing arrogance of Anglo-Saxon Protestant missionaries, and warned against borrowing Western blemishes and vices." See Dawn, "Origins of Arab Nationalism," in *Origins of Arab Nationalism*, 7.

For a general discussion and the most recent scholarship on this see Rashid Khalidi et al., Lisa Anderson, and Reeva Simons, eds., *The*

Origins of Arab Nationalism (New York: Columbia University Press, 1993).

Some of the arguments in this work are revised yet again through a new theoretical framework grounded in literary criticism, cultural anthropology, socioeconomics, and psychology in, Israel Gershoni and James Jankowski, eds., *Rethinking Nationalism in the Arab Middle East* (New York: Columbia University Press, 1997).

Stephen Paul Sheehi offers yet another revisionist take on the emergence of Arab nationalism, using psychoanalytic and post-structuralist theory to analyze the rhetoric and writings of primary Arab writers during the nineteenth century. Drawing also upon the contemporary thought of Mohammad Arkoun, he argues that Arab nationalism was preceded by "an organization and regime of knowledge that was shared by 'Christian secularists' and 'Islamic Modernists,' Arab Ottomanists and Egyptian nationalists alike." See *Foundations of Modern Arab Identity* (Gainesville: University Press of Florida, 2004), 9-10.

72. Dawn, "Origins of Arab Nationalism," in *Origins of Arab Nationalism*, 6. Hourani identifies three main forms. See *Arabic Thought*, 341. See also Amir Shakib Arslan, *Our Decline and Its Causes*, trans. M.A. Shakoor (Lahore: S. Muhammad Ashraf, 1944).

It can be argued that Arslan represented yet another mode of reform: the Islamic-nationalist mode. See William L. Cleveland, *Islam Against the West: Shakib Arslan and the campaign for Islamic nationalism* (Austin: University of Texas Press, 1985). See also Albert Hourani's review of Cleveland's work in *Bulletin of the School of Oriental and African Studies*, University of London, Vol. 50, No. 3 (1987), 555-556.

Another important intellectual associated with this mode is 'Abd al-Rahman al-Bazzaz. See for example 'Abd al-Rahman al-Bazzaz and Sylvia G. Haim, "Islam and Arab Nationalism," *Die Welt des Islams* 3 (1954): 201-218. Accessed February 13, 2014, http://www.jstor.org/stable/1570165. See also 'Abd al-Rahman al-Bazzaz, *On Arab Nationalism* (London: Embassy of the Republic of Iraq, 1965).

73. Voll, *Islam*, 158, 162.
74. Dawn, ""The Origins of Arab Nationalism," in *Origins of Arab Nationalism*, 10.

See Hisham Sharabi, *Arab Intellectuals and the West: The Formative Years, 1875-1914* (Baltimore: Johns Hopkins University Press, 1970) and Bassam Tibi, *Arab Nationalism: Between Islam and the Nation-State*, 3rd ed. (New York: St. Martin's Press, 1997).

75. Dawn, "From Ottomanism to Arabism," in *The Modern Middle East*, 375; Hourani, *Arabic Thought*, 343; Voll, *Islam*, 162.

76. Hourani, *Arabic Thought,* 176-179. See also Vatikiotis, "Ahmad Lutfi al-Sayyid," in *History,* 239-244.
77. Vatikiotis, *History,* 225-226.
78. Taha Hussein, *The Days,* trans. E.H. Paxton, Hilary Wayment, and Kenneth Cragg (Cairo: American University of Cairo Press, 1997), 126-127.
79. Hussein, *The Days,* 245.
80. Hourani, *Arabic Thought,* 326-328
81. Taha Hussein, *The Future of Culture in Egypt* (Washington, DC: American Council of Learned Societies, 1954), 1. For the Arabic see Taha Husayn, *Mustaqbal al-Thaqafa fi Misr,* 2 vols., (Cairo: Matba'at al-Ma'arif wa-Maktabatuha, 1944).
82. Ibid., 3.
83. Ibid., 5-6.
84. An example of an Islamic Modernist writing at the same time as Taha Hussein, who was not writing in the mode of secular nationalism, is Muhammad Iqbal. As John L. Esposito observes, Iqbal "Could admire the achievements of the West – its dynamic spirit, intellectual tradition, and technological advances. However, he was equally critical of the imperialism of European colonialism, the moral bankruptcy of secularism and the economic exploitation of capitalism." See John L. Esposito, "Muhammad Iqbal and the Islamic State," in *Voices of Resurgent Islam,* 188.
85. Hussein, *Future of Culture in Egypt,* 15.
86. Ibid., 17.
87. Ibid., 6.
88. Khalid Muhammad Khalid, *From Here We Start,* trans. Isma'il R. el-Faruqi (Washington, DC: American Council of Learned Societies, 1953), 28-29. For the original Arabic see Khalid Muhammad Khalid, *Min Huna Nabda',* 11th printing, (Cairo: Anglo-Egyptian Bookstore, 1969).
89. Ibid., 117, 124, 134.
90. Khalid Muhammad Khalid, *al-Dawla fi al-Islam* (Cairo: Dar al-Thabit, 1981), 9. See also Voll, "Political Islam and The State," in *Oxford Handbook,* 58.
91. Muhammad al-Ghazzali, *Our Beginning in Wisdom,* trans. Isma'il R. el-Faruqi (Washington, DC: American Council of Learned Societies, 1953), xiii. For the original Arabic see Muhammad al-Ghazali, *Min Huna Na'lam,* 5th printing (Cairo: Nahda Masr, 2005).
92. Ibid., xiii. He resumes his discussion of despotism and its destructive effects on religious vitality on page 15.
93. Ibid., 3.
94. Ibid., 22.
95. Kurzman, *Modernist Islam,* 77. See also Hourani, "Rashid Rida," in *Arabic Thought,* 222-244.

    For more on Rida's life and thought, see Muhammad Rashid Rida, *al-Manar wa al-Azhar* (Cairo: Matba'at al-Manar, 1934); Shakib

Arslan, *al-Sayyid Rashid Rida aw ikha arba'in sana* (Damascus: Matba'at Ibn Zaydun, 1937); Malcolm Kerr, *Islamic Reform: The Political and Legal Theories of Muhammad 'Abduh and Rashid Rida* (Berkeley: University of California Press, 1966).
96. Ahmad Dallal, "Appropriating the Past: Twentieth-Century Reconstruction of Pre-Modern Islamic Thought," *Islamic Law and Society* 7, no. 3 (Oct. 2000): 342.
97. Muhammad Rashid Rida, *al-Khilafah* (Cairo: Zahra lil-'Alam al-'Arabi, 1988).
98. Muhammad Qasim Zaman, *Modern Islamic Thought in a Radical Age: Religious Authority and Internal Criticism* (New York: Cambridge University Press, 2012), 9-11.
99. Voll, *Islam*, 163.
100. Rashid Rida, "Patriotism, Nationalism, and Group Spirit in Islam," in *Islam in Transition*, 42.
101. Enayat, *Islamic Political Thought*, 70.
102. Voll, *Islam*, 163.

The *salafi* label is incredibly complex and can be misleading if not used carefully. Regarding Rida, "the term Salafi is ... used for, and by, those who reject the authority of the medieval schools of law and insist on an unmediated access to the foundational texts as the source of all norms." Yet even this definition is not to mistake, for example, the Wahhabi-style insistence upon doctrinal purity. See Zaman, *Modern Islamic Thought*, 7, 15.

For a fine essay that emphasizes the adaptable nature of salafism, despite its doctrine being "highly formalized and de-culturalized," as well as its evolution throughout history, see Roel Meijjer, "Salafism: Doctrine, Diversity and Practice," in *Political Islam: Context versus Ideology*, ed. Khaled Hroub (London: Saqi, 2010), 37-60. For a broader treatment see Roel Meijer, ed., *Global Salafism: Islam's New Religious Movement* (Oxford: Oxford University Press, 2013).
103. Muhammad Rashid Rida, "Renewal, Renewing, and Renewers," in *Modernist Islam*, 78.
104. Even in Rida's fundamentalist-style thought, however, there is still recognition of a *de facto* separation in Islam between "matters of the world" and "matters of religion." As Rida wrote in his book *Yusr al-Islam*:

> That which God commands us to observe in regard to obeying the people in charge (*uli al-amr*) amongst us relates to matters of the world and its public interests, with the added condition that this [observance] does not entail disobedience to God...As for matters of religion, it has been completed, and He [God]...is the legislator of religion (*shari' al-din*)...The

people in charge amongst Muslims have no authority over anyone in matters of pure religion, either by adding to it or subtracting from it.

Rashid Rida, *Yusr al-Islam wa-usul al-tashri' al-'amm fi nahy Allah wa-Rasullhi 'an kathrat al-su'al* (Cairo: Maktabat al-Salam al-Alamiya, 1984), 160. Translation from Dallal, "Appropriating the Past," 355.

105. Rida, "Renewal, Renewing, Renewers," in *Modernist Islam*, 78-79.
106. Enayat, *Islamic Political Thought*, 76-77.
107. Dallal, "Appropriating the Past," 357; Abdelilah Belkeziz, *The State in Contemporary Islamic Thought: A Historical Survey of the Major Muslim Political Thinkers of the Modern Era*, trans. Abdullah Richard Lux (London: I.B. Tauris, 2009), 119.
108. Voll, *Islam*, 163.
109. See Mary C. Wilson, introduction to "Reforming Elites and Changing Relations with Europe, 1789-1918," in *Modern Middle East*, 23.
110. Richard P. Mitchell, *The Society of the Muslim Brothers* (New York: Oxford University Press, 1993), 5.
111. Roxanne L. Euben and Muhammad Qasim Zaman, "Hasan al-Banna," in *Princeton Readings*, 50.
112. There is a massive bibliography on the Muslim Brothers. The classic work – accepted by the original members of the Muslim Brotherhood as such – remains Richard P. Mitchell's *The Society of the Muslim Brothers*. However, Mitchell's narrative ends around the time of Nasir.

A fine analysis of the Muslim Brotherhood, and Islamic activism more broadly, during the Sadat years is Abdullah al-Arian, *Answering the Call: Popular Islamic Activism in Sadat's Egypt* (Oxford: Oxford University Press, 2014). Al-Arian's analysis is notable for describing how the Brotherhood reconstituted itself after being banned by Nasir.

Another recent work that focuses on the organization from its founding until the Arab Spring - with a comparative analysis of its subsidiaries in Jordan, Kuwait, and Morocco - is Carrie R. Wickham, *The Muslim Brotherhood* (Princeton: Princeton University Press, 2013). Wickham's book is also significant for focusing not on the extremism of some factions within the organization as a whole but rather on the changing nature of their participation in political processes.

For more on the changing nature of the Brotherhood see Shadi Hamid, *Temptations of Power: Islamists & Illiberal Democracy in a New Middle East* (New York: Oxford University Press, 2014); Khalil al-Anani, "Brotherhood Bloggers: A New Generation Voices Dissent," *Arab Insight* 2, no. 1 (Winter 2008): 29-38; Mustapha Kemal al-Sayyid, "The Other Face of the Islamist Movement," *Democracy and Rule of*

Law Project, Carnegie Paper no. 33 (January): 1-28; Gehad Auda, "The 'Normalization' of the Islamist Movement in Egypt from the 1970s to the Early 1990s," in *Accounting for Fundamentalisms: The Dynamic Character of Movements,* ed. Martin E. Marty and R. Scott Appleby, The Fundamentalism Project, vol. 4 (Chicago: University of Chicago Press, 1994): 374-412; ʿAmr Hamzawy and Nathan Brown, "The Egyptian Muslim Brotherhood: Islamist Participation in a Closing Political Environment," Carnegie Paper no. 19 (Carnegie Endowment for International Peace, March 2010); March Lynch, "Young Brothers in Cyberspace," *Middle East Report* 37, no. 245 (Winter), 2010, http://www.merip.org/.

There are many other important works in English, although to a certain extent all are somewhat outdated because of the rapid changes since the Arab Spring. For a concise yet insightful essay by a former leader of the Brotherhood, see Kamal Helbawy, "The Muslim Brotherhood in Egypt: Historical Evolution and Future Prospects," in *Political Islam: Context versus Ideology,* ed. Khaled Hroub (London: Saqi, 2010), 61-85. See also Barry Rubin, "Comparing Three Muslim Brotherhoods: Syria, Jordan, Egypt," *Middle East Review of International Affairs* 11, no. 2 (June, 2007); Abdel Azim Ramadan, "Fundamentalist Influence in Egypt: the Strategies of the Muslim Brotherhood and the Takfir Groups," in *Fundamentalisms and the State: Remaking Polities, Economies, and Militance,* ed. Martin E. Marty and R. Scott Appleby, The Fundamentalism Project, vol. 3 (Chicago: University of Chicago Press, 2004), 152-183; Hisham al-Awadi, *In Pursuit of Legitimacy: The Muslim Brothers and Mubarak, 1982-2000* (London: Tauris Academic Studies, 2004); Raymond William Baker, *Sadat and After: Struggles for Egypt's Political Soul* (Cambridge: Harvard University Press, 1990).

For some of the most important recent works in Arabic see Ahmad Ban, *al-Ikhwan al-Muslimun wa-mihnat al-watan wa-al-din* (Cairo: Markaz al-Nil lil-Dirasat al-Istiratijiyah, 2013); Amir Shammakh, *al-Ikhwan al-Muslimun wa-thawrat 25 Yanayir* (Cairo: Dar al-Tawzi wa-al-Nashr, 2013); Jamal ʿAbd al-Latif Hasan Husayn, *al-Ikhwan al-Muslimun wa-hukm Misr: tadhiyat al-Ikhwan al-Muslimun, thawrat 25 min Yanayir 2011* (Alexandria: Muʾassasat Huras al-Duwaliyah, 2012).

For older but still classic works in Arabic see Yusuf Qaradawi, *al-Ikhwan al-Muslimun: 70 ʿaman fi al-daʿwa wa-al-tarbiya wa-al-jihad bi-munasabat murur sabaʿin* (Cairo: Maktabat Wahbah, 1999); Muhammad Abdallah al-Samman, *Hasan al-Banna: al-Rajal wa al-Fikrah* (Cairo: Dar al-Iʿtisam, 1978); Raʿuf Shalabi, *Ash-Shaykh Hasan al-Banna wa madrasatuh ʿal-Ikhwan al-Muslimunʿ* (Cairo: Dar al-Ansar, 1978); Zakariyya Sulayman Buyyumi, *al-Ikhwan al-Muslimun wa-al-Jamaʿat*

al-Islamiyah fi al-hayat al-siyasiyah al-Misriyah, 1928-1948 (Cairo: Maktabat Wahbah, 1979) and *al-Ikhwan al-Muslimun bayna ʿAbd al-Nasir wa-al-Sadat: min al-Manshiyah ila al-minassah, 1952-1981* (Cairo: Maktabat Wahbah, 1987).
113. Hasan al-Banna, "The New Renaissance," in *Islam in Transition*, 59.
114. Mitchell, *Muslim Brothers*, 30.
115. Ibd., 4.
116. Scott, *Challenge of Political Islam*, 13. See note number 159 for more.
117. Muhammad Abdallah al-Samman, *Hasan al-Banna: al-Rajal wa al-Fikrah* (Cairo: Dar al-lʿtisam, 1978/1398), 62; as cited in Voll, *Islam*, 181.
118. Mitchell, *Muslim Brothers*, 321; Voll, *Islam*, 181.
119. Voll, *Islam*, 181.
120. Al-Banna, "The New Renaissance," in *Islam in Transition*, 60.
121. Mitchell, *Muslim Brothers*, 224-227.
122. Hasan al-Banna, "Toward the Light," in *Princeton Readings*, 57.
123. Al-Banna, "Toward the Light," in *Princeton Readings*, 59-60.
124. Euben and Zaman, "Sayyid Abuʾl-Aʿla Mawdudi," in *Princeton Readings*, 79-80.
125. Abu-l-ʿAlaʿ Mawdudi, "Nationalism and Islam," in *Islam in Transition*, 74-75.
126. Sayyid Abul Aʿla Mawdudi, *The Islamic Movement: Dynamics of Values, Power and Change*, ed. and trans. Khurram Murad (Leicester: The Islamic Foundation, 1984), 97.
127. Mawdudi, *Islamic Movement*, 71.
128. Ibid., 105, 111-132.
129. Maulana Maududi, "Speech delivered in a gathering of ladies at Lahore," in *Selected Speeches and Writings of Maulana Maududi*, trans. S. Zakir Aijaz (Karachi: International Islamic Publishers, 1981), 70-71.
130. For more on Mawdudi and the *Jamaʿat* see Seyyed Vali Reza Nasr, *Vanguard of the Islamic Revolution: The Jamaʿat-I Islami of Pakistan* (Berkeley: University of California Press, 1994) and *Mawdudi and the Making of Islamic Revivalism* (New York: Oxford University Press, 1996); Khurshid Ahmad and Zafar Ishaq Ansari, *Mawdudi: An introduction to his life and thought* (Leicester: The Islamic Foundation, 1979); Roy P. Jackson, *Mawlana Mawdudi and Political Islam: Authority and the Islamic State* (London: Routledge, 2011); Jan-Peter Hartung, *A System of Life: Mawdudi and the Ideologisation of Islam* (New York: Oxford University Press, 2014).
131. Maududi, "On the Occasion of the Foundation of Jamaat-e-Islami," in *Selected Speeches*, 3.
132. Syed Abul-Ala Maudoodi, *Islamic Law and Constitution*, ed. Khurshid Ahmad (Karachi: Jamaat-e-Islami Publications, 1955), 14.
133. Mawdudi, *Islamic Movement*, 73.
134. Maududi, "Speech delivered outside Delhi Gate, Lahore," in *Selected Speeches*, 89-90.

135. Emmanuel Sivan, *Radical Islam: Medieval Theology and Modern Politics* (New Haven: Yale University Press, 1990), 22-23.
136. Maududi, "On the Occasion of the Foundation of Jamaat-e-Islami," in *Selected Speeches*, 5.
137. Enayat, *Islamic Political Thought*, 85.
138. "State of Israel: Proclamation of Independence May 14, 1948," in *The Israel-Arab Reader*, eds. Walter Laquer and Barry Rubin, 7th ed. (New York: Penguin Books, 2008), 81-83.
139. Yvonne Y. Haddad, *Contemporary Islam and the Challenge of History* (Albany: State University of New York Press, 1982), 34.
140. Mitchell, *Muslim Brothers*, 55-58, 230.
141. Haddad, *Contemporary Islam*, 41-42.

 For the best history of the 1967 War and the effects it continues to have on the Middle East see Michael B. Oren, *Six Days of War: June 1967 and the Making of the Modern Middle East* (New York: Presidio Press, 2003).

 To be certain, the 1967 War also prompted a secular style response. The revered Arab poet Nizar Qabbani wrote the famous lines, "The Israelis conquer not our borders, / but thrive on our shortcomings" in his poem *"Comments on The Notebook of Defeat.* For this translation see Leo Hamalian and John Yohannan, eds., *New Writing from the Middle East* (New York: New American Library, 1978), 74.

 Among the most prominent intellectuals to respond in secular terms was Sadeq al-Azm. His views are clear from the title of one of his most stinging critiques of Arab Muslims in the 1960s, "Criticism of Religious Thought." See *Naqd al-Fikr al-Dini* (Beirut: Dar al-Tali'ah, 1969) and *al-Naqd al-Dhati ba'd al-Hazima* (Beirut: Dar al-Tali'ah, 1968). For a translation of the latter see Sadik al-Azm, *Self Criticism After the Defeat*, trans. George Stergios (London: Saqi Books, 2011).

 See also Nadim Bitar, *Min al-Naksa ila al-Thawra* (Beirut: Dar al-Tali'ah, 1968).

 For the best summary of the different intellectual responses to the 1967 defeat see Ajami, *The Arab Predicament*. Ajami summarizes the immediate secular responses to the defeat in pp. 30-59.
142. Haddad, *Contemporary Islam*, 43.
143. Raphael Israeli, ed., *The Public Diary of President Sadat*, pt. 1, (Leiden: Brill Academic Publishing, 1975), 1105. See also Ajami, *Arab Predicament*, 185.
144. Haddad, *Contemporary Islam*, 43.
145. Yergin, "The Oil Weapon," in *The Prize*, 570.
146. Pipes, "'This World is Political!'"; Voll, "Islamic Renewal," in *Decolonization*, 203, 205.
147. Al-Ghazzali, "Our Beginning in Wisdom," 21.

Part Three

1. Abu-Rabi', *Contemporary Arab Thought*, 136.
2. See Muhammad Tawfiq Barakat, *Sayyid Qutb, khulasat hayatihi: manhajuhu fi al-harakah, al-naqd al-muwajjah ilayh* (Beirut: n.d.). This is quoted in Haddad, *Contemporary Islam*, 225-226. See also Yvonne Y. Haddad, "Sayyid Qutb: Ideologue of Islamic Revival," in *Voices of Resurgent Islam*, 67.
3. Yvonne Haddad notes that Qutb's published works from the first part of his career are almost exclusively non-religious in character, and most of them he renounced later in his life. Among these are *Qissat Ashwak; Muhimat al-Sha'ir fi al-Hayat; al-Atyaf al-Arba'a;* and *Tiflun min al-Qarya*. Among works that were non-religious but he did not specifically renounce are *al-Naqd al-Adabi: Usuluh wa-Manahijuh; al-Shati' al-Majhul; Kutub wa-Shakhsiyyat; Naqd Kitab Mustaqbal al-Thaqafa;* and *al-Madina al-Mashūra*. See Haddad, *Contemporary Islam*, 225-226.

    In contrast to the almost strictly literary topics of the first period, his increasing interest in 'Islamic topics' is clear from the titles of his published works during the second period: *al-'Adala al-Ijtima'iyya fi al-Islam; Ma'rakat al-Islam wa-al-Ra'smaliyya; Dirasat Islamiyya; al-Taswir al-Fanni fi al-Qur'an; Mashahid al-Qiyama fi al-Qur'an*. See Haddad, *Contemporary Islam*, 226.
4. Euben and Zaman, "Sayyid Qutb," in *Princeton Readings*, 129-130.
5. Sayyid Qutb, "The America I Have Seen: In the Scale of Human Values," in *America in an Arab Mirror: Images of America in Arabic Travel Literature, 1668 to 9/11 and Beyond*, eds. Kamal Abdel-Malek and Mouna el-Kabla, rev. ed. (New York: Palgrave Macmillan, 2011), 11, 14.

    For the original essay see Sayyid Qutb, "Amrika allati Raayt" (The America I Have Seen)," *al-Risala*, vol. 2, no. 957 (November 5, 1951), 1245-1247; no. 959 (November 19, 1951), 1301-1306; no. 961 (December 3, 1951), 1357-1360.
6. Qutb, "America," in *America in an Arab Mirror*, 15.
7. Ibid., 18-20. For more on Qutb's years in America see John Calvert, "'The World is an Undutiful Boy!': Sayyid Qutb's American Experience," *Islam & Christian Muslim Relations* 11, no. 1 (03, 2000): 87, http://search.proquest.com/docview/218266511?accountid=11091.
8. Sayyid Qutb, "History as the Interpretation of Events," in Haddad, *Contemporary Islam*, 163.
9. Sayyid Qutb, *Social Justice in Islam*, trans. John B. Hardie, revised by Hamid Algar (Oneonta, NY: Islamic Publications International, 2000), 51.
10. Ibid., 114.
11. Ibid.

12. Haddad, "Sayyid Qutb," in *Voices of Resurgent Islam*, 74-77.
13. Mokrane Guezzou, introduction to *Return of the Pharaoh: Memoir in Nasir's Prison* by Zainab al-Ghazali, trans. Mokrane Guezzou (Leicester: The Islamic Foundation, 1994), xx-xxi.
14. Haddad, *Contemporary Islam*, 226.
15. Al-Ghazali, *Return of the Pharaoh*, 40.
16. Seyyid Qutb, *Milestones* (Damascus: Dar al-Ilm, n.d.), 10-11.
17. Ibid., 96.
18. Ibid., 7.
19. Ibid., 11, 51.
20. Ibid., 8.
21. Ibid., 8, 20-21.
22. Ibid., 21, 77, 79.
23. Sayyid Qutb, "In the Shade of the Qur'an," in *Princeton Readings*, 145.
24. Qutb, *Milestones*, 94-95. See also Qutb, "Shade of the Qur'an," in *Princeton Readings*, 148-149.
25. Wallerstein, *World-Systems Analysis*, 42.
26. Qutb, "Shade of the Qur'an," in *Princeton Readings*, 146-147.
27. Voll, "Islamic Renewal," in *Decolonization*, 206.
28. Ahmad, "Islamic Resurgence," in *Voices of Resurgent Islam*, 225.
29. Hasan al-Turabi, "The Islamic State," in *Princeton Readings*, 213; Voll, *Islam*, 290.
30. Shahram Akbarzadeh and Abdullah Saeed, eds., *Islam and Political Legitimacy* (London: RoutledgeCurzon, 2003), 2; Ayubi, *Political Islam*, 3. This concept is as new as the concept of an 'Islamic state'. While scholars differentiate who was first to call for an 'Islamic state', most agree that it began with Rashid Rida at the earliest. See Ayubi, *Political Islam*, 64; Ayubi, *Over-stating the Arab State*, 17-52; Enayat, *Modern Islamic Political Thought*, 69.
31. Al-Turabi, "The Islamic State," in *Princeton Readings*, 213.
32. Qutb, *Social Justice*, 114.
33. Voll, *Islam*, 293.
34. Hasan Turabi, "Islam, Democracy, The State and the West," ed. Arthur L. Lowrie (lecture, University of South Florida, Tampa, FL, May 10, 1992), 24.
35. As quoted by Abu-Rabi' in *Contemporary Arab Thought*, 150.
36. Cited in Euben and Zaman, *Princeton Readings*, 12.
37. Muhammad al-Mubarak, *Nizam al-Islam: al-Hukm wa al-Dawla*, 4th ed. (Beirut: Dar al-Fikr, 1981), 12-18; Belkeziz, *State in Contemporary Islamic Thought*, 122.
38. Belkeziz, *State in Contemporary Islamic Thought*, 123.
39. Rachid Ghannouchi, "The Participation of Islamists in a Non-Islamic Government," in *Islam in Transition*, 271.
40. Max Weber, *The Sociology of Religion*, trans. Ephraim Fischoff (Boston: Beacon Press, 1991), 166. See also Roxanne L. Euben, *Enemy in the Mirror: Islamic Fundamentalism and the Limits of Modern Rationalism* (Princeton: Princeton University Press, 1999), 17.

41. See Carrie Rosefsky Wickham, *Mobilizing Islam: Religion, Activism and Political Change in Egypt* (New York: Columbia University Press, 2002).
42. For the best work on Ghannouchi's life and career see Azzam S. Tamimi, *Rachid Ghannouchi: A Democrat Within Islamism* (Oxford: Oxford University Press, 2001). See also John L. Esposito and John O. Voll, "Rashid Ghannoushi: Activist in Exile," in *Makers of Contemporary Islam* (New York: Oxford University Press, 2001), 91-117.

    As with the Muslim Brotherhood, after the Arab Spring any work on Muslim politics becomes somewhat outdated nearly as soon as it is published, but a fine history and collection of primary sources on Ennahda is *The Renaissance Party in Tunisia: The quest for freedom and democracy* (Washington, DC: American Muslim Council, 1991).

    On Hasan Turabi, see Abdelwahab El-Affendi, *Turabi's Revolution: Islam and Power in Sudan* (London: Grey Seal, 1991); Mohamed El-Hachmi Hamdi, *The making of an Islamic political leader: Conversations with Hasan al-Turabi*, trans. Ashur A. Shamis (Boulder, CO: Westview Press, 1998); Esposito and Voll, "Hasan al-Turabi: The Mahdi Lawyer," in *Makers of Contemporary Islam*, 118-149.
43. Yusuf al-Qaradawi, "Islam and Democracy," in *Princeton Readings*, 243.
44. Al-Ghazali, *Return of the Pharaoh*, 7.
45. Al-Turabi, "The Islamic State," in *Princeton Readings*, 213, 219. Similarly, Fahmy Howeidy writes that, "Freedom is the right of society, where the human being exercising his freedom is the obverse side of *al-tawhid* and the enunciation of the *shahadatayn* in confirmation of the profession of his servitude to Allah alone, and his liberation from any authority of anyone among people" in "Islam and democracy," *Contemporary Arab Affairs* 3:3 (2010), 304.
46. Wallerstein, *World-Systems Analysis*, 42-43.
47. Al-Turabi, "The Islamic State," in *Princeton Readings*, 214.
48. Qutb, *Milestones*, 59, 77, 95, 103.
49. Maudoodi, *Islamic Law and Constitution*, 108.
50. Ibid., 78-79, 109-110.
51. Qutb, *Milestones*, 94-95.
52. Deina Ali Abdelkader, *Islamic Activists: The Anti-Enlightenment Democrats* (New York: Pluto Press, 2011), 62.
53. Qutb, *Milestones*, 57-58.
54. Ibid., 58.
55. Massimo Campanini, "al-Hakimiyah," in *The Oxford Encyclopedia of the Islamic World*. Oxford Islamic Studies Online, http://www.oxfordislamicstudies.com/article/opr/t236/e1033 (accessed March 29, 2013).
56. Maudoodi, *Islamic Law and Constitution*, 111-112.
57. Ibid., 114.
58. Ibid., 81-82.

59. Al-Turabi, "The Islamic State," in *Princeton Readings,* 216.
60. See Euben and Zaman, *Princeton Readings in Islamist Thought,* 35-40, 309.

    Azizah al-Hibri (ed.) presents nine essays in *Women and Islam* (Elmsford, NY: Pergamon Press, 1982) that attempt to demonstrate gender discrimination as cultural rather than religious in influence.
    For interesting critiques of the concept of social contract in Western political philosophy and history see Carole Pateman, *The Sexual Contract* (Stanford: Stanford University Press, 1988). For a similar critique along racial rather than gendered lines, see Charles W. Mills, *The Racial Contract* (Ithaca, NY: Cornell University Press, 1999).

    There is a significant body of literature challenging the widely accepted view of Middle Eastern (Muslim and non-Muslim alike) women as disinterested, uninvolved and repressed individuals. As a starting point, see Margot Badran and Miriam Cooke, eds., *Opening the Gates: An Anthology of Arab Feminist Writing,* 2nd ed. (Bloomington, IN: Indiana University Press, 2004). See also Leila Ahmed, *Women and Gender in Islam: Historical Roots of a Modern Debate* (New Haven, CT: Yale University Press, 1993); Lila Abu-Lughod, *Do Muslim Women Need Saving?* (Cambridge, MA: Harvard University Press, 2013); Amina Wadud, *Inside the Gender Jihad: Women's Reform in Islam* (Oxford: Oneworld Publications, 2006) and *Qur'an and Woman: Rereading the Sacred Text from a Woman's Perspective* (Oxford: Oxford University Press, 1999); Fatima Mernissi, *Beyond the Veil: Male-female Dynamics in Modern Muslim Society,* 2nd rev. ed. (Indianapolis: Indiana University Press, 1987).
61. Ovamir Anjum, *Politics, Law, and Community in Islamic Thought: The Taymiyyan Moment* (New York: Cambridge University Press, 2012), 51, 53-58.
62. Jeroen Gunning, *Hamas in Politics: Democracy, Religion, Violence* (New York: Cambridge University Press, 2009), 63.
63. Ibid., 67.
64. See Bettina Graf and Jakob Skovgaard-Petersen, eds., *Global Mufti: The Phenomenon of Yusuf al-Qaradawi* (New York: Columbia University Press, 2009). In this work, the second chapter problematizes Qaradawi's relationship with the Muslim Brotherhood; the seventh chapter discusses his *wasatiyya* approach; the final chapter attempts to contextualize Qaradawi's role in global Islamic activism.
65. To be certain, Qaradawi is not the only Islamist to think of his intellectual school "as an outgrowth of the centrist Islamic mainstream," or *wasatiyya*. Raymond Baker labels these Islamist thinkers as the "New Islamists," and includes among them Fahmy Howeidy, Kamal Abul Magd, the late Muhammad al-Ghazali, and Muhammad Selim el-Awa. See Raymond William Baker, *Islam Without Fear: Egypt and the New Islamists* (Cambridge, MA: Harvard University Press, 2003).

66. Abu-Rabi', *Contemporary Arab Thought*, 137-138.
67. See Yusuf al-Qaradawi, *al-Hulul al-mustawradah wa-kayfa janat 'ala ummatina* (Beirut: Mu'assasat al-Risalah, 1985); *al-Hall al-Islami faridah wa-darurah* (Cairo: Maktabat Wahabah, 1977); *Bayyinat al-hall al-Islami wa-shubuhat al-'almaniyin wa-al-mutagharribin* (Cairo: Maktabat Wahbah, 1988). See also Abu-Rabi', *Contemporary Arab Thought*, 138, 408.
68. Yousuf al-Qaradawi, *Min fiqh al-dawla fi al-Islam* (Cairo: Dar al-Sharouk, 2001).
69. Al-Qaradawi, "Islam and Democracy," in *Princeton Readings*, 239.
70. Ibid.
71. Qaradawi, *Min fiqh al-dawla fi al-Islam*, 65.
72. Ibid., 60, 63.
73. Ibid., 62.
74. Ibid., 63.
75. Ibid., 64.
76. Ibid., 62.
77. Al-Turabi, "The Islamic State," in *Princeton Readings*, 213.
78. Qaradawi, *Min fiqh al-dawla fi al-Islam*, 63, 64.
79. Nadia Yassine, *Full Sails Ahead*, trans. Farouk Bouasse (Iowa City, IA: Justice and Spirituality Publishing, 2006), 183.
80. This analysis deals only with Islamist thought regarding the place of Muslims in the community. The topic of non-Muslims in an Islamic state and their function in the social contract deserves a future work of its own.

    The basic position that is dominant within Political Islamist thought is that proper implementation of the shari'a in an Islamic state not only affirms the essential equality of men and women, but also affirms the protected status of non-Muslims and their rights to worship and live free of oppression. The exception to this is the head of state, who must be Muslim. To justify their theoretical position of tolerance of all faiths in an Islamic state, Political Islamists often cite *Surat al-Baqarah*, which reveals: "There is no compulsion in religion" (2:256). As for the Islamic origins of pluralism and religious tolerance, Islamists also cite *Surat al-Hujurat*: "Oh, mankind! We have created you male and female and made you different nations and tribes so that you might come to know one another. Verily, the most honored of you in the sight of God is he who is the most righteous of you" (49:13).

    The literature regarding non-Muslims in an Islamic state or Islamic society is extensive. For a starting point, see Rachel M. Scott, *The Challenge of Political Islam: Non-Muslims and the Egyptian State* (Stanford: Stanford University Press, 2010); Youssef Courbage and Philippe Fargues, *Christians and Jews Under Islam* (London: I.B. Tauris, 1998); Peter E. Makari, *Conflict and Cooperation: Christian-Muslim Relations in Contemporary Egypt* (Syracuse: Syracuse University Press, 2007).

Yvonne Haddad has written prolifically on this topic in contemporary times. See her "Christians in a Muslim State: The Recent Egyptian Debate," *Christian-Muslim Encounters*, eds. Yvonne Yazbeck Haddad and Wadi Zaidan Haddad (Gainesville: University Press of Florida, 1995), 381-398; "Islamist Depictions of Christianity in the Twentieth Century: The Pluralism Debate and the Depiction of the Other," *Islam and Christian-Muslim Relations* 7, No. 1 (1996), 75-93; "Islamists and the Challenge of Pluralism," Occasional Paper, Georgetown University (Washington, DC: Center for Contemporary Arab Studies), 1995.

For a treatment of minorities in early Islamic society, see C.E. Bosworth, "The Concept of *Dhimma* in Early Islam," in *Christians and Jews in the Ottoman Empire: The Functioning of a Plural Society*, eds. Benjamin Braude and Bernard Lewis, Vol. 1 (New York: Holmes and Meir Publishers, 1982), 37-51. For a treatment of minorities in the Ottoman period see Bruce Masters, *Christians and Jews in the Ottoman Arab World: The Roots of Sectarianism* (New York: Cambridge University Press, 2001).

For works written by Islamists on this topic, see Muhammad Selim el-Awa, "Ahl al-Dhimma fi al-Nitham al-Huquqi al-Islami," *al-Hayat al-Tayyiba*, no. 11 (2003), 179-185; "al-'Alaqat bayn al-Muslimin wa Ahl al-Kitab," *al-Muslim al-Mu'asir* 22, No. 85 (199?), 27-38; "al-Ta'addudiyya al-Siyasiyya min Manthur Islami," *Minbar al-Hiwar*, 6, No. 20 (1991): 129-238. See also Yusuf al-Qaradawi, *Non-Muslims in Islamic Society*, trans. Khalil Muhammad Hamad and Sayed Mahboob Ali Shah (Indianapolis: American Trust Publications, 1985). Fahmi Howeidy, *Muwatinun la Dhimmiun: Mawqi' Ghayr al-Muslimin fi Mustama'a al-Muslimin* [*Citizens not Dhimmis: Non-Muslims in Muslim Society*], 3rd ed. (Cairo: Dar al-Shuruq, 1999).

81. Fahmy Howeidy, "Islam and Democracy," *Contemporary Arab Affairs* 3:3 (2010), 302.
82. Ibid., 302.
83. Al-Qaradawi, "Islam and Democracy," in *Princeton Readings*, 235.
84. Al-Qaradawi, *Min fiqh al-dawla fi al-Islam*, 148.
85. Asma Asfaruddin, "Obedience to Political Authority: An Evolutionary Concept," in M.A. Muqtedar Khan, ed., *Islamic Democratic Discourse: Theory, Debates, and Philosophical Perspectives* (Oxford: Lexington Books, 2006), 50. See also Zaman, "Revisiting 'Those in Authority,'" in *Modern Islamic Thought in a Radical Age*, 47-55.
86. Asfaruddin, "Obedience to Political Authority," in *Islamic Democratic Discourse*, 47.

87. Ibid.
88. Ibid., 42.
89. Ibid., 45.
90. Yassine, *Full Sails Ahead*, 183.
91. Fathi Osman, "Shūra and Democracy," in *Islam in Transition*, 288. See also Fathi Osman, "Islam in a Modern State: Democracy and the Concept of Shūra," Occasional Papers Series, Center for Muslim-Christian Understanding (Washington, DC: Georgetown University, 2001), 14.
92. Ghannouchi, "The Participation of Islamists in a Non-Islamic Government," in *Islam in Transition*, 273.
93. Mohammad Hashim Kamali, *Principles of Islamic Jurisprudence* (Cambridge: The Islamic Texts Society, 2003), 415.
94. Sherman A. Jackson, "Muhtasib," in *The Oxford Encyclopedia of the Islamic World*, Oxford Islamic Studies Online, http://www.oxfordislamicstudies.com/article/opr/t236/e0555 (accessed December 10, 2013). See also Abdul Rahman Doi I, "Hisbah," in *The Oxford Encyclopedia of the Islamic World*, Oxford Islamic Studies Online, http://www.oxfordislamicstudies.com/article/opr/t236/e0310 (accessed December 10, 2013).
95. Zainab Abu Taleb, Professor of Arabic and Islamic Studies, Yemen College of Middle Eastern Studies (Sana'a, Yemen), in discussion with the author, July 2013. Scholars of Islamic theology might provide exceptions to Professor Abu Taleb's statement, but these are just that: exceptions. For the most nuanced and comprehensive treatment of this concept in the history of Islam see Michael Cook, *Commanding Right and Forbidding Wrong in Islamic Thought* (New York: Cambridge University Press, 2000).
96. Osman, "Islam in a Modern State," 12.
97. Al-Qaradawi, *Min fiqh al-dawla fi al-Islam*, 148. Qaradawi notes that it is the job of the community to "watch over him [the ruler], hold him accountable, and impeach him if they so deem" (59).
98. Gunning, *Hamas in Politics*, 66.
99. Howeidy, "Islam and democracy," 303.
100. Maudoodi, *Islamic Law and Constitution*, 199.
101. Muhamed S. El-Awa, *On the Political System of the Islamic State*, trans. Ahmad Naji al-Imam, ed. Anwer Beg (Indianapolis, IN: American Trust Publications, 1980), 114.
102. Ibid., 92-97. El-Awa provides a succinct problematization of this debate and concludes that *shūra* is obligatory. His treatment is theoretical, however, and, like most Islamists, he does not develop specific legal ramifications of the issue. See also Howeidy, "Islam and democracy," 332.
103. El-Awa, *Political System of the Islamic State*, 88.
104. Al-Qaradawi, "Islam and Democracy," in *Princeton Readings*, 244-245.
105. Ibid., 244.

106. Maudoodi, *Islamic Law and Constitution*, 117-118, 135.
107. Howeidy, "Islam and democracy," 307, 312.
108. Ibid., 310.
109. Ibid., 331.
110. Yassine, *Full Sails Ahead*, 182, 187-188.
111. Howeidy, "Islam and democracy," 325.
112. Osman, "Islam in a Modern State," 12.
113. Howeidy, "Islam and democracy," 326.
114. El-Awa, *Islamic State*, 88, 114.
115. Howeidy, "Islam and democracy," 312.
116. Ibid., 312.
117. El-Awa, *Islamic State*, 114-115.
118. Ibid.
119. Al-Qaradawi, *Min fiqh al-dawla fi al-Islam*, 148.
120. Mohamed Selim el-Awa, "Religion and Political Structures: an Islamic Viewpoint," Occasional Paper, No. 3 (Birmingham: Centre for the Study of Islam & Christian-Muslim Relations, 1999), 11.
121. Al-Azmeh, *Islams and Modernities*, 67-68.
122. Howeidy, "Islam and democracy," 316.
123. Ibid., 331.
124. Ibid., 318-319.
125. Rashid al-Ghannoushi, "Islamic Movements; Self-Criticism and Reconsideration," in *The Contemporary Arab Reader on Political Islam*, Ibrahim M. Abu-Rabi', ed. (New York: Pluto Press, 2010), 133.
126. Al-Qaradawi, *Min fiqh al-dawla fi al-Islam*, 64.
127. Yusuf al-Qaradawi, *al-Muslimun wa'l-'awlama* (Cairo: Dar al-tawzi' wa'l-nashr al-Islamiyya, 2000), 144; Zaman, *Modern Islamic Thought in a Radical Age*, 24.
128. It is not my intention here to even attempt at providing a definition of democracy in the "Western" context. However, the *Oxford English Dictionary* provides a useful conceptualization: "Government by the people; *esp.* a system of government in which all the people of a state or polity (or, esp. formerly, a subset of them meeting particular conditions) are involved in making decisions about its affairs, typically by voting to elect representatives to a parliament or similar assembly; (more generally) a system of decision-making within an institution, organization, etc., in which all members have the right to take part or vote. In later use often more widely, with reference to the conditions characteristically obtaining under such a system: a form of society in which all citizens have equal rights, ignoring hereditary distinctions of class or rank, and the views of all are tolerated and respected; the principle of fair and equal treatment of everyone in a state, institution, organization, etc." "democracy, n.". OED Online. June 2014. Oxford University Press. http://www.oed.com.proxy.library.georgetown.edu/view/Entry/49755?redirectedFrom=democracy& (accessed August 05, 2014).

129. Howeidy, "Islam and democracy," 328.
130. Nader Hashemi argues that not only is there an indigenous theory of secularism inherent in Islam, but that the widely-held belief that religious politics or religious mobilization is incompatible with liberal-democratic development is false and not rooted in historical reality. See his *Islam, Secularism, and Liberal Democracy: Toward a Democratic Theory for Muslim Societies* (New York: Oxford University Press, 2009).
131. Mawdudi, "Political Theory of Islam," in *Islam in Transition*, 264.
132. Murad Wilfried Hofmann, *Religion on the Rise: Islam in the Third Millennium*, trans. Andreas Ryschka (Beltsville, MD: amana publications, 2001), 92.
133. Al-Qaradawi, *Min fiqh al-dawla fi al-Islam*, 56.
134. Rachid Ghannouchi, "Secularism and Relation Between Religion and State from the Perspective of the Nahda Party" (lecture, Center for the Study of Islam and Democracy, Washington, DC, March 2, 2012).
135. For a concise summary of Khomeini's thought, see Euben and Zaman, "Ayatollah Ruhollah Khomeini," in *Princeton Readings*, 155-162 and Ayatollah Ruhollah Khomeini, "Islamic Government," in *Princeton Readings*, 163-180. For a collection of Khomeini's writings see Hamid Algar, trans., *Islam and Revolution: Writings and Declarations of Imam Khomeini* (Jakarta: Mizan Press, 1981). See also Baqer Moin, *Khomeini: Life of the Ayatollah* (New York: St. Martin's Press, 2000). For a masterful account that places the 1979 in the context of Iranian history see Roy Mottahadeh, *The Mantle of the Prophet*, 2nd ed. (Oxford: Oneworld Publications, 2008). For the best general history of modern Iran, see Ervand Abrahamian, *A History of Modern Iran* (Cambridge: Cambridge University Press, 2008).
136. Osman, "Islam in a Modern State," 9. Not all Muslims, of course, would agree with Osman that there is no clergy in Islam. Khalid Muhammad Khalid, for example, argued in *From Here We Start* that the rise of a priesthood in Islam contributed to the decline of Muslim society.
137. Mawdudi, "Political Theory of Islam," in *Islam in Transition*, 264.
138. Al-Qaradawi, *Min fiqh al-dawla fi al-Islam*, 57.
139. Osman, "Islam in a Modern State," 14.
140. Ibid., 15.
141. Ibid., 13, 15.
142. Al-Qaradawi, *Min fiqh al-dawla fi al-Islam*, 147.
143. Maudoodi, *Islamic Law and Constitution*, 139.
144. Al-Qaradawi, *Min fiqh al-dawla fi al-Islam*, 147.
145. Ibid.,148.
146. Al-Turabi, "The Islamic State," in *Princeton Readings*, 217.
147. *Sunan al-tirmidhi: Kitab al-fitan, bub ma ja'a fi luzum al-jama'a.*
For more on the contemporary debate in Islamic thought regarding the concept of consensus see Zaman, "Rethinking Consensus," in *Modern Islamic Thought in a Radical Age*, 45-74.

148. Al-Turabi, "The Islamic State," in *Princeton Readings*, 215, 217.
149. Osman, "Islam in a Modern State," 13, 19-20. Osman continues to note that, "Non-Muslims and secularists can have their political parties to present their views, and defend their interests and guard the human rights and dignity of all the children of Adam as the Quran teaches. Women can join or form the party they like" (20).
150. El-Awa, "Religion and Political Structures," 9.
151. Howeidy, "Islam and democracy," 326.
152. Ibid., 318-319.
153. Hofmann, *Religion on the Rise*, 93.
154. Maudoodi, *Islamic Law and Constitution*, 22-23.
155. Gunning, *Hamas in Politics*, 67-68.
156. See Zaman, "Contestations of the Common Good," in *Modern Islamic Thought in a Radical Age*, 108-142, for a treatment of the ways in which this concept has been debated in Islamic thought.
157. Muhammad Qutb, *Hawl tatbiq al-Shari'ah* (Cairo: Maktabat al-Sunnah, 1991), 39; Deina Abdelkader, *Social Justice in Islam* (Herndon, VA: International Institute of Islamic Thought, 2000), 33.
158. Abdelkader, *Social Justice in Islam*, 63.

Part Four

1. Turabi, "The Islamic State," in *Voices*, 241; Brown, *Religion and State*, 48.
2. Maududi, "Speech delivered outside Delhi Gate, Lahore," in *Selected Speeches*, 84.
3. Richard P. Mitchell, "The Islamic Movement: Its Current Condition and Future Prospects," in *The Islamic Impulse*, ed. Barbara Freyer Stowasser (London: Croom Helm, 1987), 84-85, cited in John O. Voll, foreword to *The Society of the Muslim Brothers*, by Richard P. Mitchell (New York: Oxford University Press, 1993), xvii.
4. Sayyid Qutb, *Hadha al-din* (Cairo: n.d.) 7, 37, cited in Haddad, *Contemporary Islam*, 92.
5. Louise Marlow, *Hierarchy and egalitarianism in Islamic thought* (New York: Cambridge University Press, 1997), 1-6; Robert G. Hoyland, *Arabia and the Arabs: From the Bronze Age to the Coming of Islam* (New York: Routledge, 2001), 117.
6. Qutb, *Social Justice in Islam*, 26.
7. Jonathan Berkey, *The Formation of Islam: Religion and Society in the Near East, 600-1800* (New York: Cambridge University Press, 2003), 40.
8. Ibn Khaldun, *Muqaddimah*, trans. Franz Rosenthal, ed. N.J. Dawood (Princeton: Princeton University Press, 2005), 97, 99, 107.
9. Edward Gibbon, *The Decline and Fall of the Roman Empire*, ed. J.B. Bury, vol. 5 (London: Methuen and Co., Ltd., 1911), 333-334.
10. Berkey, *Formation of Islam*, 40-41; Fred McGraw Donner, *The Early Islamic Conquests* (Princeton: Princeton University Press, 1981), 11-12, 16.

11. Brown, *Religion and State*, 28. See also Xavier de Planhol, "The Geographical Setting," in the *Cambridge History of Islam*, vol. 2, eds. P.M. Holt, Ann K.S. Lambton, and Bernard Lewis (Cambridge: Cambridge University Press, 1970), 443-468.
12. Donner, *Early Islamic Conquests*, 20.
13. Gibbon, *Decline and Fall*, vol. 5, 339, 343.
14. Hoyland, *Arabia*, 117.
15. Ibid.
16. el-Awa, *Islamic State*, 3.
17. Hoyland, *Arabia*, 119.
18. Ibid., 120.
19. Ibid., 119.
20. Ibid., 122.
21. Gibbon, *Decline and Fall*, vol. 6, 267.
22. Herodotus, *History*, ed. and trans. George Rawlinson, vol. 2 (London: John Murray: 1858), 400-401.
23. W. Robertson Smith, *Kinship & Marriage in Early Arabia* (London: Adam and Charles Black, 1903), 61.
24. Herodotus, *History*, vol. 2, 401.
25. Ibid.
26. Hoyland, *Arabia*, 251, 115.
27. R.B. Serjeant, "The 'Sunnah Jami'ah," Pacts with the Yathrib Jews, and the 'Tahrim' of Yathrib: Analysis and Translation of the Documents Comprised in the So-Called 'Constitution of Medina,'" *Bulletin of the School of Oriental and African Studies, University of London*, Vol. 41, No. 1 (1978), 1; Berkey, *Formation of Islam*, 66.
28. Marshall Hodgson, *Rethinking world history: Essays on Europe, Islam, and World History*, ed. Edmund Burke, III (New York: Cambridge University Press, 1993), 115-116. It is instructive to note that Nadia Yassine cites this passage in formulating her arguments for politics of an Islamic state in *Full Sails Ahead* p. 157.
29. Anjum, *Politics, Law, Community*, 51.
30. W. Montgomery Watt, "Hidjra," in *Encyclopedia of Islam, Second Edition*.
31. Ibn Ishaq, *The Life of Muhammad: A Translation of Ishaq's Sirat Rasul Allah*, trans. A. Guillaume, ed. Ibn Hashim (London: Oxford University Press, 1955), 119, 130.
32. Ishaq, *Sirat Rasul Allah*, 222.
33. Ibid.
34. Patricia Crone, *Meccan Trade and the Rise of Islam* (Princeton: Princeton University Press, 1987), 217.
35. Marco Scholler, "Medina," in *Encyclopedia of the Qur'an*. Similarly, Michael Lecker notes that at the time of Muhammad's arrival "the main Jewish clans were still the dominant political and military power in Medina" (3) in *The 'Constitution of Medina': Muhammad's First Legal Document* (Princeton: Darwin Press, 2004).

36. Serjeant, "Constitution of Medina," 3.
37. Ibn Hashim, *al-Sirah al-nabawiyah*, 2:71 as cited in Michael Lecker, *People, Tribes and Society in Arabia Around the Time of Muhammad* (Burlington, VT: Ashgate Publishing Company, 2005), 37.
38. Al-Waqidi, *Kitab al-maghazi*, ed. Marsden Jones, vol. 1 (London: Oxford University Press, 1966), 184. Cited in Serjeant, "Constitution of Medina," 2.
39. Ali Bulaç, "The Medina Document," in *Liberal Islam*, ed. Charles Kurzman (New York: Oxford University Press, 1998), 170.
40. Ishaq, *Sirat Rasul Allah*, 201-202.
    The days of the *tashriq* are from the *Fajr* prayer on the ninth day of *Dhul HIjjah* (the twelfth and final month of the Islamic year) through the *Asr* prayer on the thirteenth day of *Dhul Hijjah*.
41. Gibbon, *Decline and Fall*, vol 5, 380-381. See also Ishaq, *Sirat Rasul Allah*, 201-207.
42. Ishaq, *Sirat Rasul Allah*, 222.
43. Text as preserved in Ibn Ishaq's version and as cited in Lecker, *Constitution of Medina*, 32. Mu'minun has proven difficult for scholars to translate, but it generally is accepted to mean "believers." For an innovative interpretation of this see Fred M. Donner, *Muhammad and the Believers: At the Origins of Islam* (Cambridge: MA, Harvard University Press, 2012).
44. Lecker, *Constitution of Medina*, 32.
45. Ibid., 32, 102.
46. Bulaç, "The Medina Document," in *Liberal Islam*, 173.
47. Yassine, *Full Sails Ahead*, 179.
48. Zayd bnu 'Ali al-Wazir, *al-Fardiya* (Yemeni Heritage and Research Center, 2000) cited in Yassine, *Full Sails Ahead*, 179-180.
49. Ashgar Ali Engineer, "Islam and Secularism," in *Islam in Transition*, 140.
50. Yassine, *Full Sails Ahead*, 182.
51. Mottahadeh, *Loyalty and Leadership*, 42.
52. Muhammad Salim al-Awa, "Political Pluralism from an Islamic Perspective," in *Islam in Transition*, 283.
53. Osman, "Shūra and Democracy," in *Islam in Transition*, 289.
54. Ishaq, *Sirat Rasul Allah*, 684-685.
55. "Khalifa," *Encyclopedia of Islam, Second Edition*.
56. Ishaq, *Sirat Rasul Allah*, 687.
57. El-Awa, *Islamic State*, 115.
58. Qaradawi, "Islam and Democracy," in *Princeton Readings*, 236. Qaradawi also mentions this in *Min fiqh al-dawla fi al-Islam*, 56.
59. Engineer, "Islam and Secularism," in *Islam in Transition*, 141.
60. Martin Hinds, "The Murder of the Caliph 'Uthman," *International Journal of Middle East Studies*, Vol. 3, 4 (October 1972), 450, 457.
61. Gibbon, *Decline and Fall*, vol. 5, 410.

62. Hinds, "The Murder of the Caliph 'Uthman," 458.
63. Ibid., 458-459.
64. El-Awa, *Political System*, 40-41.
65. Engineer, "Islam and Secularism," in *Islam in Transition*, 141.
66. Ibid., 137.
67. Mottahadeh, *Loyalty and Leadership*, 40-41.
68. Ibid., 41.
69. Yassine, *Full Sails Ahead*, 179.
70. Sayyid Qutb, "History as the Interpretation of Events," in *Contemporary Islam*, 165.
71. Qutb, *Milestones*, 15.
72. Ibid., 17.

Part Five

1. Francis Fukuyama, "The End of History?" *The National Interest* (Summer 1989).
2. Francis Fukuyama, *The End of History and the Last Man* (New York: The Free Press, 1992), 46.
3. Abdelkader, *Social Justice in Islam*, 149, 63.
4. Wael B. Hallaq, *The Impossible State: Islam, Politics, and Modernity's Moral Predicament* (New York: Columbia University Press, 2013), 48.
5. Ahmad, "The Nature of Islamic Resurgence," in *Voices of Resurgent Islam*, 220. Emphasis in original. To be sure, use of the term 'Islamic resurgence' is not to imply that Islam ever seceded from the lives of Muslims; rather, it is used to describe the primacy of Islam in the reformist vision of contemporary Islamists.
6. There is an extensive body of literature on the global religious resurgence. As a starting point see Monica Duffy Tott, Daniel Philpott and Timothy Samuel Shah, *God's Century: Resurgent Religion and Global Politics* (New York: W.W. Norton, 2011); Scott M. Thomas, *The Global Resurgence of Religion and the Transformation of International Relations: The Struggle for the Soul of the Twenty-First Century* (New York: Palgrave Macmillan, 2005); Mark Juergensmeyer, *The New Cold War? Religious Nationalism Confronts the Secular State* (Berkeley: University of California Press, 1993) and *Global Rebellion: Religious Challenges to the Secular State, from Christian Militias to al Qaeda* (Berkeley: University of California Press, 2009); Timothy Samuel Shah, Alfred Stepan and Monica Duffy Toft, eds., *Rethinking Religion and World Affairs* (New York: Oxford University Press, 2012).
7. José Cassanova, *Public Religions in the Modern World* (Chicago: University of Chicago Press, 1994), 6.
8. Abdelkader, *Social Justice in Islam*, 150.
9. Peter L. Berger, "The Desecularization of the World: A Global Over-

view," in *The Desecularization of the World: Resurgent Religion and World Politics,* ed. Peter L. Berger (Washington, DC: Ethics and Policy Center, 1999), 2.
10. Nader Hashemi, *Islam, Secularism, and Liberal Democracy: Toward a Democratic Theory for Muslim Societies* (New York: Oxford University Press, 2009), 1-3.
11. John O. Voll, "Bin Laden and the New Age of Global Terrorism," *Middle East Policy,* Vol. VIII, No. 4 (December 2001), 2.
12. Jürgen Habermas, "New Social Movements," *Telos,* No. 49 (Fall, 1981), 33; also quoted in Voll, "New Age of Global Terrorism," 2. Emphasis in original.

 For more on 'new social movement theory' see Sidney Tarrow, *The New Transnational Activism* (Cambridge: Cambridge University Press, 2005); Steven M. Buechler, "New Social Movement Theories," *The Sociological Quarterly,* Vol. 36, No. 3 (Summer 1995), 441-464.
13. Ronald Inglehart, "Values, Ideology, and Cognitive Mobilization in New Social Movements," *Challenging the Political Order: New Social and Political Movements in Western Democracies,* eds. Russell J. Dalton and Manfred Kuechler (Cambridge: Polity Press, 1990), 44-45; also quoted in Voll, "New Age of Global Terrorism," 2.
14. Jean-Francois Lyotard, *La Condition postmoderne: rapport sur le savoir* (France: Les Editions de Minuit); *The Postmodern Condition: A Report on Knowledge,* trans. Geoff Bennington and Brian Massumi (Minneapolis: University of Minnesota, 1984).
15. See Jürgen Habermas, trans. Seyla Ben-Habib, "Modernity versus Postmodernity," *New German Critique* No. 22 (Winter, 1981): 3-14; Jürgen Habermas, *The Structural Transformation of the Public Sphere: An Inquiry into a Category of Bourgeois Society,* trans. Thomas Burger and Frederick Lawrence (Cambridge, MA: MIT Press, 1991); Jürgen Habermas, *The Philosophical Discourse of Modernity: Twelve Lectures,* trans. Frederick G. Lawrence (Cambridge, MA: MIT Press, 1990).
16. Anthony Giddens, *The Consequences of Modernity* (Stanford: Stanford University Press, 1990), 3, 7.
17. Ibid., 37. Emphasis added.
18. Ibid., 134-137.
19. S.N. Eisenstadt, "Multiple Modernities," *Daedalus,* Vol. 1, No. 1 (Winter, 2000), 1-29, quotations from pp. 1, 2.
20. Dilip Parameshwar Gaonkar, ed., *Alternative Modernities* (Durham, NC: Duke University Press, 2001), 1.
21. Birgit Schaebler and Leif Steinberg, eds., *Globalization and the Muslim World: Culture, Religion, and Modernity* (Syracuse: Syracuse University Press, 2004), 4.
22. Richard T. Antoun and Mary Elaine Hegland, eds., *Religious Resurgence: Contemporary Cases in Islam, Christianity, and Judaism* (Syracuse: Syracuse University Press, 1987), 4.

23. Hallaq, *Impossible State*, 13.
24. Talal Asad, "The Idea of an Anthropology of Islam," Occasional Papers Series, Center for Contemporary Arab Studies (Washington, DC: Georgetown University, 2004), 13.
25. Hobsbawm and Ranger, eds., *Invention of Tradition*, 1.
26. John Micklethwait and Adrian Wooldridge, *The Fourth Revolution: The Global Race to Reinvent the State* (New York: Penguin Press, 2014), 17; John Micklethwait and Adrian Wooldridge, "Can China Best the West at Statecraft?" *Wall Street Journal*, May 16, 2014, accessed August 6, 2014, http://online.wsj.com/news/articles/SB10001424052702304547704579562230042916694.
27. Ulrich Beck, *The Reinvention of Politics: Rethinking Modernity in the Global Social Order*, trans. Mark Ritter (Cambridge: Polity Press, 1997), 6.

Afterword

1. Allal al-Fasi, *In Defense of Shari'a* (Rabat: Manshūrat al-Asr al-Hadeeth, 1972).
2. Sayyid Qutb, *Toward an Islamic Society* (Cairo: Dar al-Shuruq, 1988), 48-49.
3. Ibid., 49-50.
4. Sayyid Qutb, *History: Thought and Discourse* (Cairo: Dar al-Shuruq, 1983), 132-133.
5. Yusef al-Qaradawi, *The Islamic Awakening: Between Rejection and Extremism* (Qatar: Dar al-Umma, 1981), 60-61.
6. Ibid.
7. Yusef Qaradawi, *Islamic Shari'a: Its Applicability Regardless of Time and Place*, (Beirut: al-Maktab al-Islami, 1973), 11-12.
8. The term "conservative liberals" is meant to connote primarily the elites/intelligentsia who hold on to "western liberal" ideals, but fail to listen or accept others opinions regarding governance. i.e. they are liberal in name but do not follow one of the formative practices of liberalism: pluralism.

Bibliography

Abdelkader, Deina. *Islamic Activists: The Anti-Enlightenment Democrats.* New York: Pluto Press, 2011.
—— *Social Justice in Islam.* Herndon, VA: International Institute for Islamic Thought, 2000.
ʿAbduh, Muhammad. *The Theology of Unity.* Translated by Ishaq Musa'ad and Kenneth Cragg. Kuala Lampur: Islamic Book Trust, 2004.
Abu-Lughod, Ibrahim. "Retreat from the Secular Path? Islamic Dilemmas of Arab Politics." *The Review of Politics* 28, no. 4 (Oct. 1966), 447-476.
Abu-Rabiʿ, Ibrahim M. *Contemporary Arab Thought: Studies in Post-1967 Arab Intellectual History.* London: Pluto Press, 2004.
—— *Intellectual Origins of Islamic Resurgence in the Modern Arab World.* Albany: State University of New York Press, 1996.
—— ed. *The Blackwell Companion To Contemporary Islamic Thought.* Oxford: Blackwell Publishing, 2006.
—— *The Contemporary Arab Reader on Political Islam.* London: Pluto Press, 2010.
Al-Afghani, Jamal al-Din and Muhammad ʿAbduh. *Al-Urwa al-Wuthqa.* 2nd ed. Beirut: Dar al-Kitab al-Arabi, 1980.
Agoston, Gabor. "Military Transformation in the Ottoman Empire and Russia, 1500-1800." In *Kritika: Explorations in Russian and Eurasian History* 12, no. 2 (2011): 281-319. doi 10.1353/kri.2011.0018.
Ahmed, Jamal Mohammed. *The Intellectual Origins of Egyptian Nationalism.* London: Oxford University Press, 1960.
Al-Ahsan, Abdullah. *Ummah or Nation? Identity Crisis in Contemporary Muslim Society.* Leicester: The Islamic Foundation, 1992.
Aijaz, S. Zakir, trans. *Selected Speeches and Writings of Maulana Maududi.* Karachi: International Islamic Publishers, 1981.
Ajami, Fouad. *The Arab Predicament: Arab Political Thought and Practice since 1967.* New York: Cambridge University Press, 1992.
Akbarzadeh, Shahram and Abdullah Saeed, eds. *Islam and Political Legitimacy.* New York: RoutledgeCurzon, 2003.
Anjum, Ovamir. *Politics, Law, and Community in Islamic Thought: The Taymiyyan Moment.* New York: Cambridge University Press, 2012.

Antoun, Richard T. and Mary Elaine Hegland, eds. *Religious Resurgence: Contemporary Cases in Islam, Christianity, and Judaism.* Syracuse: Syracuse University Press, 1987.

Antoun, Richard T. *Understanding Fundamentalism: Christian, Islamic, and Jewish Movements.* Lanham, MD: Rowman & Littlefield Publishers, 2008.

Asad, Talal. *Formations of the Secular: Christianity, Islam, Modernity.* Stanford: Stanford University Press, 2003.

— "The Idea of an Anthropology of Islam." *Occasional Papers Series.* Washington, DC: Center for Contemporary Arab Studies, Georgetown University, 1986.

El-Awa, Muhamed S. *On the Political System of the Islamic State.* Translated by Ahmad Naji al-Imam. Edited by Anwer Beg. Indianapolis: American Trust Publications, 1980.

El-Awa, Mohamed Selim. "Religion and Political Structures: an Islamic Viewpoint." Occasional Paper No. 3. Birmingham: Centre for the Study of Islam and Christian Muslim Relations, 1999.

Ayubi, Nazih. *Over-Stating the Arab State: Politics and Society in the Middle East.* London: I.B. Tauris, 2009.

— *Political Islam: Religion and Politics in the Arab World.* New York: Routledge, 1991.

Al-Azmeh, Aziz. *Islams and Modernities.* 3rd ed. London: Verso, 2009.

Baker, Raymond William. *Islam Without Fear: Egypt and the New Islamists.* Cambridge, MA: Harvard University Press, 2003.

Bairoch, Paul. "International Industrialization Levels from 1750 to 1980." In *Journal of European Economic History* 11 (1982): 290-296.

Barakat, Muhammad Tawfiq. *Sayyid Qutb, khulasat hayatihi: manhajuhu fi al-harakah, al-naqd al-muwajjah ilayh.* Beirut, n.d.

Bech, Ulrich. *The Reinvention of Politics: Rethinking Modernity in the Global Social Order.* Translated by Mark Ritter. Cambridge: Polity Press, 1997.

Belkeziz, Abdelilah. *The State in Contemporary Islamic Thought: A Historical Survey of the Major Muslim Political Thinkers of the Modern Era.* Translated by Abdullah Richard Lux. New York: I.B. Tauris, 2009.

Bennabi, Malek. *Islam in History and Society.* Translated by Asma Rashid. Kuala Lumpur: Berita Publishing, 1991.

Berger, Peter L., ed. *The Desecularization of the World: Resurgent Religion and World Politics* (Washington, DC: Ethics and Policy Center, 1999).

Berkey, Jonathan. *The Formation of Islam: Religion and Society in the Near East, 600-1800.* New York: Cambridge University Press, 2003.

Bickerton, Ian J. and Carla L. Klausner. *A History of the Arab-Israeli Conflict.* 6th ed. Boston: Prentice Hall, 2010.

Brown, L. Carl. *Religion and State: The Muslim Approach to Politics.* New York: Columbia University Press, 2000.

Burke, III, Edmund. Introduction to *Rethinking world history: Essays on Europe, Islam, and World History* by Marshall G.S. Hodgson. Edited by Edmund Burke, III, ix-xxi. New York: Cambridge University Press, 1993.

Cassanova, Jose. *Public Religions in the Modern World.* Chicago: University of Chicago Press, 1994.
Crone, Patricia. *Meccan Trade and the Rise of Islam.* Princeton: Princeton University Press, 1987.
Dallal, Ahmad. "Appropriating the Past: Twentieth Century Reconstruction of Pre-Modern Islamic Thought." In *Islamic Law and Society 7*, no. 3 (October 2000): 325-358.
Dalton, Russell J. and Manfred Kuechler, eds. *Challenging the Political Order: New Social and Political Movements in Western Democracies.* New York: Oxford University Press, 1990.
Al-Din, Khayr. *The Surest Path.* Translated by Leon Carl Brown. Cambridge, MA: Harvard Center for Middle Eastern Studies, 1967.
Donner, Fred McGraw. *The Early Islamic Conquests.* Princeton: Princeton University Press, 1981.
Donohue, John J. and John L. Esposito, eds. *Islam in Transition: Muslim Perspectives.* 2nd ed. New York: Oxford University Press, 2007.
Eisenstadt, S.N. "Multiple Modernities." *Daedalus*, Vol. 1, No. 1 (Winter, 2000): 1-29.
Enayat, Hamid. *Modern Islamic Political Thought.* Austin: University of Texas Press, 1982.
Esposito, John L. *Islam and Politics.* 4th ed. Syracuse: Syracuse University Press, 1984.
—— ed. *Voices of Resurgent Islam.* New York: Oxford University Press, 1983.
Esposito, John L. and John O. Voll. *Makers of Contemporary Islam.* New York: Oxford University Press, 2001.
Euben, Roxanne L. *Enemy in the Mirror: Islamic Fundamentalism and the Limits of Modern Rationalism.* Princeton: Princeton University Press, 1999.
Euben, Roxanne L. and Muhammad Qasim Zaman, eds. *Princeton Readings in Islamist Thought: Texts and Contexts from al-Banna to Bin Laden.* Princeton: Princeton University Press, 2009.
Evans, Peter. "The Eclipse of the State? Reflections on Stateness in an Era of Globalization." *World Politics*, Vol. 50, No. 1 (October 1997): 62-87.
Filali-Ansary, Abdou. Introduction to *Islam and the Foundations of Political Power*, by Ali Abdel Razeq. Translated by Maryam Loutfi, edited by Abdou Filali-Ansari. Edinburgh: Edinburgh University Press, 1982.
Findley, Carter Vaughn. *Turkey, Islam, Nationalism, and Modernity.* New Haven: Yale University Press, 2011.
Foucault, Michel. "What is Enlightenment?" In *The Foucault Reader.* Edited by Paul Rabinow. New York: Vintage Books, 2010.
Fukuyama, Francis. *The End of History and the Last Man.* New York: The Free Press, 1992.
—— "The End of History?" *The National Interest*, Summer 1989.
Galwash, Ahmad A. *The Religion of Islam: A Standard Book*, 5th edn, Volume 1. Cairo: Imprimerie Misr, 1958.
Gaonkar, Dilip Parameshwar, ed. *Alternative Modernities.* Durham, NC: Duke University Press, 2001.

Gelvin, James L. *The Modern Middle East: A History.* 3rd ed. New York: Oxford University Press, 2011.

Ghannouchi, Rachid. "Secularism and Relation Between Religion and State from the Perspective of the Nahda Party." Lecture given at the Center for the Study of Islam and Democracy, Washington, DC, March 2, 2012.

al-Ghazali, Muhammad. *Min Huna Na'lam.* 5th printing. Cairo: Nahda Masr, 2005.

—— *Our Beginning in Wisdom.* Translated by Isma'il R. el-Faruqi. Washington, DC: American Council of Learned Societies, 1953.

al-Ghazali, Zainab. *Return of the Pharaoh: Memoir in Nasir's Prison.* Translated by Mokrane Guezzou. Leicester: The Islamic Foundation, 1994.

Gibbon, Edward. *The Decline and Fall of the Roman Empire.* Edited by J.B. Bury. Volumes V, VI. London: Methuen & Co. Ltd., 1912.

Giddens, Anthony. *The Consequences of Modernity.* Stanford: Stanford University Press, 1990.

Goldfrank, David M. *The Origins of the Crimean War.* New York: Longman Publishing, 1994.

Graf, Bettina and Jakob Skovgaard-Peterson, eds. *Global Mufti: The Phenomenon of Yusuf al-Qaradawi.* New York: Columbia University Press, 2009.

Gunning, Jeroen. *Hamas in Politics: Democracy, Religion, Violence.* New York: Cambridge University Press, 2009).

Habermas, Jürgen. "Modernity versus Postmodernity." Translated by Seyla Ben-Habib. *New German Critique* 22 (Winter, 1981): 3-14.

—— "New Social Movements." *Telos* 49 (Fall 1981): 33-37.

—— *The Philosophical Discourse of Modernity: Twelve Lectures.* Translated by Frederick G. Lawrence. Cambridge, MA: The MIT Press, 1990.

Haddad, Yvonne Y. *Contemporary Islam and the Challenge of History.* Albany: State University of New York Press, 1982.

—— "Islamists and the Challenge of Pluralism." Occasional paper. Washington, DC: Center for Contemporary Arab Studies, Georgetown University, 1995.

Hallaq, Wael. *The Impossible State: Islam, Politics, and Modernity's Moral Predicament.* New York: Columbia University Press, 2013.

Hashemi, Nader. *Islam, Secularism, and Liberal Democracy.* New York: Oxford University Press, 2009.

Hay, Stephen, ed. *Sources of Indian Tradition: Modern India and Pakistan.* Vol 2. 2nd ed. New York: Columbia University Press.

Herodotus. *History.* Translated and Edited by George Rawlinson. Volume II. London: John Murray, Albemarle Street, 1860.

Hinds, Martin. "The Murder of the Caliph 'Uthman." *International Journal of Middle East Studies,* Vol. 3, 4 (1972): 450-469.

Hodgson, Marshall. *Rethinking world history: Essays on Europe, Islam, and World History.* Edited by Edmund Burke, III. New York: Cambridge University Press, 1993.

—— *The Venture of Islam: Conscience and History in a World Civilization*. 3 vols. Chicago: University of Chicago Press, 1977.
Hofmann, Murad Wilfried. *Religion on the Rise: Islam in the Third Millennium*. Translated by Andreas Ryschka. Beltsville, MD: amana publications, 2001.
Hourani, Albert. *A History of the Arab Peoples*. Cambridge, MA: Harvard University Press, 2002.
—— *Arabic Thought in the Liberal Age: 1798 – 1939*. Cambridge: Cambridge University Press, 1983.
—— Introduction to *The Modern Middle East*, 2nd ed., by Albert Hourani, Philip Khoury and Mary C. Wilson, eds., 1-23. London: I.B. Tauris: 2011.
Hourani, Albert, Philip Khoury and Mary C. Wilson, eds. *The Modern Middle East*. 2nd ed. London: I.B. Tauris: 2011.
Howeidy, Fahmy. "Islam and democracy." *Contemporary Arab Affairs* 3:3 (2010):297-333. doi 10.1080/17550912.2010.494405.
Hoyland, Robert G. *Arabia and the Arabs: From the Bronze Age to the Coming of Islam*. New York: Routledge, 2001.
Hunter, Shireen T. and Huma Malik, eds. *Modernization, Democracy, and Islam*. Westport, CT: Praeger Publishers, 2005.
Hunter, F. Robert. *Egypt Under the Khedives, 1805-1879: From Household Government to Modern Bureaucracy*. Cairo: The American University in Cairo Press, 1999.
Hussein, Taha. *The Days*. Translated by E.H. Paxton, Hilary Wayment, and Kenneth Cragg. Cairo: American University in Cairo Press, 1997.
—— *The Future of Culture in Egypt*. Washington, DC: American Council of Learned Societies, 1954.
—— *Mustaqbal al-Thaqafa fi Misr*. 2 vols. Cairo: Matba'at al-Ma'arif wa-Maktabatuha, 1944.
Ibn Ishaq, *The Life of Muhammad: A Translation of Ishaq's Sirat Rasul Allah*. Translated by A. Guillaume. Edited by Ibn Hashim. London: Oxford University Press, 1955.
Ibn Khaldun. *The Muqaddimah*. Translated by Franz Rosenthal. Edited by N.J. Dawood. Princeton: Princeton University Press, 2005.
Imarah, Muhammad, ed. *al-A'mal al-kamilah li-Rifa'ah Rafi' al-Tahtawi*. Cairo: Dar al-Shuruq, 2010.
Israeli, Raphael, ed. *The Public Diary of President Sadat*. Part 1. Leiden: Brill Academic Publishing, 1975.
Kadafar, Cemal. "The Question of Ottoman Decline." In *Harvard Middle Eastern and Islamic Review* 4, 1-2 (1997-98): 30-75.
Kamali, Mohammad Hashim. *Principles of Islamic Jurisprudence*. Cambridge: The Islamic Texts Society, 2003.
Kant, Immanuel. "An Answer to the Question: 'What is Enlightenment?'" In *Kant: Political Writings*. Edited by Hans Reiss. Translated by H.B. Nisbet. 2nd ed. Cambridge: Cambridge University Press, 1991.
Keddie, Nikkie R. *An Islamic Response to Imperialism: Political and Religious*

Writings of Sayyid Jamal ad-Din "al-Afghani." Berkeley: University of California Press, 1968.
―― *Sayyid Jamal ad-Din "al-Afghani."* Berkeley: University of California Press, 1972.
Kennedy, Paul. *The Rise and Fall of the Great Powers.* New York: Random House, 1987.
Kenny, L.M. "Al-Afghani on Types of Despotic Government." *Journal of the American Oriental Society* 86, No. 1 (1966): 19-27.
Kepel, Gilles. "Islamism Reconsidered: A Running Dialogue with Modernity."*Harvard International Review* 22, No. 2 (Summer 2000): 22-27.
Kerr, Malcom. *Islamic Reform: The Political and Legal Theories of Muhammad ʿAbduh and Rashid Rida.* Berkeley: University of California Press, 1966.
Khalid, Muhammad Khalid. *Al-Dawla fi al-Islam.* Cairo: Dar al-Thabit, 1981.
―― *From Here We Start.* Translated by Isma'il R. el-Faruqi. Washington, DC: American Council of Learned Societies, 1953.
―― *Min Huna Nabda'.* 11th printing. Cairo: Anglo-Egyptian Bookstore, 1969.
Khalidi, Rashid and Lisa Anderson, Muhammad Muslih, Reeva Simon, eds. *The Origins of Arab Nationalism.* New York: Columbia University Press, 1993.
Khan, M.A. Muqtedar, ed. *Islamic Democratic Discourse: Theory, Debates, and Philosophical Perspectives.* Oxford: Lexington Books, 2006.
Knauft, Bruce M., ed. *Critically Modern: Alternatives, Alterities, Anthropologies.* Bloomington, IN: Indiana University Press, 2002.
Kurzman, Charles, ed. *Liberal Islam: A Sourcebook.* New York: Oxford University Press, 1998.
Kurzman, Charles, ed. *Modernist Islam: A Sourcebook.* New York: Oxford University Press, 2002.
Laquer, Walter Z., ed. *The Middle East in Transition.* New York: Frederick A. Praeger, 1958.
Laquer, Walter and Barry Rubin, eds. *The Israel-Arab Reader.* 7th ed. New York: Penguin Books, 2008.
Laroui, Abdallah. *The Crisis of the Arab Intellectual: Traditionalism or Historicism?* Translated by Diarmid Cammell. Berkeley: University of California Press, 1976.
Lawrence, Bruce B. *Defenders of God: The Fundamentalist Revolt Against the Modern Age.* New York: Harper & Row, 1989.
Lecker, Michael. *People, Tribes and Society in Arabia Around the Time of Muhammad.* Burlington, VT: Ashgate Publishing Company, 2005.
―― *The 'Constitution of Medina': Muhammad's First Legal Document.* Princeton: The Darwin Press, Inc., 2004.
Lewis, Bernard. *Islam and the West.* New York: Oxford University Press, 1993.

—— *The Emergence of Modern Turkey*. 3rd ed. New York: Oxford University Press, 2002.
—— *The Muslim Discovery of Europe*. New York: W.W. Norton, 2001.
Malek, Kamal Abdel and Mouna el-Kabla, eds. *America in an Arab Mirror: Images of America in Arabic Travel Literature, 1668 to 9/11 and Beyond*. Rev. ed. New York: Palgrave Macmillan, 2011).
Marlow, Louise. *Hierarchy and Egalitarianism in Islamic Thought*. New York: Cambridge University Press, 1997.
Marsot, Afaf Lutfi al-Sayyid. *Egypt in the Reign of Muhammad Ali*. Cambridge: Cambridge University Press, 1984.
Maudoodi, Syed Abul-Ala. *Islamic Law and Constitution*. Edited by Khurshid Ahmad. Karachi: Jamaat-e-Islami Publications, 1955.
al-Mawardi, 'Ali ibn Muhammad. *Al-Ahkam al-sultaniyyah wa-al-wilayat al-diniyah*. Edited by 'Ali ibn Muhammad ibn Habib al-Basri al-Mawardi and Muhammad Fahmi al-Sirjani. Cairo: al-Maktabah al-Tawfiqiyah, 1978.
Mawdudi, Sayyid Abul A'la'. *The Islamic Movement: Dynamics of Values, Power, and Change*. Edited and translated by Khurram Murad. Leicester: The Islamic Foundation, 1984.
McNeill, William H. *The Rise of the West: A History of the Human Community*. Chicago: University of Chicago Press, 1991.
Micklethwait, John and Adrian Wooldridge. *The Fourth Revolution: The Global Race to Reinvent the State*. New York: Penguin Press, 2014.
Mitchell, Richard P. "The Islamic Movement: Its Current Condition and Future Prospects." In *The Islamic Impulse*. Edited by Barbara Freyer Stowasser. London: Croom Helm, 1987.
—— *The Society of the Muslim Brothers*. New York: Oxford University Press, 1993.
Moaddel, Mansoor. *Islamic Modernism, Nationalism, and Fundamentalism: Episode and Discourse*. Chicago: University of Chicago Press, 2005.
Moaddel, Mansoor and Kamran Talattof, eds. *Contemporary Debates in Islam: An Anthology of Modernist and Fundamentalist Thought*. New York: St. Martin's Press, 2000.
Mottahedeh, Roy P. *Loyalty and Leadership in an Early Islamic Society*. Princeton: Princeton University Press, 1980.
Al-Mubarak, Muhammad. *Nizam al-Islam: al-Hukm wa al-Dawla*. 4th ed. Beirut: Dar al-Fikr, 1981.
Nettl, J. P. "The State as a Conceptual Variable." *World Politics*, Vol. 20, No. 4 (July, 1968): 559-592.
Osman, Fathi. "Islam in a Modern State: Democracy and the Concept of Shūra." Occasional Paper Series, Center for Muslim-Christian Understanding, Georgetown University, Washington, DC, 2001.
Owen, Roger. *State, Power and Politics in the Making of the Modern Middle East*. 3rd ed. New York: Routledge, 2004.
Owen, Roger. *The Middle East in the World Economy, 1800-1914*. New York: I.B. Tauris, 2002.

Parker, Geoffrey. *The Military Revolution: Military innovation and the rise of the West, 1500-1800.* 2nd ed. New York: Cambridge University Press, 1996.
Pipes, Daniel. "'This World is Political!' The Islamic revival of the seventies," *Orbis*, 24 (Spring 1980): 9-41.
Piscatori, James P. *Islam in a World of Nation-States.* New York: Cambridge University Press, 1986.
Al-Qaradawi, Yousuf. *Min fiqh al-dawla fi al-Islam.* Cairo: Dar al-Sharouk, 2001.
—— *al-Muslima wa'l-awlama.* Cairo: Dar al-tawzi' wa'l-nashir al-Islamiyya, 2000.
Qutb, Muhammad. *Hawl tatbiq al-Shari'a.* Cairo: Maktabat al-Sunnah, 1991.
Qutb, Sayyid. *Social Justice in Islam.* Translated by John B. Hardie. Revised by Hamid Algar. Oneonta, NY: Islamic Publications International, 2000.
Qutb, Seyyid. *Milestones.* Damascus: Dar al-Ilm, n.d.
Rahman, Fazlur. *Islam.* 2nd ed. Chicago: Chicago University Press, 1979.
—— *Major Themes of the Qur'an.* 2nd ed. Chicago: University of Chicago Press, 2009.
—— *Revival and Reform in Islam.* Edited by Ebrahim Moosa. Oxford: Oneworld Publications, 2000.
Ramadan, Tariq. *Islam, the West and the Challenges of Modernity.* Translated by Said Amghar. Leicester: The Islamic Foundation, 2004.
—— *Radical Reform: Islamic Ethics and Liberation.* Oxford: Oxford University Press, 2009.
al-Raziq, 'Ali 'Abd. *Al-Islam wa-usul al-hukm: bahth fi al-Khilafah w-al-hukumah fi al-Islam.* 3rd ed. Cairo: Matba'at Misr, 1925.
Raziq, Ali Abdel. *Islam and the Foundations of Political Power.* Edited by Abdou Filali-Ansari. Translated by Maryam Loutfi. Edinburgh: Edinburgh University Press, 2012.
Rida, Muhammad Rashid. *Al-Khilafah.* Cairo: Zahra lil-'Alam al-'Arabi, 1988.
—— *Ta'rikh al-Ustadh al-Imam al-Shaykh Muhammad 'Abduh.* Vol 2. 2nd ed. Cairo: al-Manar, 1926.
—— *Yusr al-Islam wa-usul al-tashri' al-'amm fi nahy Allah wa-Rasullhi 'an kathrat al-su'al.* Cairo: Maktabat al-Salam al-Alamiya, 1984.
Robinson, Chase. *Islamic Historiography.* Cambridge: Cambridge University Press, 2003.
Roy, Olivier. *The Failure of Political Islam.* Translated by Carol Volk. Cambridge, MA: Harvard University Press, 1994.
Rutherford, Bruce, K. *Egypt After Mubarak.* Princeton: Princeton University Press, 2008.
Ruthven, Malise. *Fundamentalism: The Search for Meaning.* Oxford: Oxford University Press, 2009.
Salame, Ghassan, ed. *The Foundations of the Arab State.* New York: Routledge, 1987.

Salim, Arskal. *Challenging the Secular State: The Islamization of Law in Modern Indonesia.* Honolulu: University of Hawai'I Press, 2008.
Al-Samman, Muhammad Abdallah. *Hasan al-Banna: al-Rajal wa al-Fikrah.* Cairo: Daral-l'tisam. 1978/1398.
Schaebler, Birgit and Leif Steinberg, eds. *Globalization and the Muslim World: Culture, Religion, and Modernity.* Syracuse: Syracuse University Press, 2004.
Scott, Rachel M. *The Challenge of Political Islam: Non-Muslims and the Egyptian State.* Stanford: Stanford University Press, 2010.
Serjeant, R.B. "The 'Sunnah Jami'ah," Pacts with the Yathrib Jews, and the 'Tahrim' of Yathrib: Analysis and Translation of the Documents Comprised in the So-Called 'Constitution of Medina.'" *Bulletin of the School of Oriental and African Studies, University of London*, Vol. 41, 1 (1978): 1-42.
Sharabi, Hisham. *Arab Intellectuals and the West: The Formative Years, 1875-1914.* Baltimore: Johns Hopkins University Press, 1970.
Shaw, Stanford J. and Ezel Kural Shaw. *History of the Ottoman Empire and Modern Turkey.* Vol 2. Cambridge: Cambridge University Press, 1977.
Sheehi, Stephen Paul. *Foundations of Modern Arab Identity.* Gainesville: University Press of Florida, 2004.
Sivan, Emmanuel. *Radical Islam: Medieval Theology and Modern Politics.* New Haven: Yale University Press, 1990.
Smith, Wilfred Cantwell. *Islam in Modern History.* Princeton: Princeton University Press, 1957.
Smith, W. Robertson. *Kinship & Marriage in Early Arabia.* Edited by Stanley A. Cook. London: Adam and Charles Black, 1903.
Stewart, Charles. *Westward Bound: Travels of Mirza Abu Taleb.* Edited by Mushirul Hasan. Translated by Charles Stewart. Oxford: Oxford University Press, 2005.
Al-Tahtawi, Rifa'a Rafi'. *Al-Murshid al-amin lil-banat wa-al-banin.* Edited by 'Imad Badr al-Din Abu Ghazi. Cairo: Majlis al-A'la lil Thaqafah, 2002.
Al-Tahtawi, Rifaa Rafi. *An Imam in Paris: Account of a Stay in France by an Egyptian Cleric (1826-1831).* Edited and translated by Daniel L. Newman. London: Saqi Books,2004.
Al-Tahtawi, Rifa'ah Badawi Rafi'. *Takhlis al-ibriz fi talkhis Bariz.* Cairo: Dar al-Kutub, 2005.
Tamimi, Azzam. "Islam and Democracy from Tahtawi to Ghannouchi." *Theory, Culture & Society* 24 (2007): 39-58. doi: 10.1177/02632706407074994.
—— *Rachid Ghannouchi.* New York: Oxford University Press, 2001.
Tibi, Bassam. *Arab Nationalism: Between Islam and the Nation-State.* 3rd ed. New York: St. Martin's Press, 1997.
Tignor, Robert L., ed. *Napoleon in Egypt; al-Jabarti's Chronicle of the French Occupation, 1798.* Translated by Shmuel Moreh. Expanded ed. Princeton: Markus Wiener Publishers, 2006.
Tilly, Charles, ed. *The Formation of National States in Western Europe.* Princeton: Princeton University Press, 1975.

Al-Tunisi, Khayr al-Din. *Aqwam al-masalik fi ma'rifat ahwal al-Mamali.* Edited by Monsef al-Shannufi. Vol 1. Tunis: Bayt al-Hikmah, 2000.
Turabi, Hasan. "Islam, Democracy, the State and the West." Edited by Arthur L. Lowrie. Lecture given at the University of South Florida, Tampa, Florida, May 10, 1992.
Vatikiotis, P.J. *The History of Egypt.* 2nd ed. Baltimore: The Johns Hopkins University Press, 1980.
Voll, John O. "Alternative Modernities: Modernized Muslims and Islamized Modernities." Paper presented at the World History Association Meeting, 26 June 2009.
—— "Bin Laden and the New Age of Global Terrorism." *Middle East Policy,* Vol. VIII, No. 4 (December 2001). doi 10.1111/j.1475-4967.2001.tb00001.x.
—— Foreword to *The Society of the Muslim Brothers,* by Richard P. Mitchell, vii-xxii. New York: Oxford University Press, 1993.
—— *Islam: Continuity and Change in the Modern World.* 2nd ed. Syracuse: Syracuse University Press, 1994.
—— "Islamic Renewal and the 'failure of the West'." In *Decolonization: Perspectives from Now and Then,* edited by Prasenjit Duara, 199-217. New York: Routledge, 2003.
—— "Political Islam and the State." In *The Oxford Handbook of Islam and Politics,* edited by John L. Esposito and Emad el-Din Shahin, 56-67. New York: Oxford University Press, 2013.
Wahba, Wafaa H, trans. *The ordinances of government: a translation of Al-Ahkam al-Sultaniyya w' al-Wilayat al-Diniyya of al-Mawardi.* London: Garnet Publishing Limited, 1996.
Wallerstein, Immanuel. *World-Systems Analysis: An Introduction.* Durham, NC: Duke University Press, 2004.
Weber, Max. *The Protestant Ethic and the Spirit of Capitalism.* Edited and translated by Stephen Kalberg. Rev. ed. New York: Oxford University Press, 2011.
—— *The Sociology of Religion.* Translated by Ephraim Fischoff. Boston: Beacon Press, 1991.
Wickham, Carrie Rosefsky. *Mobilizing Islam: Religion, Activism and Political Change in Egypt.* New York: Columbia University Press, 2002.
Yassine, Nadia. *Full Sails Ahead.* Translated by Farouk Bouasse. Iowa City, IA: Justice and Spirituality Publishing, 2006.
Yergin, Daniel. *The Prize: The Epic Quest for Oil, Money and Power.* New York: Free Press, 2009.
Zaman, Muhammad Qasim. *Modern Islamic Thought in a Radical Age: Religious Authority and Internal Criticism.* New York: Cambridge University Press, 2012.

Index

Note: Readers are encouraged to also consult the glossary.

al-'Aas, Sa'id ibn 152
Abbas I (Shah) 3
Abbasid dynasty 11, 152
Abdelkader, Deina 103, 159, 169–74
'Abduh, Muhammad 51–57, 73, 163; biographer of 70; consultation with community 117; and fundamentalist-style mode of renewal and reform 77; influence on Hussein 65; and modernist mode of renewal and reform 16
Abdulhamid II (Sultan) 50, 51
"Abode of Sorrows" (al-Afghani) 47
al-Abras, 'Abid ibn 135
absolutism. *See* despotism and absolutism
Abu Bakr 144, 149–51. *See also* caliphate; Ottoman Empire
Abu-Lughod, Ibrahim 16
Abu-Rabi', Ibrahim M.: Arab intellectuals and crisis 8; and concept of Political Islam 33, 183n32; impact of Napolean's invasion of Egypt 11; Islamist movement 87–88; and Muslim attitudes toward the West 14; on Qaradawi's vision 108

al-Afghani, Jamal al-Din 46–51, 163; conceptualization of Islam 24–25; criticism of 190n40; and fundamentalist-style mode of renewal and reform 77; influence on Rida 70; and modernist mode of renewal and reform 16; strength and unity of the *umma* 52
Agarthicides of Cnidus 139–40
al-Ahkam al-Sultaniyya (al-Mawardi) 58
Ahmad, Khurshid 35, 96, 160
al-Ahsan, Abdullah 59
Ajami, Fouad xiii, 26
Akbar (Babur's grandson) 3
'Ali, Ben (president of Tunisia) xiii, 99
'Ali, Muhammad 37–39, 41, 45
Alternative Modernities (Gaonkar) 164
"The America I Have Seen" (Qutb) 89
Americans. *See* United States
Anglo-Egyptian Treaty of 1936 66
Anjum, Ovamir 143
Antoun, Richard 165
Anwar, Zainah 106
al-'Aqqad, Abbas Mahmud 122
Aqwam al-masalik fi ma'rifat ahwal al-Mamalik (Khayr al-Din) 42–43
Arab cultural achievements 3–4, 30, 48, 141

Arab League Summit (1964) 87
Arab nationalism xiii, 62–64, 195n71; criticism of 70–71, 73, 94; decline of 87; Pan-Arabism xiii, 64, 65, 87; and Young Turks movement 60–61. *See also* nation-states; Pan-Islamic unity; patriotism and love of country
Arab revolt (1936–1939) 82. *See also* Arab Spring; Arab-Israeli wars
Arab Spring xii–xiii, 21, 169. *See also* Arab revolt
Arab tribal society 136–43; and group feeling 136–37; nepotism in 151; political authority in 138–43. *See also* social contract
Arabia and the Arabs (Hoyland) 138–39
Arab-Israeli wars 83, 84–85, 201n141. *See also* Arab revolt; war with Russia; world wars
Arkoun, Mohammad 195n71
Arslan, Amir Shakib 63
art and culture. *See* Arab cultural achievements
Asad, Talal 165
Asfaruddin, Asma 111–12, 113
asymmetric development and modernization 1–11; concept of decline 4–7; emergence of Muslim nation-states 59; and industrialization 7–8, 10; of Muslim society 158; and Napoleon's invasion of Egypt 11; prosperity of House of Islam 3–4; rise of Western naval power 35–36; of the *umma* 8–10, 13, 162–63. *See also* crisis of Muslim intellectuals; renewal and reform; *individual modes of renewal and reform*

Ataturk, Mustafa Kemal 61, 63, 70, 75
el-Awa, Muhammad Salim: political authority 139; political parties 128–30; *shūra* as binding 120, 121, 122, 149, 150, 208n102
Ayubi, Nazih 20, 58
al-Azhar education 38, 39, 41, 65
"al-Azhar Official Organ" (periodical) xix
al-Azm, Sadeq 201n141
al-Azmeh, Aziz 22, 24, 25, 122

Baathism 158
Babur (King of Kabul) 3
al-Baghdadi, Abu Bakr xxi, 169
Bairoch, Paul 7, 182n15
al-Banna, Hasan 20, 74–78, 159; and conceptualization of Islamic state 73, 98; death of 92, 99; and imperialism 82–83; and Muslim Women's Association 106; on political parties 127
Barakat, Muhammad Tawfiq 88
bayʿa (oath of allegiance) 126–27, 165; *bayʿa* of al-'Aqaba 146; Caliph al-Muqtadar's letter 153; foundation of Medinan governance 143; in pre-Islamic Arab society 140–41, 142; reinvention of 22, 160; successor to the Prophet 149. *See also shūra*
The Beacon (Rida) 70
Beck, Ulrich 167
Belkeziz, Abdelilah 98
Ben Bella, deposition of 87
Ben-Gurion, David 83
Bennabi, Malek 8–9, 10
Berger, Peter xii, 161
Berkey, Jonathan 137

Bhutto, Benazir (prime minister of Pakistan) 106
binary of Islam and the West xi, xxii, 23, 56–57, 169
Bonaparte, Napoleon. *See* Napoleon's invasion of Egypt
Bourguiba, Habib (president of Tunisia) 99
British control of Muslim territories 45, 56, 66
British role in spreading modernity 26–27
Brown, L. Carl 62
Bulaç, Ali 146, 147–48
Burke, Edmund, III 28
Burnt Notion (poem) 23
al-Bustani, Butrus 63
Byzantine Empire, destruction of 12

caliphate: conception of 149–55; consensus of the community 110–11; dismissal of governors 152; dissolution of 13, 17, 57, 59, 60; responsibility of 58. *See also* Abu Bakr; Ottoman Empire; Umayyad empire
The Caliphate (Rida) 70
capitalism 18, 30, 31. *See also* economic dominance; Western hegemony
Casanova, José 160–61
clergy in Islam 125–26, 210n136
colonialism: colonizability 1, 8–9, 11, 70; and nationalism 67, 71. *See also* Western domination
communism 18, 19, 77–78, 94
community. *See* asymmetric development and modernization; *bayʿa*; crisis of Muslim intellectuals; decline of the *umma*; *dīn wa dawla*;

ḥisba; Islamic state; leadership; Muslim evaluation of the West; nation-states; Political Islam; popular vicegerency; Prophet at Medina; reinvention of Islamic thought; renewal and reform; *shūra*; sovereignty; unitary linear model of development; *individual modes of renewal and reform*
La condition postmoderne: rapport sur le savoir (Lyotard) 162
consensus. *See* democracy; *ijmāʿ*; political authority
The Consequences of Modernity (Giddens) 162
Constitution of Medina 147–48
consultation. *See shūra*
contracts and contractual authority: as basis for governance 44, 49–50, 51, 59; and caliphate 150, 153; Constitution of Medina 147–48; divine contract 131–33; and the Prophet's flight from Mecca 143; in tribal society 138, 140–42; vision of Islamic government 44. *See also* political authority; social contract
countermodernity 28, 31. *See also* Islamic countermodernity
Crimean Tatars and first non-Muslim control over Muslim people 5
crisis of Muslim intellectuals 1–10; critique of the West 1–2; and decline of Ottoman Empire 4–7, 9–10; malaise of modern Islam 13; and prosperity of the House of Islam 3–4; role of rise of industrialism 7–8; success

of Political Islam xxi, xxiii; tradition v. modernity 8–9. *See also* asymmetric development and modernization; renewal and reform
The Crisis of the Arab Intellectual (Laroui) 9
critical interpretation of Islam 53–56
Crone, Patricia 144–45
Crusades 11
cultural revolution (China) 94

dar al-Islam (House of Islam): and caliphs 58; and Crusades 11; prosperity of 3–4
dawla (state): reinvention of 58; shift from *umma* 17, 57–58, 62, 73, 158–59. *See also dīn wa dawla*
Dawn, C. Ernest 63, 193n64
The Decline and Fall of the Roman Empire (Gibbon) 137
decline of the *umma* 5, 68–69, 119, 148, 152
Defenders of God (Lawrence) 31, 32
de-legitimization of Islamist efforts 173
democracy 87; and consensus of the community 110–11, 172, 173; defined 209n128; "divine democratic government" 109; as fundamentally Islamic xx, xxii, 122–24, 164; issues for Islamic scholars 173; Nabataean kingship 140; Political Islam as challenge to 157; principles of Islamic political system xix, 130; and religious activism 161, 167, 210n130; and secularism 124–25. *See also* freedom; political participation; representative government; separation of "church" and state
Democracy in Islam (al-'Aqqad) 122
"Despotic Government" (essay) 50–51
despotism and absolutism xix; al-Afghani critique 50–51; of Ali''s government 41; as antithetical to Islamic government 101; and colonialism 64, 67–68; evils of 49–51, 52–53, 55–56, 95–96; liberation from 36–37; military enforcement of 87; Muslim resistance to xix, xx, xxi; and neglect of *shūra* 117, 119; opposition to 99–100, 106; and political diversity 129; in post-Medinan period 152; in pre-Islamic Arab society 140; Qur'anic verse 4:59 112–14. *See also* renewal and reform
dīn wa dawla (religion and state) 75–76, 159; characteristic of Islamic state 97–100; debate 61–62, 67, 68. *See also dawla*; Islamic state; religion
divine contract 131–33
domestic imperialism. *See* decline of the *umma*
domination-subordination. *See* binary of Islam and the West; colonialism; *ijmā*; Western domination; Western hegemony
Donner, Fred 137, 138

"the Eastern Question" 5–6, 31, 181n10
economic dominance: Arab oil embargoes 84–85, 158; and moral corruption 54; Muslim trade routes and expansion 3; third caliphate 151;

Western 2, 5–8, 12, 38, 163.
See also capitalism; Western
domination; Western hegemony
Egypt: and de-legitimization
of reform efforts 173; and
drive toward modernity
37–39; imitative renewal in 72;
Islamization of 74–78, 92; and
nationalism 64, 65, 66, 68, 76;
need for social transformation
91–92; and Pan-Arab
reawakening xiii; and President
al-Nasir 17, 84, 87, 96, 158, 163;
Westernization of 45, 74, 88
Eisenstadt, Shmuel 164
Eliot, T.S. 23
Enayat, Hamid 71–72, 73, 83
The End of History and the Last Man
(Fukuyama) 157
Engineer, Ashgar Ali 148, 150–51,
152
"Enlightenment complex" 173
Ennahda ("Renaissance") 99
*L'Esprit des lois: l'amour de la patrie
conduit à la bonté des moeurs*
(Montesquieu) 39
Euben, Roxanne 88–89
Europe Through Arab Eyes (Matar)
15
European power, rise of 2, 5–8, 10.
See also Western domination;
Western hegemony
extremism xiv, 33, 171, 172, 173.
See also al-Qa'ida; ISIS; militant
activists

The Failure of Political Islam (Roy)
21
failure of the West and modernity
14, 19, 35, 77, 158–59;
countermodernity 130; and

discriminatory reading of
Islamic history 153–54; Islamic
modernity 14, 19, 33, 77–78,
158–59; and militarism 89–90;
and Political Islam 96–97, 164;
Qutb's indictment 89–90, 93–
94; religious primitivism 90–91;
role of Maryam Jameelah 106
"Fanaticism" (al-Afghani) 52
al-Fanjari, Ahmad Shawqi xx
Faruq I, King, message to 78
al-Fasi, Allal 170
Fi zilal al-Qur'an (Qutb) 92
Filali-Ansary, Abdou 62
fiqh (jurisprudence) 170, 172
Foucault, Michel 27–28, 29
Foucaultian analysis 32, 33
*The Fourth Revolution: The
Global Race to Reinvent the
State* (Micklethwait and
Wooldridge) 166
freedom xx; as justice 204n45; in
pre-Islamic Arab society 136,
139; in the Prophet's Medina
145; as required by Islam 36,
95–96, 100–103; Tahtawi's
description of 41. See also
democracy; social justice
French control of Muslim
territories 45, 56
French role in spreading
modernity 26–27, 36, 42. See
also Napoleon's invasion of
Egypt
From Here We Learn (al-Ghazali) 68
From Here We Start (Khalid) 67–68
Fukuyama, Francis 157, 160
Full Sails Ahead (Yassine) 119,
153–54, 212n28
fundamentalism, relationship to
modernity 31–33

fundamentalist-style mode of renewal and reform 14, 68–74; and changes in Arab world 81, 87; emergence of 17–19, 57; intellectual foundations of 20–21; and Islamic countermodernity 96; Qutb's place in 95; split from Islamic Modernism 63; success of 32–33; transition to Political Islam 76–77, 158–59, 160, 163–64. *See also* renewal and reform; *other individual modes of renewal and reform*

The Future of Culture in Egypt (Hussein) 66, 67

Gaonkar, Dilip Parameshwar 164
Gause, Gregory xiii
geopolitical power, shifts in 1–2, 8
Ghanim, Khalil 62–63
al-Ghannouchi, Rachid xxi; democracy 123–24; Islamic state 99; and "Islamic Tendency Movement" 99; political power 115; secularism 125; and social contract 34
al-Ghazali, Muhammad 68–69, 85–86
al-Ghazali, Zainab 93, 100, 106
al-Ghazzali, Abu Hamid 70
Gibbon, Edward 137, 139, 140–41, 146, 151
Giddens, Anthony 162–63
Goldfrank, David 6
Great Powers 5, 6
"Great Western Transmutation" (GWT) 28–30
group feeling (*asabiyya*) 137
Guillaume, Alfred 149
Guizot, François 47
Gunning, Jeroen 131–32

Habermas, Jürgen 162
Habib, Kemal al-Sa'id 22
Haddad, Yvonne 18, 83, 84, 92
hākimiyya (God's sovereignty on Earth): and the Islamic state 101–4; and social contract 131–32; types of 108–9. *See also* Islamic state; social contract; sovereignty
Hallaq, Wael 159, 165
Hamas 106, 107, 131. *See also* Muslim Brotherhood
Harakat al-ittijah al-islami (founded by Ghannouchi) 99
Hashemi, Nader 161, 210n130
Hasina, Sheikh (prime minister of Bangladesh) 106
Hay, Stephen 15
head of state. *See* political authority
Herodotus 141
Hinds, Martin 151
ḥisba (promotion of good, prevention of evil) 115–17, 172. *See also* political participation; *shari'a*; *shūra*
historical time, quickening of 30–31
History: Thought and Discourse (Qutb) 170–71
Hizb al-Umma (political party) 64
Hobbes, Thomas 22, 34, 159
Hobsbawm, Eric 20, 166
Hodgson, Marshall: Ataturk modernizers 61; European power 5; Isma'il policies 45; labels in world historical analyses 24, 25; modernity 28–29, 30, 31; Muslim culture 4; pre-Islamic concepts and Islam 142
Hodgsonian analysis 33

Hoffman, Murad Wilfried 1, 131–33
holistic view of Islam. *See* Islam as comprehensive world view; Islam as religion or state
The Honest Guide for Girls and Boys (al-Tahtawi) 39–40
Hourani, Albert: Arab nationalism 64; changing Middle East 12; "destiny of the mind" 65; Islam and modern thought 53–54; Ottomans 5, 6–7, 180n8; al-Raziq's goals 61; on Tahtawi 39; Tanzimat reforms 44–45
House of Islam. *See* dar al-Islam
Howeidy, Fahmy: Islam and democracy 120–21, 122–23, 124, 130; *shūra* and ruling 118–21; social contract 34; *tawhid* and freedom 204n45; trusteeship of the *umma* 111–12
Hoyland, Robert 138–39, 141
al-Hudaybi, Hassan 93, 172
al-Hukumah al-Istibdadiyah (essay) 50–51
human agency on Earth. *See* "popular vicegerency"
human rights 172, 211n149. *See also* social justice
Hussein, Taha 64–67

Ibn Hashim 145–46
Ibn Ishaq: Constitution of Medina 146–47; dissent in Mecca 143–45; successor to the Prophet 149–50
Ibn Khaldun 137
Ibn Taymiyya 11, 70, 113, 114
Ibrahim, Anwar 106
Ibrahim, Nurul 106
ijmā' (consensus) 172; function in Islamic state 128–29; and nepotism 151; in pre-Islamic history 140, 142, 143, 149, 150–52; reinvention of 22, 160, 165. *See also ḥisba*; political authority; *shari'a*; *shūra*
An Imam in Paris: Account of a Stay in France by an Egyptian Cleric (al-Tahtawi) 39
importance of to Khayr al-Din 44
imprisonment and shaping of political philosophies 92, 99–100
In the Shade of the Qur'an (Qutb) 92, 93
India 3, 45, 78, 79
industrialization 7–8. *See also* economic dominance; Western domination
Inglehart, Ronald 162
The Interpreter of the Qur'an (Mawdudi, publisher) 79
invented traditions. *See* reinvention in Islamic thought
The Invention of Tradition (Hobsbawm and Ranger) 166
Iqbal, Muhammad 196n84
Iran, Islamic Revolution in 86
Iran, rule of clerics 125, 126
ISIS (the "Islamic State") xxi, 169, 170, 173. *See also* extremism; militant activists
Islah (political party) 106
Islam and Modernities (al-Azmeh) 24
Islam and the Foundations of Political Power (al-Raziq) 61–62
Islam and the West. *See* binary of Islam and the West; colonialism; renewal and reform
Islam and the World 9
Islam as civilization 47–48

Islam as comprehensive world view xi, xix, 19–20, 69, 75–78, 84
Islam as religion or state xi, 61–62, 75–76. *See also dīn wa dawla*; separation of "church" and state
Islam in History and Society (Bennabi) 8–9
Islambouli, Khalid 20
Islamic activism 166–67; contributions to modern Islamic political thought xx–xxii, 13, 16, 19, 21–22, 33–34; and gender 105–6; role of modernity and countermodernity 28; social justice 159. *See also* extremism; militant activists; *individual modes of renewal and reform*
Islamic countermodernity 32–33, 81–82, 159, 160; and discriminatory reading of Islamic history 154–55; intellectual framework for 94, 96; and Islamic state 97, 123, 130, 165; Muslim Brotherhood 77; and Political Islam 164, 165; as true countermodernity 108. *See also* countermodernity; Islamic state; Islam's compatibility with modernity; modernity; Muslim Brotherhood
Islamic Group. *See Jama' at-i Islami*
Islamic history as unrelieved autocracy xix
Islamic Modernism. *See* modernist mode of renewal and reform
Islamic Modernism, Nationalism, and Fundamentalism (Moaddel) 14
Islamic morality 80, 97, 119, 125, 154. *See also* moral practice, revival of; religion

"Islamic resurgence" 214n5
Islamic Society. *See Jama'at-i Islami*
Islamic state 33, 159; concept and importance of 20, 73, 96, 98–99, 108; consensus of the community 128–29; Constitution of Medina 148; countermodernity 130; and democracy 122; establishment of 21, 80, 159, 165, 203n30; and example of Israel 82–86; non-Muslims in 206n80; and religion 126; as social contract xx, 22; sovereignty 104; and the *umma* 110–11. *See also dīn wa dawla*; *hākimiyya*; Islamic countermodernity; Political Islam; religion; social contract; sovereignty
the "Islamic State." *see* ISIS
"Islamic Tendency Movement" 99
Islamic unity. *See* Muslim solidarity; Pan-Islamic unity; *tawhid*
"Islamic Unity" ('Abduh and al-Afghani) 53
Islamically-oriented adaptation 14, 37, 56–57
Islamism, Weberian concept of 99
Islam's compatibility with modernity xiv, 48, 70, 82. *See also* science and rationality
Ismail I 3
Isma'il (Khedive) 45
Isma'iliyya and evils of Western influence 74–75
Israel: as alternative to Western modernity 19; control of Jerusalem 84; establishment and Islamist cause 82–83, 85–86; success of 158. *See also* Jewish immigration

Index   235

Jaamat-e-Islami, women in 106
al-Jabarti 15, 35, 37
jahaliyya (age of ignorance) 20, 93, 95, 141–42
Jamaaʿat al-Sayyidaat al-Muslimaat (Muslim Women's Association) 106
Jamaʿat-i Islami (Islamic Society) 80–82
Jameelah, Maryam 106
al-Jamiʿ at (periodical) 79
Jamʿiyyat al-ʿUlama-yi-Hind (organization) 79
al-Jaridah (newspaper) 64
Jerusalem, Israeli control of 84
Jewish immigration, impact on Qutb 88
Jewish tribes in Medina 10–11, 144–45, 146, 147, 148, 212n35
al-Jisr, Shaykh Husayn Abu 69
jurisprudence. See fiqh; shariʿa
Justice and Spirituality Association 106

Kant, Immanuel 27
Karman, Tawakkol 106
Kathir, Ibn 113
Keddie, Nikkie R. 49, 52, 189n29
Kemal, Mustafa 60
Kemal, Namik 189n29
Kennedy, Paul 2, 8
Kenny, L.M. 51
Kepel, Gilles 21
Khalid, Khalid Muhammad 67–68
Khan, Abu Taleb 1–2, 15
Khan, Sayyid Ahmad 46
Khayr al-Din Pasha 42–46, 49–50, 53, 159
Kipling, Rudyard 25
Kissinger, Henry 19, 84, 85
Korany, Baghat 59
Kurzman, Charles 16, 61

labeling of historical concepts 23–34; "the Eastern Question" 31; fundamentalism 31–32; "Great Western Transmutation" (GWT) 28–30; Islam and its variants 24–25, 33–34; "modernity" 26–33; nation-states 26; social contract 34; "sons of the East" 25; "technicalism" 28, 29–30; "the West" 24, 25–27, 30–31. See also renewal and reform
Laroui, Abdallah 9, 10
Lawrence, Bruce 31, 32
leadership 58; and divine guidance 80; failure of 88; and improving condition of the umma 43; and Islam's role 82, 91, 94. See also political authority
Lecker, Michael 147
legislative sovereignty 109, 111
Lewis, Bernard xix, 26, 40–41, 182n13
The Lighthouse (Rida) 70
Locke, John 22, 34
love of country. See patriotism and love of country
loyalty. See Arab nationalism; patriotism and love of country
loyalty, reinvention of 59
Loyalty and Leadership in Early Islamic Society (Mottahadeh) 152–53
Lyotard, Jean-François 162

Maʿalim fi al-Tariq (Qutb) 92
Mabruk, Muhammad Ibrahim 98–99
Magharibi 15
Magritte, René 23
Mamluk dynasty 36–37

Manahij al-albab al-misriyya fi mabahij al-adab al-'asriyya (al-Tahtawi) 39–40, 40–41
al-Manar (Rida) 70
maslaha (public interest) 22, 44, 111. *See also ḥisba; ijmā*
Masmoudi, Radwan 87
Matar, Nabil 15, 26
al-Mawardi 58, 113
Mawdudi, Sayyid Abu'l-A'la 74, 79–83, 96, 159; consultation with community 117; democracy 122, 124; human agency on Earth 104; imprisonment of 99; Islamic state 98, 126; Medinan period 135; modern legislature 118; political parties 128; "popular vicegerency" 108; and Qaradawi 107, 109, 110; Qur'anic verse 4:59 114; sovereignty 102, 131
Mecca and birth of Islam 137–38
media accounts of Political Islam movement xii, 21, 169
Medina. *See* Medinan period; Prophet at Medina
Medinan period: conceptual foundation of community xi, 143; as model xiii, 135–36. *See also* Constitution of Medina; Islam as comprehensive world view; Prophet at Medina
Micklethwaite, John 166–67
Milestones, Milestones Along the Way (Qutb) 92, 93, 102–3, 110, 154
militant activists xii, xiv, xxi, 33, 88, 169. *See also* extremism; Hamas; ISIS; Islamic activism
Mitchell, Richard P. 77
Moadddel, Mansoor 14
al-Modallal, Isra 106

modern critical scholarship, suspicion of 65–66
The Modern Middle East (Hourani) 12
modernist mode of renewal and reform 14, 46–60, 158, 163, 196n84; call for Pan-Islamic unity 46–48, 52; and critical interpretation of Islam 53–57; emergence of nationalism 63; emergence of Political Islam 117; evils of despotism 49–51; and fit with Western intellectual hegemony 16–17; influence on Hussein 65; and Islamic civilization 47–48; revival of the *umma* 51–53, 54, 56; and transition to fundamentalism 77; in the twentieth century 191n54. *See also* renewal and reform; *other individual modes of renewal and reform*
modernity: Lawrence's definition of 31; Qutb's disavowal of 96; as world view 24, 27–28. *See also* countermodernity; Islamic countermodernity; Islam's compatibility with modernity
modernization. *See* asymmetric development and modernization
modernization and unitary linear model of development 8, 14, 17, 29
Moghul Empire 3–4, 12
Mongol invasions 11
Montesquieu 39
moral authority 112, 113, 115
moral practice, revival of 52, 53, 54, 64, 89, 165. *See also* Islamic morality

morality. *See* Islamic morality; moral authority; moral practice, revival of
Morocco 15
Mottahadeh, Roy 152–53
Mubarak, Hosni (president of Egypt) xiii
al-Mubarak, Muhammad 98–99
Muqaddimah (Ibn Khaldun) 137
al-Muqtadar, Caliph 152–53
al-Murshid al-amin li'l-banat wa'l-banin (al-Tahtawi) 39–40, 41
Muslim Brotherhood 20, 73, 75–77, 95, 172. *See also* Hamas; Qutb, Sayyid
"Muslim Decadence and Revival" (Nadwi) 9
Muslim declaration of faith. *See shahada*
Muslim evaluation of the West 10–23; attitude of apathy 14–16; discriminatory evaluations 17–19; domination by the West 11–13; emergence of Political Islam 19–23; and renewal of the *umma* 10–11. *See also* crisis of Muslim intellectuals
Muslim history, discriminatory reading of 153–54, 159–60, 166
Muslim identity, primacy of Islam 65, 86, 98. *See also* national identity as framed by religious heritage
Muslim society: degradation of 9–10, 69, 81–82; failure of community 47–48, 51–52, 54–55, 94–95; restructuring of 96; social organization in 138, 140–43; and subordination of faith 72, 74. *See also* decline of the *umma*

Muslim solidarity 46–47, 49, 52, 71, 73. *See also* Pan-Islamic unity
Muslim Women's Association 106
Mu'tazila philosophy 53–54
Nadwi, Sayyid Abu'l Hasan 'Ali 9–10
Nahda 173
Nahnah, Shaykh Mahfoudh 131–33
Napoleon's invasion of Egypt: and modern Middle East 11–13; and Muslim apathy 15–16; opening of reform initiatives 38–39; and Western hegemony 35–37. *See also* French role in spreading modernity; Tanzimat mode of renewal and reform
al-Nasir, Jamal 'Abd (president of Egypt) 17, 84, 87, 96, 163
Nasirism 158
"The Nation and the Authority of the Despotic Ruler" ('Abduh and al-Afghani) 53
national identity as framed by religious heritage 85–86. *See also* Muslim identity
nationalism: and fundamentalist attitudes 19; and Mawdudi 79. *See also* Arab nationalism; *din wa dawla*; fundamentalist-style mode of renewal and reform; secular-nationalist mode of renewal and reform
nation-states: as alien to Muslim experience 26, 40, 57–60, 62; imposition of 13, 17, 135; Islamic activism and 21, 166; role of Islam in 61, 73; Turkey 183n29. *See also* Arab nationalism; Pan-Islamic unity; patriotism and love of country

nepotism of the third caliphate 151
Nicholas I (emperor of Russia) 5–6

oath of allegiance. *See bay'a*
oil embargoes 19, 84–85, 158. *See also* vulnerability of the West
On Pre-Islamic Poetry (Hussein) 65
On the Political System of the Islamic State (el-Awa) 117
oneness of God. *See tawhid*
opposition as theme in Political Islam 99–100
oriental despotism 169
Osman, Fathi: *bay'a* and the caliphate 149; clergy 125–26; political parties 129, 211n149; Qur'anic verse 4:59 114, 115; *shūra* and ruling 116, 118–19, 127
Ottoman Empire: and caliphate 11, 59; decline and collapse of 5–7, 9–10, 42, 59, 62, 180n8; and despotism 25, 48–51; European penetration of 46, 188n8; as European-type state 58, 72; failure to defend Egypt 16, 35–36; as "Great Power" 2–3; military of 3, 6–7, 12, 182n13, 187n1; and reform 12, 37–39, 42–46, 63. *See also* caliphate; Tanzimat mode of renewal and reform; Young Turks
Our Beginning in Wisdom (al-Ghazali) 68, 69
Owen, Roger 38

Pakistan 26, 80
Palestine 26; Jewish immigration 88; leftist groups 158
Pan-Islamic unity 52, 189n29; appeal for 46–47; transition to nationalism 64; used by despots 50. *See also* Arab nationalism; nation-states; patriotism and love of country; *tawhid*
Parker, Geoffrey 35, 187n1
Party of the Nation (Egypt) 64
Pasha, Midhat 50
The Paths of Egyptian Hearts in the Joys of Contemporary Arts (al-Tahtawi) 39–40
patriotism and love of country 39–42. *See also* Arab nationalism; nationalism; nation-states; Pan-Islamic unity; *watan*
The People's Party (Egypt) 64
pluralism *(ta'adudiyya)* 22, 128–30, 206n80, 216n8. *See also* tolerance of all faiths
political authority: in an Islamic state xx, 103–4; in Arab tribal society 138–43; and Caliph al-Muqtadar's letter 153; deriving from the community 109–11, 116–17; jurisprudence and creed 98; natural limits on 101–2; Prophet's vision of 111–15; right to depose rulers 53, 109; rulers' relationship to community 44; and selection of rulers 122, 127, 148. *See also* contracts and contractual authority; *ijmā;* leadership; representative government
Political Islam: al-Banna's role in 74–78; borrowing from European liberal philosophy 22–23; and discriminatory reading of Islamic history 154–55; emergence and conceptualization of 19–23, 32–34, 96–98, 159; father of 74; Mawdudi's role in 79–82; as

modernity in the global Muslim community xi; opposition as theme 99–100; as rejection of modernity 164. *See also* fundamentalist-style mode of renewal and reform; Islamic state; Islam's compatibility with modernity; Political Islamists; reinvention in Islamic thought
Political Islamists: defined xx–xxii, 19, 33–34; *vs. takfiri* militants xxi; view of Islamic sociopolitical organization 19–20. *See also* Political Islam
political participation 39, 99, 101, 127–29, 211n149. *See also* democracy; *hisba*; representative government; *shūra; shūracracy*
political parties. *See* democracy; political participation
"popular vicegerency" 104–11; consensus of the community 104–5, 109–11; head of state 107; Islamic state as civil state 108–9; role of women 105–6
The Postmodern Condition: A Report on Knowledge (Lyotard) 162
postmodernism 27–28, 162, 164, 167
power. *See* asymmetric development and modernization; European power, rise of; geopolitical power, shifts in; Great Powers; Muslim power and prosperity; political authority; Western domination
pre-Islamic Arabic thought. *See* Arab tribal society
Principles of Government (al-Mawardi) 58

Prophet at Medina 138; choice of successor 149–50; concept of Islamic state 20; consensus of the community 128; flight from Mecca 143–45; *hisba* and *shūra* 115, 116, 118, 119; as ideal model xiii, xxi; Islam revealed as civilization 54; and patriotism 40; and political system at Medina 145–48; Qur'anic verse 4:59 112–13, 114, 115; reform of the *umma* 10; unity under xi, 62. *See also* Medinan period
The Protestant Ethic and the Spirit of Capitalism (Weber) 27
Protestantism 27, 31–32
public interest. *See maslaha*
Public Religions in the Modern World (Casanova) 160–61

Qabbani, Nizar 201n41
Qaddafi, Muammar (colonel, of Libya) xiii
al-Qaʿida 32, 33, 170, 173. *See also* extremism; militant activists
al-Qaradawi, Yousuf xx; and democracy 124; Islamic extremism 171; Islamic state 126–27; as Islamist 205n65; opposition to despotism 99–100; political parties 127, 128; rulers and the community 112, 116, 121–22, 150; and secularism 124–25; *shūra* as binding 117–18; and the social contract 34; sovereignty and the state 108–10, 111; and transformation of Muslim society 107–8
Queen of Sheba 142

Qur'anic verses: conception of the community 116–17; consent of the governed 105; contracts and obligations 132; diversity 129–30, 206n80; obligation to question rulers 121; Qur'anic verse 3:104 129; Qur'anic verse 4:59 111–15; *shari'a* as contractualistic 142–43; sovereignty 108

Qutb, Muhammad 133

Qutb, Sayyid 88–97, 202n3; on birth of Islam 136, 137; concept of Political Islam 97–98; death of 96, 99; de-legitimization of reform efforts 173; democracy 122; disavowal of modernity 93–96; on failure of the West 89–91; and Hamas 107; and historical inspiration for Islamists 154; al-Hudaybi as *Murshid* 93; human agency on Earth 110; and Muslim Brotherhood 91–93; and Muslim women 93, 106; political power and authority 101, 102–4, 114; politicization 82–83; and Qaradawi 107, 109; Qutb's influence 91, 92; *shari'a* as framework 170; transformation of 88–89; vision of reform 20–21, 159. *See also* Muslim Brotherhood

al-Radd 'ala Dahriyyi (al-Afghani) 47

Ranger, Terence 20, 166

Rawlinson, George 141

al-Rayyis, Muhammad Diya' al-Din 123, 130–31

al-Razi, Fakhr al-Din 113

al-Raziq, 'Ali 'abd 61–64, 68, 70, 75

reform. *See* renewal and reform

Refutation of the Materialists (al-Afghani) 47

reinvention in Islamic thought: as characteristic of intellectual history 13–14; at core of Political Islam xii, xiv, 20–23, 159–60, 163–67; and Islamic state xx, xx–xxi. *See also* Political Islam; tradition and invention of the caliphate

reinvention of 22, 115–21, 160, 165

relative societal ascension and decline 30–31

religion: clergy in Islam 125–26, 210n136; and democracy 167, 210n130; and freedom xx; and Islamic state 126, 159; religio-moral reform 73–74; religious conservatism 70; resurgence of xii, 85–86, 160–61, 162, 165; and separation from state 32, 44, 62, 170, 193n65, 197n104. *See also* *dīn wa dawla*; Islamic morality; Islamic state

Renan, Ernest 16

"Renewal, Renewing, and Renewers" (Rida) 72

renewal and reform: development and emergence of Political Islam xii–xiii, xxi, xxiii, 19–23, 158; foreshadowed by Abu Taleb Khan 1–2; "Islamic resurgence" 183n28; modes of reform 13–19, 195n72; and Napoleon's invasion of Egypt 36–39; and uneven development of *umma* 10–11; and Western hegemony 12–13. *See also* asymmetric development and modernization; despotism and absolutism; labeling of

historical concepts; *individual modes of renewal and reform*
representative government: Muslim intellectual thought xix–xx, xxi, 41, 50, 169; Napoleon's efforts 36–37; in Turkey 59–60. *See also* democracy; political authority; political participation
Return of the Pharaoh: Memoir in Nasir's Prison (al-Ghazali) 100
Rida, Muhammad Rashid 69–74; and al-Raziq 75; and fundamentalist-style of reform 77; and Islamic State 203n30; on political authority 114; and separation of religion and state 198n104
The Rise and Fall of the Great Powers (Kennedy) 2
Rousseau, Jean-Jacques 22, 34, 39, 42, 157
Roy, Olivier 21
rule of law. *See* legislative sovereignty; *shariʿa*
rulers, relationship to community. *See* al-Qaradawi; *ḥisba*; political authority; *shariʿa*; Tanzimat mode of renewal and reform
Russia: and "the Eastern question" 181n10; control of Muslim territories 2, 16, 45–46; decline of Ottomans 5–6; part of the "Great Powers" 182n12
Ruthven, Malise 31–32

al-Sadat, Anwar (president of Egypt) 20, 84
Safavid dynasty 3, 12
salafi xiii–xiv, 72, 95, 99, 197n102
Sargon II (King of Assyria) 138
al-Sayyed, Ahmed Lutfi 64
Saʾid (Khedive) 45

Scholler, Marco 145
science and rationality 48, 55. *See also* Islam's compatibility with modernity
Second World War. *See* world wars
sectarianism of Muslim community 52–53
secularism 160, 167, 170; and democracy 124–25; Islamic concept of 148, 210n130; and Western influence 57, 74, 100, 119; in Young Turks movement 60. *See also* separation of "church" and state
secularization theory xii, xiii
secular-nationalist mode of renewal and reform 14, 60–68; and Arab nationalism 62–64; criticism of 69, 70–73, 75, 79, 82, 124; decline of 87; in Egypt 64–68, 76; emergence of 17, 57, 158; and Political Islam 164; and separation of "church" and state 61–62; and Young Turks 60–61, 193n64. *See also* nationalism; renewal and reform; *other individual modes of renewal and reform*
Selim III (sultan) 12, 183n25, 188n8
separation of "church" and state 20, 32, 44, 62, 170, 193n65, 197n104. *See also* democracy; secularism
Serjeant, R.B. 142, 145
Seymour, Hamilton 5–6
shahada (declaration of faith) 95, 204n45
Shannab, Ismail Abu 107, 116
Sharabi, Hisham 63
shariʿa (Islamic law): and *bayʿa* 127, 142–43, 149; equality of all men and women 206n80; and

evidence that *shūra* is binding 117–18; and hegemony 119; important principles of 44, 170; and Islamic state 98, 100, 101, 126–27, 129, 130, 159, 165; and man-made laws 109–10, 111, 118, 170; Muslims straying from 47–49; and questioning rulers 121; reinvention of 116, 117–22, 130, 165; and social justice 133, 172. *See also ḥisba; ijmā; shūra*

Sheehi, Stephen Paul 195n71

shūra (consultation) 172; and democracy 123–24, 125; importance to Khayr al-Din 44; Islamists' reinvention of 160, 165; as obligatory 117–18, 208n102; and opposition to the third caliph 151; political system at Medina 143, 148, 149; pre-Islamic Arab society 140, 142; and selection of rulers 127. *See also bay'a; ḥisba; ijmā;* political participation; *shari'a; shūracracy*

shūracracy 131–33. *See also* political participation; *shūra*

Signposts Along the Road. See Milestones, Milestones Along the Way

Silk Road 3

"Sisters in Islam" 106

Smith, Wilfred Cantwell 13

social contract 34; as basis of Political Islam xx, xxi, xxii; and *bay'a* 127, 141; and the caliphate 149–50, 153; concept of 22, 34, 104; as fundamentally Islamic 164; *ḥisba* and *shūra* as notion of 115–23; and Islamic government 100, 114, 165, 166; and political authority 109–11;

and *shūracracy* 131–33. *See also* Arab tribal society; contracts and contractual authority; *hākimiyya;* Islamic state

The Social Contract (Rousseau) 39, 42, 157

social justice: failure of the West 130; in Islamic society 133, 159; and Political Islam 169; and *shūra* 118–20. *See also* freedom; human rights

Social Justice in Islam (Abdelkader) 159

Social Justice in Islam (Qutb) 91–92

social movement theory 161–62

social transformation 91–92, 95, 107–8

socialism 18, 19

The Society of the Muslim Brothers. *See* Muslim Brotherhood

The Society of the Muslim Brothers (Mitchell) 77

sovereignty 96; in an Islamic state 101–4; legislative sovereignty 109, 111; and political authority 111–12; and social contract 131–32. *See also hākimiyya;* Islamic state

Spanish *Reconquista* 11–12

The State in Islam (Khalid) 68

Suez Canal 45

Suez Canal Company 74–75

Sukarno (president of Indonesia) 87, 158

Sukarnoputri, Megawati (president of Indonesia) 106

sultan. See caliphate

Sunni Islam, intellectual history of 13

Surat al-Baqarah 105, 121, 132, 142–43, 206n80

Surat al-Hujurat 206n80
Surat al-Imran 116, 132
Surat al-Khaf 121
Surat al-Ma'idah 121, 143
Surat al-Naml 142
Surat al-Ra'd 108
Surat al-Shūra 116–17
Surat an-Nur 105
Surat as-Sad 121
Surat Hud 121, 129–30
Surat Ibrahim 132
The Surest Path (Khayr al-Din) 42–43
The Suspicions of the Secularists and Westernizers for the Islamic Solution (Qaradawi) 108
Syria 26, 70

al-Tahtawi, Rifaʿa Rafiʿ 39–42, 44–45, 49–50, 53, 159
tajdid and *islah*. *See* renewal and reform
al-Tajdid wa al-tajaddud wa al-mujaddidun (Rida) 72
Takhlis al-Ibriz fi Talkis Bariz aw al-Diwan al-Nafis bi-iwan Baris (al-Tahtawi) 39
Taleb, Zainab Abu 116
Taliban 32
Tanzimat mode of renewal and reform 14, 37–46, 158; emergence of 16; political participation and *watan* 39–42; and responsibility of rulers 42–46; to strengthen Ottoman society 38–39, 50, 163; transition from 45–46, 48. *See also* Egypt; Napoleon's invasion of Egypt; Ottoman Empire; renewal and reform; *other individual modes of renewal and reform*

taqlid (imitation) 54–55, 56, 158
Tarjuman al- Qurʾan (Hind, publisher and editor) 79
tawhid (unity): dissent in Mecca 143–44; as element of a complete political system 92; and freedom 204n45; and the Islamic state 100–104; as political imperative 79, 92, 95–96; social contract and 131. *See also* Islamic unity; Pan-Islamic unity
taʿadudiyya. *See* pluralism
Taʿassub (al-Afghani) 52
technicalism 28, 29–30
technology and military strength 6–7, 10
terrorism. *See* extremism; shariʿa
theocracy 103, 108, 110, 125–26
Third World 7–8
Tibi, Bassam 63
Tilly, Charles 7
tolerance of all faiths 4, 206n80. *See also* pluralism
"Toward the Light" (al-Banna) 78
tradition and invention of the caliphate 166. *See also* reinvention in Islamic thought; traditionalism
traditionalism 9, 49, 56, 163. *See also* tradition and invention of the caliphate
La trahison des images (Magritte) 23
The Travels of Mirza Abu Taleb Khan (Khan) 1–2, 15
Treaty of Kucuk-Kaynarca 5
Tunisia xiii, 45, 46, 99, 173
al-Turabi, Hasan: concept of Islamic government 97; on foundation of Islamic state 100–101; imprisonment of 99; model of Medinan period 135;

political parties 128–29; *umma* as primary institution in Islam 110–11; women in politics 105
Turkey 26, 59–60, 60–61, 183n29. *See also* Ottoman Empire

Umayyad empire 152. *See also* caliphate
umma (community). *See* asymmetric development and modernization; *bay'a;* crisis of Muslim intellectuals; decline of the *umma; dīn wa dawla; ḥisba;* Islamic state; leadership; Muslim evaluation of the West; nation-states; Political Islam; popular vicegerency; Prophet at Medina; reinvention of Islamic thought; renewal and reform; *shūra;* sovereignty; unitary linear model of development; Western domination; *individual modes of renewal and reform*
al-Umma wa-Sultat al-Hakim al-Mustabidd ('Abduh and al-Afghani) 53
The Unique and Necessary Islamic Solution, How Imported Solutions Were Accepted by Our Umma (Qaradawi) 108
unitary linear model of development 8, 14, 17, 29
United Arab Republic 87
United States 18, 88–92
unity of God. *See tawhid*
"universal theory of Islam" 91–92
al-Urwa al-Wuthqa (Arabic periodical) 52
'Uthman (third caliph) 150–52

Vatikiotis, P.J. 37, 38–39
Vienna 3, 7, 182n13

Voll, John: foreword xi–xiv; Islamic fundamentalism 32–33; modernity 19; office of *caliph* 58–59; religious resurgence 161; restoring the *umma* 73; split of Islamic Modernists 63; Western political models 18
vulnerability of the West 19, 85. *See also* oil embargoes
al-Wahda al-Islamiyya ('Abduh and al-Afghani) 53
Wahhabists 33
al-Walid ibn 'Uqbah 152
Wallerstein, Immanuel 12, 26, 96
al-Waqidi, Muhammad ibn 'Umar 145–46
war with Russia 5. *See also* Arab-Israeli wars; world wars
watan (fatherland) 39–41. *See also* patriotism and love of country
Watt, W. Montgomery 143
al-Wazir, Zayd bnu 'Ali 148
Weber, Max 29, 99; modernity 27, 28, 29, 30, 33
Western domination 2, 16, 45–46, 88; and Islam as vehicle for change 56–57; and Israel 83; and the rise of naval power 35; threat to *umma* 46. *See also* colonialism; economic dominance; European power, rise of; industrialization
Western education, influence on al-Tahtawi 39–42
Western hegemony 2; and affirmation of Islamic ideals 57; defense against 52; European model of modernity 82; Great Western Transmutation 28–29; and Israel 83; renewal and reform 12–13, 16, 17; and success of Political Islam 32–33.

See also capitalism; economic dominance; European power, rise of

Western liberal democracy. *See* democracy

Western society: critique by Abu Taleb Khan 2; morality in 2, 17, 18, 29, 82, 196n84; Qutb's assessment of 88–92. *See also* Muslim evaluation of the West

Westernization. *See* secular-nationalist mode of renewal and reform; Tanzimat mode of renewal and reform

What Did the World Lose with the Decline of Islam? (Nadwi) 9

women and political participation 105–6, 211n149

Wooldridge, Adrian 166–67

World War I. *See* world wars

world wars: and changing view of modernity 163; and nation-states 13, 57–60, 135; and Qutb's view of America 90; and renewal and reform 17, 19, 158, 163–64; and Western political and military model 18. *See also* Arab-Israeli wars; war with Russia

Yassin, Ahmed 106–7

Yassine, Nadia 106, 107; ignorance of Muslim history 153–54; Islamic state 148, 212n28; political authority 111, 114, 115; social justice 119–20

Young Turks movement 60–61, 193n64. *See also* Ottoman Empire

Zaman, Muhammad Qasim 89

al-Zawahiri, Ayman xxi

Zia, Khaleda (prime minister of Bangladesh) 106

Zuhayr on *shūra* councils 140

www.ingramcontent.com/pod-product-compliance
Lightning Source LLC
Chambersburg PA
CBHW020750160426
43192CB00006B/288